Treasures of the Taylorian

Series One: Reformation Pamphlets

Volume 3

Martin Luther

Von der Freiheit eines Christenmenschen

On the Freedom of a Christian

Edited by Howard Jones and
Henrike Lähnemann

Taylor Institution Library, Oxford, 2020

First published in November 2020 by Taylor Institution Library.
Reprinted with corrections in February 2021.

https://www.bodleian.ox.ac.uk/taylor

A number of digital downloads to accompany this edition are available from the Taylor Institution Library website. They include:

A podcast of the edition
Facsimiles of all four Taylorian copies of the text
Additional articles and blog posts
An Open Access version of this book

The facsimile is of the first edition of Martin Luther, *Von der Freiheit eines Christenmenschen.* Taylor Institution Library, ARCH.8°.G.1520(25)

The cover image is from the title page of the same edition.

Typesetting and cover design by Emma Huber, Subject Consultant for German, Taylor Institution Library

ISBN 978-0-9954564-5-7

Taylor Institution Library, St Giles, Oxford OX1 3NA

https://editions.mml.ox.ac.uk/editions/freiheit-1520/

Table of Contents

The Taylor Reformation Pamphlet Series

Emma Huber and Henrike Lähnemann

1520 was a momentous year for the Reformation – and for printing as an effective medium of propaganda. The developments of the previous years had led to a dramatic increase in theological publishing, from the '95 Theses' in 1517 via its German version, the 'Sermon von Ablass und Gnade', in 1518 and a number of shorter texts in 1519, to three momentous pamphlets in 1520, culminating in November in 'Von der Freiheit eines Christenmenschen', the best-seller of the 16th century. At a distance of 500 years, the 'Taylor Reformation Pamphlet Series' has been charting this publication schedule, starting in late 2015 with preparations for the quincentenary of the publication of the '95 Theses', which was re-enacted on 31 October 2017 with a copy typeset by Oxford students and printed on the Bibliographical Press of the Bodleian Library. Then came the publication of 'Sermon on Indulgences and Grace' in 2018, followed by the present edition of 'On the Freedom of a Christian' (the *Freiheitsschrift*) in November 2020.

The latest edition comes not only at a time when Luther's advice on how to behave during a plague is particularly poignant[1] but also as digital media have become more relevant as a means of communication, inviting us to experiment with new formats, just as the printers did when they published Luther's increasingly popular output. This new edition of the *Freiheitsschrift* is the first, not only to be published online,[2] but also to be fully launched online, with 33 speakers in 32 locations (one couple sharing a camera) taking part in a round table and relay-reading, streamed live via YouTube.

---

[1] 'Reformation Advice on Dealing with Pandemics' on the Taylor Reformation Blog https://blogs.bodleian.ox.ac.uk/taylor-reformation, 'When plague came to Wittenberg' by Lyndal Roper on https://www.history.ox.ac.uk/pandemics-and-plagues.

[2] https://editions.mml.ox.ac.uk/editions/freiheit-1520; all related blogposts and the recording of the launch linked from there.

This seems therefore an opportune moment to review how the project developed and to draw lessons for other initiatives which aim to combine Modern Languages and Digital Humanities.

The project to make the Taylor Institution Library Reformation pamphlets more widely available started in 2015, when Henrike Lähnemann was asked to teach the Method Option 'Palaeography and History of the Book' for the Faculty of Medieval and Modern Languages. Edmund Wareham had been using the Taylor Institution Library's Reformation Pamphlet collection for a while for his teaching on the Reformation courses run by Lyndal Roper in the History Faculty, and he recommended having a look at these for student projects. Emma Huber, the German subject librarian, not only helped make these pamphlets available, but also suggested using them as a test case for developing digital editions. Howard Jones agreed to act as linguistic adviser and translator.

The first cohort of History of the Book students presenting the pamphlets they had chosen for their projects, from left to right: Lucas Eigel with 'De captivitate', Kezia Fender with the coloured-in copy of the 'Wunderliche Weissagung von dem Papsttum', Klaus Meyer with the 'Hortulus animae', Jennifer Bunselmeier with a Karlstadt 'Disputacio', Charlotte Hartmann presenting the exhibition in the Voltaire Room of the Taylor Institution Library. All of the featured pamphlets are now available at https://editions.mml.ox.ac.uk/topics/reformation.shtml

A prototype of the website was presented at a workshop on the 'Future of German Studies' in January 2016, taking as a starting point Martin Luther's 'Sendbrief vom Dolmetschen' of 1530, a core text for translation theory and historical linguistics which had been on the Oxford syllabus since the early 20th century. This was done as a joint presentation by the History of the Book students and Charlotte Schwarzer, Cultural Attaché at the German Embassy in London. The Embassy generously funded the launch of the full version as part of the events around the quincentenary. Since 2017 also marked the 70th anniversary of the twinning of Bonn and Oxford, the publication of the new edition of the 'Sendbrief', the first in the new series of 'Reformation Pamphlets', was attended by a delegation from Bonn.

It is worth recording the full list of speakers for the crowd-sourced performance, since it represented such a wide variety of backgrounds and voices, from two Oxford schoolgirls via the Mayor of Bonn and members of the German Lutheran congregation to Dutch, French, German, and British colleagues from the Faculty of Medieval and Modern Languages.

> Readers of the 'Sendbrief' in order of appearance: Henrike Lähnemann, Howard Jones, Nigel Palmer, Catriona Seth, Andrew Allen, Alexandra Lloyd, Helmut Kollig, Kathrin Luddecke, Ed Wareham, Alderik Blom, John Partridge, Johanneke Sytsema, Ulla Weinberg, Ewa Węgrzyn, Jennifer Bunselmeier, Brigitta Poppe, Christine Baro-Hone, Patrizia Zachhuber, Hans Hahn, Elsa Voak, Eleanor Voak , Charlie Louth, David Murray, Franziska Kohlt, Katrin Kohl, Hannah Jackson, Claudia Piller, Tiziana Imstepf, Emma Huber, Sophie Hall, Maren Fichter, Susanne Herrmann-Sinai, Lena Vosding, Martin Christ, John Flood.

What followed for the Bonn group (and what became a blueprint for community engagement) was a print workshop with Richard Lawrence and Alexandra Franklin at the Bibliographical Press of the Bodleian Library where the visitors could use the typeset material provided by the History of the Book students.

Cooperation with groups and congregations around Oxford developed in three strands: Translating, Printing, and Singing the Reformation. With the last of these strands we returned to Germany, integrating Reformation theology and heritage in the journey by the Oxford Bach Soloists to Northern Germany and the roots of J S Bach's music. The collaboration had started at the beginning of the project, with Tom Hammond-Davies and Alexandra Lloyd performing from the cantata 'Christ lag in Todesbanden' at the launch of the website.[3]

The second print-on-demand publication in the series paid particular attention to the materiality of the pamphlets since it combined a side-by-side facsimile of the Taylorian copies of two different editions of the short 'Sermon von Ablass und Gnade'. The 'print-your-own-pamphlet' instructions, on how to produce facsimile booklets of eight pages from the double-sided sheets of paper folded twice, proved popular with students and visitors at the Open Days.

Display of Reformation pamphlets (and the Martin Luther Playmobil figure to show the relationship to coloured-in metalcuts) from the Taylorian collection for a 'Spot the Difference' session with an Open Day group.

[3] https://editions.mml.ox.ac.uk/topics/reformation-music.shtml

The collaboration for this second print-on-demand publication went further afield and included colleagues from Germany, with Martin Keßler (Göttingen, now Basel) contributing a theological introduction and Ulrich Bubenheimer helping to date and locate Reformation autographs. The translation of the text was again done by Howard Jones, who also provided a linguistic introduction to the Early New High German features of the pamphlet. An appendix included Luther's '95 Theses' in Latin together with an English translation. For the history of the copies, Henrike Lähnemann cooperated with a former History of the Book student, Christina Ostermann, who was researching the acquisition policy of the Taylorian for her doctoral thesis.

> Readers of the 'Sermon von Ablass und Gnade' in order of appearance: Ritchie Robertson, Emma Huber, Jack Stuart, Johanneke Sytsema, Molly Ford, Martin Keßler, Florence Butterfield, Andrew Allen, Jennifer Bunselmeier, Felix Kraft, Eleanor Voak, Elsa Voak, Charles Russ, Jenny Russ, Olivia Kobiela, Linus Ubl, Rudolf Smend, Kathrin Luddecke, Christina Ostermann, Mette Ahlefeldt-Laurvig, Henrike Lähnemann.

Over the course of 2018 and 2019, the Reformation editions website expanded rapidly. Digital Humanities became an official part of the History of the Book teaching, and Emma Huber developed a Digital Editions course which was first tested with other librarians across the Bodleian Libraries and then rolled out to students and members of the public; on the Taylorian website there are now 55 editions online – and counting. The present volume, the third in the series, profited from this collaborative approach. Two Erasmus+ interns, Julia Bouquet and Kiara Hart, encoded the xml-text of the transcription from the digital facsimile done by Emma Huber; the translation was prepared by two early modernist colleagues in London, Anna Linton and Sharon Baker,[4] and tested while it was still a work-in-progress

[4] An account of the translation process can be found in the blog post by Julia Bouquet on https://blogs.bodleian.ox.ac.uk/taylor-reformation/2020/05/14/translating-the-spirit-of-freedom/

by final year students in Oxford practising for their final exam on 'translation from pre-modern sources'. The demanding process of establishing an accurate and consistent English translation of key terms such as 'frum' or 'Christen mensch' (how to render this in a non-gendered way in English?) also fed into Howard Jones's chapter comparing the German and Latin versions of the text, addressing the relationship between the two which has puzzled scholars for generations. Howard Jones also helped with the translation and the linguistic footnotes which were developed as an extended essay by a second-year German and Linguistics student, Ari Warrington who is also going to contribute a longer version as a blog post.

The historical and philosophical introduction was written by Hannah Clemens, Theology Student at the HU Berlin, another Erasmus+ Intern in Oxford (with Andrew Allen at Exeter College Chapel in 2019), with the philosophical side provided by her husband Dennis Clemens. It was translated by Raluca Vasiu and Florence Butterfield, two Oxford Modern Languages graduates who took the early modern German period option for their finals, and copy-edited by Samuel Heywood, a master's student working on Luther's hymns.

The chapter on the history of the Taylorian copies grew out of another student project: Maximilian Krümpelmann's History of the Book project, first published on the History of the Book blog[5] which was started by Modern Languages master's students Lena Zlock and Caroline Godard as an attempt to bring the Digital Humanities and book-historical side of their coursework together.

The three German and one Latin copies of Luther's 'On the Freedom of a Christan' in the Taylor Institution reflect not only Reformation history, but also the history of the physical copies – from their first readers to their acquisition by the library. All items show various later additions which clearly mark them as historical objects in the Taylorian's holdings: ownership marks, stamps, and pencil notes help

[5] https://historyofthebook.mml.ox.ac.uk/

to further our understanding of the development of the library as a teaching collection and the role of its Reformation pamphlets as teaching material. It was therefore a fitting paradox that the restrictions imposed by Covid-19 on teaching large groups in fact opened up the event to a much wider audience than the previous events. At the Taylorian itself the four copies of the text were presented by Henrike Lähnemann who was joined online by speakers from all across Oxford, England, and Germany, including two readers from Heidelberg, the city were three of the copies had been based before they were bought for the Taylorian (cf. chapter 2).

The launch started off with a round-table discussion chaired by Edmund Wareham who spoke via Zoom with Lyndal Roper, Henrike Lähnemann, and Howard Jones about the significance of the text, the links with the Peasants War, the opportunities and dangers of celebrating anniversaries – and the importance of an interdisciplinary approach to overcome this challenge.

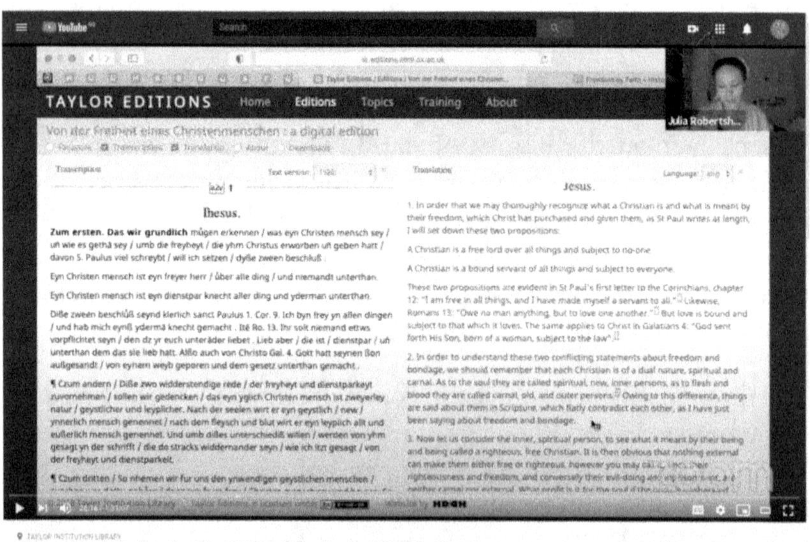

Screenshot of the relay reading stream from Zoom to YouTube with Julia Robertshaw, a second-year German Sole student taking the course 'Luther as Special Author', reading the opening paragraph.

Part of the challenge was also technical: Tom Revell, Events Organiser for Oxford Medieval Studies, acted as 'cameraman' on the Zoom account of Medium Aevum, highlighting each speaker in turn, sending 'requests to unmute' reminders – and it went without a glitch.

> Readers for the 'Von der Freiheit' launch in order of appearance: Howard Jones, Julia Robertshaw, Eleanor Voak, Samuel Schulenburg, Emma Huber, Hannah Clemens, Dennis Clemens, Raluca Vasiu, Julia Bouquet, Lena Vosding, Marlene Schilling, Thomas Henderson, Kate Shore, Maximilian Krümpelmann, Kiara Hart, Carolin Gluchowski, Josephine Bewerunge, Caroline Lehnert, Anna Linton, Molly Ford, Susanne Herrmann-Sinai, Reinier van Straten, Ruth Görnandt, Elijah Ferrante, Mai-Britt Wiechmann, Linus Ubl, Luise Morawetz, Ari Warrington, Konstantin Winters, Timothy Powell, Alexandra Burgar, and Anhad Arora as a reserve reader in case somebody could not go live.

The website for the edition is a work-in-progress, making use of the open format to add further resources e.g. on the Latin edition and more detailed linguistic analysis. Other strands of the Reformation project include Oxford's TORCH network, which plans to look at monuments of the Reformation and their heritage, making use of the Reformation Walking Tour through Oxford which was developed as part of the Taylor Editions website.[6]

Thanks to all of our more than one hundred relay readers, colleagues, students, printers, librarians, members of various congregations, Germanists, visitors from abroad, and citizens who in one way or another took part in the project to make the Reformation pamphlets accessible and relevant for future readers and listeners. The project is set to continue charting the publication history of the Reformation and, with it, a piece of European heritage.

Oxford, 23 November 2020

---

[6] http://oxfordstories.ox.ac.uk/reformation-walking-tour.

Introduction

This introduction highlights the theological, philosophical, material, linguistic, and stylistic importance of the work. The Bibliography at the end lists only literature cited and references in footnotes are by short title.

For a fully hyperlinked version of these chapters, cf. the online version https://editions.mml.ox.ac.uk/editions/freiheit-1520

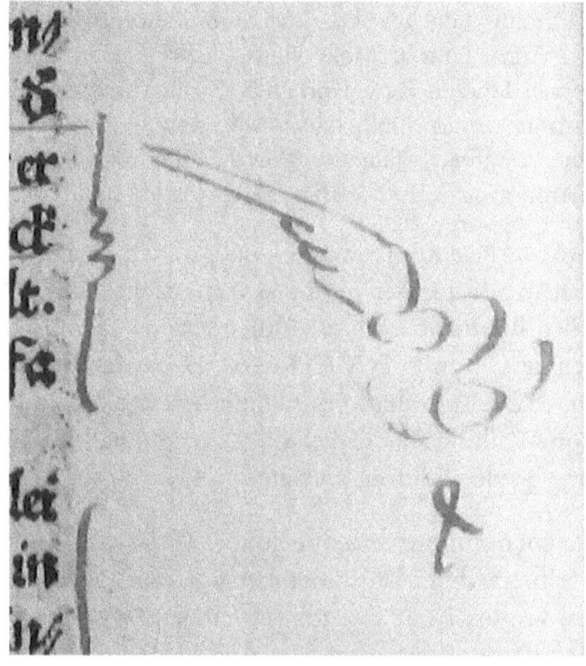

Manicule in the Speyer edition of 'Von der Freiheit', highlighting article 4. ARCH.8°.G.1519(11/2), fol. Aijr

1. The Historical and Philosophical Background

Dennis and Hannah Clemens[7]

> Gerhard Ebeling: *No theologian – we may even go further and say no other thinker – has spoken in such compelling terms of the freedom of man on the one hand, and with such terrifying force of the bondage of man on the other.*[8]

If the Reformation is closely linked to the person of Martin Luther, it is also closely linked to the notion of freedom. For Luther the ideological shift of the Reformation was a liberation. When a theological insight turned into a movement of political reform, Luther changed his name, and 'Luder' became 'Luther', the short form of the Greek 'eleutherios', a name derived from the Greek for 'free'.[9]

Martin Luther's letter to Georg Spalatin with his signature *Mártinos eleuthérios* in Greek, 20 January 1519 (Landesarchiv Sachsen-Anhalt [Z 8, Nr. 36], edited in WA.B, No. 138, p. 310).

---

[7] The chapter was originally written as a blog post and translated into English by Raluca Vasiu and Florence Butterfield. With thanks to Frauke Thees for her critical reading of the text.
Full version https://historyofthebook.mml. ox.ac.uk/2020/10/29/freedom-by-faith/

[8] Ebeling (1980: 211).

[9] Kingreen (2017: VII). It was common practice among humanists to adopt a Latin or Greek form of their family name, cf. Philipp Melanchthon (from Schwartzerdt), and Johannes Cochläus (from Dobeneck).

But what role did Luther assign himself by this new name – liberated or liberator? In any case, this new-found freedom concerned his relationship with God and his faith as well as his relationship with authority, both secular and ecclesiastical. After gradually becoming more radical, Luther's reform programme culminated in his three major writings of 1520. These were derived from his original understanding of the relationship between the divinity and the individual, a concept most effectively summarised in the *Freiheitsschrift*, which Roper describes as *the most beautiful writing of that time.*[10]

The Historical Background

In 1520, when Luther issued this key text, he found himself in a precarious situation. All attempts to resolve the conflict with Rome had failed and the trial for heresy against him, which had begun in June 1518 but then paused, was being pursued again. Luther was aware of the threat to his own life if he were to fall into the hands of the papal authorities. But in the two intervening years much had happened that would shape Luther personally and theologically.

Shortly after the commencement of the trial (as a result of the publication of the '95 Theses'), Luther was interrogated by the Thomist cardinal Cajetan following the Diet of Augsburg in 1518. As was to be expected given Luther's tendency to radicalise his stance when facing opponents, the debates with Cajetan soon went beyond the issue of indulgences. Among other things, they discussed the traditional concept of the *thesaurus ecclesiae (treasure of grace)* – a theoretical prerequisite of indulgences. The treasure of grace, which comprised the merits of Christ, provided clerics with the means to reduce punishments for repentant sinners.

During the discussion Luther made his famous statement that he had to *obey God more than men* and do nothing against his conscience

[10] Roper (2016: 216).

(WA 2, 16: 11–12, 19).[11] He refused to revoke his Theses and hence effectively completed the break with Rome. The significance of this break is highlighted by Luther's long-time confessor Staupitz's decision to relieve Luther of his monastic vows in order to prevent the General Vicar of the Augustinian hermits from forcing Luther to resign. In the aftermath, Luther reckoned with imminent martyrdom. Thus, on October 11, the day before his interrogation, Luther wrote to Melanchthon from Augsburg that he would rather die than revoke what was right (WA 1, No. 98, 11. Oct. 1518, 213: 11–14). But the possibility of martyrdom did not hold Luther back: rather, it brought him closer to Christ. In the recounting of the Reichstag of Worms, the link to Christ's passion is taken to extremes by the humanist Hermann Busche who published a pamphlet *Passion Doctor Martins Luthers, oder seyn lydung durch Marcellum beschriben.* In this, Luther's journey and stay in Worms are retold as a parallel to Christ's suffering.[12] Luther's quandary as to how to proceed also spurred his theological thinking: *Each new argument left him at once more isolated and more elated. Every new step he took theologically was freighted with intense feeling, for it genuinely was a matter of life and death as he followed Christ's progress to martyrdom.*[13]

The promises of his Reformation theology, which freed him from his old theological ideas, had a stronger effect on Luther than the threats from the papal curia. For him, it meant preferring to die as a just man than to live as an unjust one. Given Luther's ability to draw theological inspiration from a life-threatening situation, it is not surprising that he wrote the *Freiheitsschrift* immediately after receiving the papal bull 'Exsurge Domine'. After the interrogation at Augsburg, Luther's situation would turn out to be less dramatic than feared. Rome suddenly changed course and Luther's heresy trial lost momentum.

---

[11] In the following chapters, quotations from Martin Luther's texts are referenced following the *Weimarer Ausgabe* (WA); cf. Bibliography.

[12] Sammel (1996: 157–74).

[13] Roper (2016: 163).

The reason for this sudden change was political. Maximilian I, the Holy Roman Emperor, wanted to have his grandson Charles of Burgundy elected as his successor, which would have confronted the Pope with a German emperor who was powerful in Italy. The Pope also suspected that the alternative candidate, Francis I of France, had interests in conflict with his own. He wanted Frederick the Wise, Elector of Saxony and Luther's patron, to help him at least block Charles's election, and sought to cultivate Frederick, even for a brief period supporting his nomination as Emperor. Thus, in the autumn of 1518, the Pope despatched Karl von Miltitz to try and win Frederick over, and at the same time put the trial against Luther on hold. The Pope even honoured Frederick with the golden papal rose.[14]

Militz, however, did not limit his efforts to pleasing the Elector, but he tried to reach an agreement with Luther as well. In January 1519, they came to a standstill agreement, the so-called Altenburg Pact. Luther promised to refrain from speaking out publicly, having been assured that this would be reciprocated by the papal side. The proposal to leave the matter in the hands of an erudite bishop offered new hope for a peaceful settlement in the dispute with Rome. Luther honoured the agreement for a few months, although his opponents continued to publish. He resorted to a cautious position until the famous confrontation that would open the literary floodgates – the dispute with the Ingolstadt theology professor Johannes Eck (1486–1543) in Leipzig.[15]

Eck, one of the humanists and theologians who had originally sided with Luther, became one of the latter's most vocal opponents. In the spring of 1518 Eck had written a refutation of Luther's '95 Theses', the Obelisci (printers' marks for errors), which prompted Luther to respond with the Asterisci (marks for additions). Both texts were

---

[14] Wallmann (2012: 25).

[15] Iserloh (1981).

intended for academic discussion and not for the general public. On Luther's side, the Wittenberg theologian Andreas Bodenstein von Karlstadt (1486–1541) published 406 theses when Eck went public with his arguments, paving the way for the Leipzig dispute in June 1519.[16] Eck's unabating criticism of the '95 Theses' made Luther insist on taking part in the dispute himself, travelling to Leipzig with Karlstadt and Melanchthon. The reformers failed to turn the dispute to their advantage. Eck's exceptional memory and rhetorical skills made him a formidable opponent, and he provoked Luther into making radical statements. Eck had realised early on that the '95 Theses' meant a fundamental challenge to the traditional church and its doctrine and managed to tease this out in the course of the debate. Luther denied the biblical basis for papal primacy and drew attention to what he saw as the errors of the Council of Constance, particularly the condemnation of Jan Hus.[17] Luther got carried away, supporting theological arguments far more radical than his '95 Theses'.

So the cat was out of the bag. Luther directed his criticism not just at isolated church failings, but at the entire ecclesiastical superstructure and its claim to be the sole administerer of faith. Eventually, without a clear conclusion, both sides claimed victory, but that did not really matter.[18] The pamphlet literature flourished thanks to Luther's growing popularity, and the humanists who dominated public opinion stood behind him. Luther's humanist credentials dated back before 1517, and the rapid spread of '95 Theses' can be ascribed almost exclusively to the activity of his humanist supporters. For example, the Nuremberg humanist Christopher Scheurl appears to have worked as an agent and to have passed the Theses on to various humanist circles.[19] While Luther's pastoral writings appealed to the general public, his polemical ones convinced the humanists. They

---

[16] https://www.archiv.sachsen.de/leipziger-disputation-vom-februar-1519-4901.html

[17] More on the debate in WA 2 und WA 59: 427–605.

[18] Wallmann (2012: 27).

[19] Moeller (1991: 102).

were the only discrete group who stood behind Luther in the first few years, and Luther's cause would not have prevailed without them. As the conflict between Luther and Rome progressed, the humanist movement was divided into the faction supporting Luther and the Catholic faction. And it was particularly the younger generation which took Luther's side: the struggle against the 'old' theology was at once a struggle against the ecclesiastical establishment and an emancipation of the new generation.

Eventually the Leipzig Disputation spread the 'Luther-case' so widely that by 1520 the whole of Germany was caught up in it. In the aftermath of the dispute, Luther entered his most creative intellectual phase. It was the feeling of empowerment and responsibility, of having a nation behind him, that motivated him. The theological argument with Eck represented an important step in Luther's process of liberation from ecclesiastical control. This process also resulted in a change in his spirituality. He gave up the traditional hour-long prayers, dedicating his time to his writings instead (WA.TR 2, No. 1253: 11). As his relationship with Staupitz became more distant, Luther drifted away from Staupitz's spirituality, which Luther deemed less and less reconcilable with his own theology and relationship to the church. He would later attribute his reformatory breakthrough to the aftermath of the Leipzig Dispute (WA 54: 185–86).

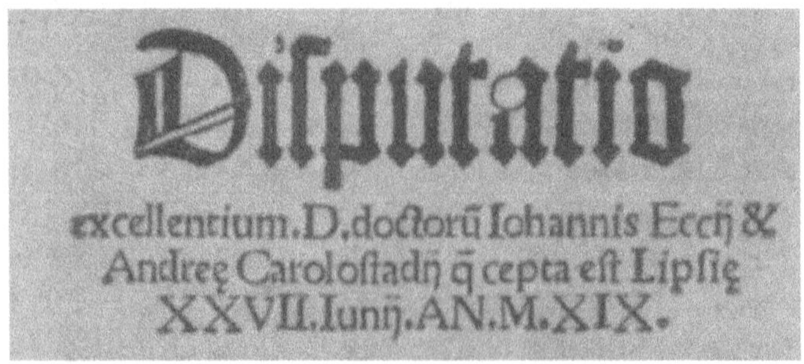

Disputatio
excellentium.D.doctorũ Iohannis Eccij &
Andreę Carolostadij q̄ cepta est Lipsię
XXVII.Iunij.AN.M.XIX.

Copy of Karlstadt's pamphlet on the Leipzig Dispute in the Taylor Institution Library ARCH. 8°.G.1519(1) https://editions.mml.ox.ac.uk/editions/theses/

The Three Treatises of 1520

Of the many texts that Luther wrote after the dispute, the three Reformation manifestos from the second half of 1520 are the most significant. They set out Luther's theological beliefs as well as proposing the far-reaching demands of the Reformation movement. All three revolve around the concept of freedom – the *Freiheitsschrift* providing the most thoroughgoing analysis.

The first major treatise of 1520 – *An den christlichen Adel deutscher Nation von des christlichen Standes Besserung* 'To the Christian Nobility of the German Nation Concerning the Improvement of the Christian Estate' (WA 6: 404–469, published in August) called on the German princes to reform the church, since the clergy was proving less reliable than ever. The fundamental medieval view favouring spiritual over secular authorities was thus called into question. The treatise complained about alleged exploitation by the Catholic Church. Such complaints had been circulating since the middle of the 15th century – since the publication of the *Gravamina der deutschen Nation gegen den Stuhl zu Rom* 'Grievances of the German nation against the Holy See at Rome'.[20] The *Gravamina* represented a collection of complaints exposing abuses of papal authority, many of which had already been addressed at the Imperial Diet. Above all, such voices reflected German dissatisfaction with the papal church. There was thus a ready audience for Luther's criticism, but it was an audience which tended to interpret his writings in a one-sided, political way, notably on the subject of freedom. For the concept of freedom was primarily introduced in humanist circles as a defence against external political and financial means of oppression. The overlap between Luther's spiritual freedom and the political freedom of the humanists lay in the repudiation of Rome. Ulrich von Hutten, humanist and leader of the Imperial Knights of the Holy Roman Empire (1488–1523) called on Luther to join his mission of rescuing

---

[20] Scheible (1996: 393–409).

this freedom, which he saw as breaking away from Roman political oppression.[21] In the imperial election, the desire for political freedom had been used as an argument against Francis I of France.[22] It was in this context that interpretations of Luther's definition of a free man became polarised, with a number of readers seeing his work as a statement on political liberty.[23]

An even more radical essay followed in October – the Latin treatise *De captivitate Babylonica ecclesiae praeludium* 'Prelude on the Babylonian Captivity of the Church' – in which Luther called into question the doctrinal stance of the Catholic Church on the sacraments. He demanded a biblical foundation for the sacraments, which he argued existed only for baptism and Holy Communion (and to a lesser extent penitence). In addition, Luther tied the power of the sacraments to the act of faith. He opposed religious and priestly vows, which he regarded as unnecessary burdens that deprived Christians of the freedom acquired through baptism. This piece of writing cost Luther several followers who were not prepared to join in his criticism of church institutions.[24]

The election of Emperor Charles V left the Pope without any further reasons to defer to the Elector of Saxony or to spare Luther. As his heresy trial resumed, Luther felt that he had less and less to lose. In October 1520 he was threatened with the papal ban and excommunication and a deadline of 60 days to retract his teaching. Seeing that his efforts to reconcile Luther with the church were in jeopardy, Karl von Miltitz persuaded him to write a letter of reconciliation and address a treatise to Pope Leo X.[25] In it, Luther reassured the Pope that he had never intended to attack him personally and blamed the controversy on Eck. The letter was backdated to 6

---

[21] Böcking (1854: 356).
[22] Schmidt (2010: 14–15).
[23] Schmidt (2010: 22–23).
[24] Wallmann (2012: 31).
[25] Rieger (2007: 2).

September 1520 so that it would not be interpreted as a response to the papal bull. This is what led to the publishing of the *Freiheitsschrift*.

The positive recpetion of this treatise can be linked to its radically different content: *At the time Luther was in the eye of the storm. His other writings of this period are full of furious accusation, defence and argumentation. Strangely, at this moment of gathering clouds and impending doom, this piece is a pool of tranquillity, an eirenic piece of writing that breathes peace, delight and security.*[26]

In the *Freiheitsschrift,* Luther elaborates his recent theological thinking in a single treatise. The bull aroused public interest, preparing the ground for the wide reception of the treatise. Having severe doubts regarding the envisaged reconciliation, Luther probably wrote the letter mainly to please the Elector.[27] As Hamm argues, the letter 'is practically a short sermon' in which he explains his attitude towards the papacy.[28]

The *Freiheitsschrift* stands out in a number of ways from the two other major texts of 1520. It was his first work written in both German and Latin (cf. chapter 4 for a comparison). Luther was not responding to a theological controversy, but writing on his own initiative on a chosen topic. He was thus sharing what he cared about most while he still could, writing for his own physical survival as well as for the spiritual survival of Christians.[29]

Luther had the Latin text published together with the papal letter. In their German versions, however, the letter and treatise were published separately, the latter with an added dedicatory letter to the Zwickau mayor Hermann von Mühlpfordt. This was intended to get

---

[26] Tomlin (2017: 147).

[27] Kaufmann argues that Luther still had hope of reconciliation and that the letter was not meant ironically, cf. Kaufmann (2017: 45).

[28] Hamm (2014: 173).

[29] Kaufmann (2017: 44).

the mayor to support the local Reformation movement led by Thomas Müntzer. The separate German version of the letter only made it to two print runs while the Latin was included in 13 printed editions. Mainly thanks to Luther, printing was booming in Wittenberg. In 1517 there was only one printer there, while by 1525 there were eight. With Luther honouring his agreement with Miltitz, the Latin version came out after the German text, but it was in the Latin form that the text spread beyond the German-speaking lands. The first edition of the German version ran to 3,000–4,000 copies, and there had already been reprints before the year was out.[30] Printers from all German-speaking areas were distributing Luther's works: between 1518 and 1525 Luther's vernacular writings outnumbered the combined total of the 17 next most prolific writers of the time. In fact, Luther accounts for 20 percent of all German works printed between 1500 and 1520.[31]

The *Freiheitsschrift* played a vital role in the development of the printing industry, representing Luther's most successful piece of writing: no other book enjoyed greater circulation in the 16th century.[32] But the reception of the work was also striking. It was clear that Luther's notion of freedom was largely misunderstood by his contemporaries. Thirteen treatises with 'Freiheit' in the title were published in the third largest printing centre of Straßburg between 1520 and 1533, but only three of these authors even vaguely follow Luther's notion of freedom.[33] Most of them rather embraced freedom as rejection of secular authorities, favouring the supremacy of divine over man-made law. Luther's rejection of human works, derived from his strong emphasis on faith, was on the whole ignored. An example is the text 'New Karsthans', allegedly written by Bucer.[34]

---

[30] On the further distribution of the work, cf. Kaufmann (2017: 56–57).
[31] Roper (2016: 187).
[32] Slenczka (2017: VIII).
[33] Edwards (1995: 105).
[34] Cf. Stupperich (1960: 406–44).

One of Luther's critics, Thomas Murner (a 'foolish cat'[35] according to Luther) characterised Luther's notion of freedom as a call for chaos and upheaval. In his 1522 piece *Von dem grossen lutherischen Narren* 'On the Great Lutheran Fool' he caricatures Luther's position as basically liberating Christians from any form of loyalty, since baptism precedes any secular authority: *Der cristlich glaub gibt vnß freiheit, / zu erkennen hie kein oberkeit. / Wir sein im tauff al frei geboren, / Ee keiser / kunig / fursten woren* ('Christian faith gives us freedom to recognise no earthly authority. We were all born free in baptism before there were emperors, kings, or princes').[36] The satirical poem can be found alongside an image of a mercenary flying the banner of 'Fryheit' (cf. the illustration on the next page).

Catholic opponents also accused Luther of jeopardising social order and spreading chaos with his new theology.[37] A more positive image of Luther as a liberator is to be found in the pamphlets preceding the Peasant War. The third of the 12 articles of the Swabian peasantry in 1525 in particular echo Luther's intertwining of freedom and servitude:

> '[...] it has until now been the custom for the lords to own us as their property. This is deplorable for Christ redeemed and bought us all with his precious blood, the lowliest shepherd as well as the greatest lord, with no exceptions. Thus the Bible proves that we are free and want to be free. Not that we want to be utterly free and subject to no authority at all; God does not teach us that. We ought to live according to the commandments, not according to the lusts of the flesh. But we should love God, recognise him as our Lord in our neighbor, and willingly do all the things God commanded us at his Last Supper.'[38]

---

[35] Roper (2016: 202). 'Murr' sounds like the noise a tom cat is supposed to make and 'ner' sounds like 'narr' ('fool').

[36] Merker (1918: 242, 3787–90).

[37] Numerous examples in the analysis by Edwards (1995: 112–18).

[38] Blickle (1981: 197–98).

Der nit mit disem fenlin wist
Das evangelium ligt vnß an
Wie es der groß nar zöget dan.
Das reissig fenlin:
Zů hertzen fassen die freiheit
Dan sie ist vnß im tauff zů geseit.

Thomas Murner, *Von dem grossen Lutherischen Narren wie in doctor Murner beschworen hat*, Straßburg: Johann Grüninger 1522, VD16 M 7088, fol. P1v. BSB Munich, Rar. 870, urn:nbn:de:bvb:12-bsb00033099-0

Although peasant alliances had been organised as early as the 15th century, these groups were still lacking in ideological coherence. Several factors led to the alignment of peasant demands with the ideas of the Reformation movement. The national audience created by the printing press, pamphlet literature, and the self-confidence of a nation strengthened by Luther's appearance seems to have shifted the movement into the mainstream and helped it to spread across Germany.[39] Thus it is unsurprising that Luther was accused of inciting the peasants to revolt. In April 1525, Luther even tried to mitigate such accusations through his *Ermahnung zum Frieden auf die zwölf Artikel der Bauernschaft* 'Admonition to Peace, concerning the Twelve Articles of the Peasantry' – an attempt to clear up the misunderstanding on Christian freedom, refuting the reading of Christian freedom as a political matter (WA 18: 326, 32–327,23). In his later writing, *Wider die räuberischen und mörderischen Rotten der Bauern* 'Against the Murderous, Thieving Hordes of Peasants', Luther's criticism of the peasants became barbed and acerbic. He could have hardly distanced himself more clearly from their movement and their understanding of freedom.

The aftermath of the *Freiheitsschrift*

Miltitz's attempt at reconciliation failed and Luther was excommunicated by an imperial ban at the Council in Worms on the 3rd of January 1521. Nevertheless, Luther had gained precious time since the beginning of the heresy trial and had secured for himself not only a significant number of active followers but the support of the general public through the growing popularity of his writings.

This became evident when Eck's attempt to use the threat of a ban to deter people from following Luther was resisted in many cities. In addition, Luther had been further developing his theology thinking, and the '95 Theses', which had originally been banned, had long

[39] Wallmann (2012: 57).

since been superseded by more radical writings. Thus, Luther's Reformation movement survived his excommunication. Luther himself burned the bull together with his students at the end of the 60-day period he had been given to recant by the bull *Exsurge Domine*, showing once again that he had never really believed in a reconciliation with the Pope.[40]

The Philosophical Argument

By 1520 Luther had brought his own personal struggle for freedom to a provisional conclusion. He was now a free man. The document which confirmed his emancipation like no other was the *Freiheitsschrift*. He described it as the sum of what constitutes a Christian life. In it, Luther summarises his theology of justification, according to which the righteousness of the Christian flows only from faith, and he describes its liberating implications and its moral consequences.

The text starts with an apparent paradox, which Luther expresses in the two central theses: *A Christian is a free lord over all things and subject to no-one. A Christian is a bound servant of all things and subject to everyone* (§1).[41] Luther immediately offered the means to resolve this contradiction. He characterised every person as consisting of a holy, spiritual nature on the one hand and a physical nature on the other (§2). Thus freedom can be understood as characterising the spiritual nature, and servitude the physical nature.[42]

The theme of the first part of the text is the spiritual nature of

---

[40] Cf. Roper (2016: 219–23).

[41] Paragraph references are to the text and English translation in this edition.

[42] By comparison in Plato, Socrates asks: 'Yet once more consider the matter in another light: When the soul and the body are united, then nature orders the soul to rule and govern, and the body to obey and serve. Now which of these two functions is akin to the divine? and which to the mortal? Does not the divine appear to you to be that which naturally orders and rules, and the mortal to be that which is subject and servant?' Plato, *Phaidon* 79e–80a.

humanity – an examination of what the freedom of a Christian entails and how it comes into being. In the discussion of the physical nature which follows, Luther elaborates the thesis of the servitude of human nature. When one examines Luther's handling of the theme of freedom beyond the treatise, it is not clear whether he affirms freedom or not, for his rejection of human free will, as discussed below, raises the question of what kind of freedom he actually ascribes to a Christian.

In the treatise however, the answer is clear. Freedom consists in the unconditional determination of the human condition through belief in God and trust in Jesus Christ: 'You should give yourself over to him with firm faith and trust in him directly. Then for the sake of this faith all your sins shall be forgiven ..., and you will be ... freed from all things.' (§6)

Being directed by God and trusting in Christ are psychological states of the human condition. As such, they are independent from bodily existence and are not determined by anything physical. Only through words can the soul be influenced in a way which brings about change in one's thoughts and one's will.[43]

For Luther, 'nothing external can make [people] either free or righteous.' (§3 but qualified in §21 which states that the body needs to be 'chastened', since otherwise it inhibits the soul from being governed by God). The significance of a freedom which proceeds only from the individual relationship of faith in Christ can be viewed against the backdrop of late medieval devotional piety. According to this view, those who are corrupted by sin can only stand before a God who seeks justice through the sacrament of penance.

True penance consists of the threefold acts of oral confession (*confessio oris*), correctional work (*satisfactio operis*), and honest,

---

[43] Slenczka (2017: 27).

heartfelt repentance (*contritio cordis*).[44] The need to balance out the sins on one's own shoulders with good deeds took many colourful forms in the late Middle Ages, for example holding private requiems, pilgrimages, the veneration of the saints and holy relics, and relief of the burden of sin by the purchase of indulgences.[45] Luther's understanding of freedom defines the soul's relationship with God as faith alone and thereby makes it independent of all outward things, leading to a rejection of penance in the form inherited from the Middle Ages, namely as a financial transaction rather than an inward act of repentance.[46] However, the treatise does not limit itself to discrediting works carried out for the purpose of becoming justified before God. It also questions the theological legitimacy of all church institutions which are supposed to mediate between God and the faithful Christian, in that it pronounces all Christians to be kings and priests (§15).

Luther's depiction of Christian freedom is therefore a consequence of his theology of justification of the sinner. By faith alone, justification frees us from all our efforts to gain favour with God.

Luther and Augustine

Luther starts out from the medieval theology of penance (Thesis 1 of the '95 Theses': *When our Lord and master Jesus Christ said, 'Do penance, etc.', he meant the whole life of the faithful to be penance*) but then proposes the alternative of justification by faith. However, he remains trapped by humanity's enslavement to sin, which necessitated the theology of justification in the first place. Luther regards the individual's relationship with God as dependent on justification, because of the individual's 'bad and corrupted nature' (WA 1, 224: No. 9). Humans, by their very nature, can therefore do nothing good. This anthropology of the bad nature also appears in

---

[44] Leppin (2014: 56).

[45] Hauschild (2001: 22).

[46] Dingel (2014: 127–28).

the *Freiheitsschrift*. Here, Luther portrays humans' inability to do good in connection with the role of Old Testament laws. For Luther the Bible consisted of two parts: the law, which illustrates one's own sinfulness and leads to despair, and the promise, which proclaims grace and redemption through faith alone. This ultimately leads the individual to despair about the law and forms the foundation of a relationship with God (§8).

Here, the influence of Augustine on Luther's conception of freedom becomes clear. With Augustine's help, Luther was, like St Paul, able to reach the insight, crucial for the Reformation, that God's justice does not judge sinners, but clothes them in justice (WA 54, 186: 16–18). In the writings of Augustine which influenced Luther, freedom is described, much as in Luther's text, as a result of justice, which itself is a consequence of faith.[47] As Augustine states, 'Whereas through the law we come to a recognition of sin, through faith we attain grace against sin; through grace, the healing of the soul from sin's disease; through the recovery of the soul, freedom; through freedom, a love of justice; and through justice, the fulfilment of the law'.[48]

In Augustine, as in the *Freiheitsschrift*, the same purification of the soul is sketched out, from humanity's damnable nature in the sight of the law through to the attainment of justification. In Augustine's writings liberation from sin is depicted as healing the soul from an illness from which it is suffering. The sick soul finds its remedy in the gift of grace. Both in Augustine and in Luther, liberation from sin has two dimensions. The first is characterised by the fact that it erases the sins which burden every human being. But since human sinfulness is also an inability to aspire to good, justice must above all consist in the reorientation of the sinner from evil to good.

---

[47] It was primarily Augustine's later writings to/against the Pelagians which helped Luther to achieve a 'Breakthrough': *De spiritu et littera*, *De nuptiis et concupiscentia*, and *Contra Iulianum*, cf. Anderas (2017: 4).

[48] Augustinus, *De spiritu et littera*, in: CSEL 60, 30: 52.

Elsewhere, Augustine describes this notion in the context of lust (*concupiscentia*): the law is something good to which humans cannot aspire without God because evil lives in the form of lust in their will. Humans can only be 'genuinely free' through the grace of God, through which it becomes possible to feel joy in God's law voluntarily.[49] The law (or the 'good') which without faith remains out of reach can, through faith, be fulfilled. This insight is the central point of the treatise. The freedom of a Christian is not only freedom from sin, but also and above all, freedom to attain goodness.[50]

With the help of a metaphor, Luther illustrates the notion of the faith that frees believers from all sins. After describing liberation from sin and the attainment of justification from a unification of the soul with Christ (§10), he symbolises this unification by the metaphor of the relationship of bride and bridegroom (§12). Just as married couples make their property communal, so also Christian and Christ form a union in which the characteristics of the soul, its 'bad habits and sins', are transferred to Christ, and the characteristics of Christ, 'all goodness and salvation', are transferred to the soul.

The image of the *matrimonium christi et christiani* is interesting in many respects. Since a marriage is characterised only by the two partners that constitute it, Luther could use this image to underline the exclusivity of the relationship between the individual soul and Christ. In addition, the legal status as well as the identity of the partner are transformed in marriage. In the same way, the moral status and identity of the soul are transformed through the community in faith.

---

[49] Augustinus, *De nuptiis et concupiscentia*, in: CSEL 42, 30: 33.

[50] Freedom is not freedom of choice for Augustine. In one of his later writings Augustine allows an opponent to ask why God would reward those who have the will to believe, and punishes others, if it is God's grace alone which creates the will to believe. Augustine states that he cannot solve this puzzle. Augustinus, *De dono perseverantiae*, in: CSEL 105, 8: 18.

Moreover, the metaphor demonstrates the influence on Luther of the mystical theology which flourished alongside medieval Scholasticism.[51] In mystical theology, from the time of Bernard of Clairvaux and his reading of the Song of Songs, the image of the bride was used to portray the intimacy of the relationship between the soul and God.[52] Luther valued not only Bernard's message of the mercy and love of God, which was oriented towards Christ, but also the fact that Bernard developed his theology by constantly referring to the word of God.[53]

Luther probably also encountered the image of bride and bridegroom in the theology of his former father confessor and mentor Johann von Staupitz, who used it frequently. The role of the metaphor for his 'Frömmigkeitstheologie' (theology inspired by devotion) can be seen, for example, in Staupitz's Passion sermons from the year 1512 in which he draws up a theology of repentance, oriented towards Christ's suffering.[54] In the third sermon, he illustrates this by using the image of the marital bond between soul and Christ. Here, the 'poor, common, suffering, helpless bride' has nothing to bring but her sins and is only able to acquire high standing through the rich possessions of the bridegroom.[55] Only through the inner-empathetic appropriation of Christ's suffering does the sinful soul become capable of true repentance.[56] In his

---

[51] For more on the argument between the *via antiqua* and *via moderna*, cf. Dieter (2014: 32).

[52] Gerleman (2011).

[53] Zimmerling (2017); Leppin (2014: 52–53).

[54] Luther had possibly read the bride metaphor in Staupitz's *Libellus de Executione Aeternae Praedestinationis*, C.9, cf. Zu Dohna (2012: 142–49).

[55] Schneider-Lastin (1990: 129).

[56] The important difference for Luther is that the soul, through the union with Christ, does not receive Christ's suffering and the repentance flowing from it, but justification and freedom. That Luther had outgrown the theology of Staupitz by

accompanying writings to the *Resolutiones*, the explanation of his '95 Theses' against indulgences which Luther dedicated to Staupitz, Luther recalls conversations with him about penance. Luther describes his teacher's insight that true repentance begins with a love of justice and love of God hitting him like an arrow, transforming that hated word 'penance' into the sweetest of words (WA 1, 525, 4–23). From these conversations, Luther gained the insight that the individual's direct, inner bond with Christ, founded on love and repentance, is more important for the forgiveness of sins than the outward practices of confessing and the performance of good works. The change in Luther's understanding of penance was a landmark on the way towards *sola fide* and, in a reminiscence, makes an appearance in the *Freiheitsschrift* in the image of the marital bond.

As clear as the metaphor of the bridal couple may be, it is difficult to understand the theological theory behind it. For Luther, the transformation of those who believe is connected with their faith in Christ, in which they appropriate Christ's justification. It is at least possible that he is processing Thomistic theories of knowledge and mind. In the Aristotelianism of Thomas Aquinas, all natural creatures consist of forms, which constitute the creature's features, and matter, which constitutes the creature's individuality. According to this view, every perception or recognition of an object is linked to a change of the form of that which perceives it.[57] As such, the cognitive form of the perceiver changes in order to align itself with the perceived object. For Thomas, to relate to something though faith or awareness means to become spiritually similar to it.[58] Likewise,

---

1520 is shown in a remark in the *Freiheitsschrift* on repentance, §25: 'There are indeed still preachers who preach repentance for sin, and also grace, but they do not emphasise God's commandments and promises so that one might learn whence and why repentance and grace come. For repentance flows from the commandments, and faith from the promises of God'.

[57] By seeing a red object the observer receives the shape of the redness of the object and thereby the cognitive shape of the red becomes manifest in some way.

[58] Brower and Brower-Toland (2008: 193–243).

Luther says that the believer becomes like Christ in the sense that the believer receives righteousness and salvation through faith.[59]

Aside from all this, the metaphor of Christ as bridegroom in characterising the relation of the soul to Christ is useful, as it draws on medieval and early modern expectations about the natural and proper relation between wife and husband. At that time, the marital relationship between husband and wife was to a large extent a hierarchical one, in which the wife, according to canon law, was subordinate to the husband and was obliged to be obedient to him.[60] Alongside the mystical associations of intimacy and unity, the parallel of the soul and the bride on the question of a Christian's freedom also evokes the soul's dependence on Christ.

Luther's Rejection of Free Will

This brings us to a key qualification of Christian freedom: freedom of a Christian is not freedom of the will. In accordance with tradition, Luther tackles the notion of human free will in the context of the question of the individual's role in attaining faith and grace.[61]

Luther makes unambiguously clear at many stages of his career that the freedom of a Christian cannot be free will, that is, it cannot be freedom in the sense of total self-determination and independence to choose between good and evil, salvation and damnation. As early as 1517, in his 'Theses against Scholastic Theology' (WA 1, 224–28), he sets out the arguments which he goes on to develop in the

---

[59] It would not have pleased Luther that the theological core of his justification doctrine, which describes the mechanisms of justification by faith, are reduced to Thomas's theory of mental reference. As Luther said in 1532: *There is not one word in Thomas that inspires reliance on Christ.* (WA.TR 2, 192: 5–6). But the similarity is still striking.

[60] McDougall (2013: 171).

[61] In the reply to Erasmus, Luther said that it is necessary to be clear about the existence of free human will, for otherwise nothing would be known about Christians and their role in the attainment of salvation or about God. WA 18, 614: 1–12.

controversy with Erasmus in 1525.

Luther rejects human initiative in attaining salvation for three reasons. First, he derives the impossibility of human free will from the classical attributes of God: omniscience and omnipotence.[62] Secondly, he argues on the grounds of divine grace. If God's turning towards humans is an act of grace, then humans can take on only a passive role, since any active role on their part would be an appropriation of salvation and a usurpation of grace.[63]

Luther's third argument against free will is that the will is constituted in such a way that it is either directed towards good or towards evil, and that no third option is possible (*tertium non datur*). In this way, will is predestined by that towards which it is directed. If will were not predestined, it would be empty in content, and a will without content is not a will. In a famous passage, Luther depicts this graphically: human will is like a riding animal, with either God or Satan holding the reins. Without one or the other, the animal never gets very far in any direction of its own accord (WA 18, 635: 17–22).

This rejection of human free will is wholly in line with Luther's theological programme of justification. Not only are people incapable of altering their status as sinners through the performance of good works: they cannot even attain faith of their own accord. Luther's rejection of free will thus carries the idea of human passivity in salvation to an extreme.

The freedom of Christians is thus not grounded in some self-determination through which, by their own efforts, they can choose the object of their faith and their will. Instead, freedom exists for Luther in the specific way thoughts and wishes are determined, that is, through Christ alone. Freedom is not achieved by an act of faith or an act of will, but by the object to which faith and the will relate.

---

[62] Dieter (2014: 41–42).

[63] WA 18, 668: 2–3.

Luther was neither the first nor the last not to link freedom and responsibility to the condition of complete self-determination but considered it compatible with the determinism of humans.[64]

Luther's Ethics

The freedom which we have discussed so far pertains to the soul. Servitude, which is the subject of the second opening proposition, pertains to the body. There is, however, a crucial difference. While it is possible for the soul to become justified independently from the body, it is not possible for the body to act without receiving instructions from the soul. There is a certain incongruity between the two dichotomies, as *the opposition [between freedom and servitude] is already there with the clergy.*[65] If servitude applies only to the outward person (§19), then the body cannot be in servitude on its own, and the liberated soul is placed in the world together with the body and is also required to act. The servitude caused by the body's dependence on the world is an obligation to good behaviour and to the performance of good works, so that Christians can 'govern their own bodies and deal with people' (§20). The freedom of a Christian is therefore not freedom from morality.

Luther wrote about morality in the *Sermon von den guten Werken* 'Sermon on Good Works' shortly before the *Freiheitsschrift*. In this work, *sola fide* takes on the character of a commandment, in which faith in Christ is the ultimate and most noble work (WA 6, 204: 25–26). In this definition the ultimate work is not identified as a work to be performed, but as a state of mind, to which all performed works are morally subordinate. Accordingly, no work, whatever its positive consequences, can be good if it does not stem from belief in God: something as minor as picking up a straw can be called good if done in belief, while raising the dead would not be good if done in

[64] For an overview of Compatibilism cf. McKenna and Coates (2020).
[65] Rieger (2007: 74).

unbelief (WA 6, 206: 9–13).

In this way, Luther's moral code in the *Sermon von den guten Werken* focuses not on what the doer brings about in the world, but on the attitude with which it is done.[66] The condition for any deed to be good is that it originates in faith in Christ. For some deeds, like picking up a straw, faith is not simply a necessary condition, but a sufficient one for it to be good. But is faith the only precondition for a good deed? In other words, can faith sanctify every reprehensible and evil deed? Luther would answer the first question with a 'yes', the second with a 'no'. The solution lies in the definition of faith. For him, certain guiding principles such as anger, revenge, and jealousy exclude true faith (WA 6, 266: 32–33). Actions which stem from such motives are thus not actions that are practised in good faith, and are therefore not good. In order to classify every motive that is incompatible with genuine belief in Christ, Luther refers to the state of meekness (*Sanftmut*, as exemplified in II Corinthians 10,1) which excludes all bad intentions. Meekness for him is fundamentally good, since it does not damage anything or anybody even if one is robbed of one's possessions, honour, life, and friends (WA 6, 266: 14–17).

Consequently, faith is the only condition and it is sufficient to make works good. Indeed, faith in its ideal form leads the believer to a way of thinking which is free from anger, revenge, and jealousy. For Luther, actions prompted by this way of thinking cannot be reprehensible or evil. Faith, properly understood, is therefore incompatible with bad deeds.

Faith does not just exclude bad behaviour, though: it can even lead to a life of charity. In the *Freiheitsschrift* Luther does not speak of meekness, but characterises the state in which correct behaviour is possible as a one of love: 'Behold, in this way love and longing for God flow out of faith, and from this love flows a free, willing, joyful

---

[66] Gerhardt (2018: 21).

life serving one's neighbour without reward'. (§27) Only when individuals put themselves fully in the service of others are they truly secure through faith and through their trust in Christ. Since only those who are in every way turned towards Christ through faith are also free, freedom is only possible through service to one's neighbour, that is, in servitude.

The freedom of a Christian is thus ultimately characterised by the individual's moral responsibility with respect to the interests, needs, and demands of one's neighbour. With the pairing of freedom and ethics, Luther's theology is an early blueprint of modern theories in which freedom only thrives in responsibility and morality. This thought becomes prominent in Kant's critical philosophy: 'Freedom and absolute practical law point reciprocally to one another'.[67] Even more important, however, are the implications of Reformation theology for ethical discourse in general. In overcoming the self-interest inherent in the pursuit of justification before God, one's field of vision becomes clear, and is reoriented to the needs of one's neighbour.[68]

Conclusion

So, was Luther liberated or liberator? He saw himself as liberated, as is shown in the emphasis he places on the passivity of the believer in attaining justification. His gradual separation from the papal church

---

[67] The source from which both freedom and moral obligation flow is not faith in Kant, but practical reason. Immanuel Kant: KpV, AA 05: 29.24–25.

[68] Of particular interest is Susan Wolf's philosophy on the question of the relevance of Luther's understanding of freedom. For her, a concept of freedom which grants people absolute autonomy over themselves is irreconcilable with the fact that people always make their decisions against a background of numerous connections and influences. Taking these circumstances into consideration, Wolf defines freedom as the ability to do the correct thing for the right reasons. Free decisions are aimed at *the true and the good*. As for Luther, freedom in Wolf consists of allowing oneself to be guided to act in the right way. Unlike for Luther, truth and good are not universal for Wolf, but dependent on context. Cf. Wolf (1990).

was something he similarly perceived as his own liberation. Nevertheless, his activity as a writer indicates that he was eager to impart his liberating insights to all Christians. As a result of his own liberation, Luther believed it to be his duty to free his neighbours from the chains that had shackled him for half his life.

It is important, however, to remember that Luther exclusively addresses spiritual freedom. To regard him as a pioneer of our modern political conception of freedom, which encompasses an equality of all people in the physical world, would be false. Ultimately, Luther connected freedom with Christian faith and service to one's neighbour.

2. The History of the Taylorian Copies

Maximilian Krümpelmann[69]

The success of the *Freiheitsschrift* was partly made possible by the rapid development of printing technology, especially the rising popularity of 'pamphlets', short texts usually consisting of fewer than 20 pages, produced with a quick turn-around in successive editions and large print-runs.[70]

Johannes Rhau-Grunenberg, who had already published Luther's '95 Theses' in his Wittenberg workshop, produced 3,000 to 4,000 copies of the first edition, a large number compared to the average print-run of the period which amounted to between of 500 to 1,500.[71] The German version was reprinted five times in that year in three places – Wittenberg, Augsburg, and Strasbourg – and the Latin in Antwerp and Vienna. Soon after, the texts were reissued in further cities such as Speyer, Nuremberg, and Zürich. Additionally, the work was translated into several other national languages in the following decades: Czech (1521), French (1525), Italian (1547), Spanish (1540), and English (1579).[72]

The Taylor Institution Library houses copies of four different editions of the *Freiheitsschrift*, printed in Wittenberg and Speyer between 1520 and 1522. These copies constitute a case in point for the major role that printing played in the dissemination of Luther's theology. Each of the four editions in the Taylorian tells a slightly

---

[69] The chapter was originally written as a post for the History of the Book blog https://historyofthebook.mml.ox.ac.uk/2020/10/18/eleutheria-luthers-freiheitsschrift-as-a-publishing-phenomenon/ and shortened for this context.

[70] Köhler (1986: 256) calculates that in 1524 alone, 2,400 pamphlets with a total print-run of 2.4 million copies were produced.

[71] Kaufmann (2017: 56). Comparator numbers from Gaskell (2015) and Gilmont (2016).

[72] Cf. the overview on the inside cover of exhibition catalogue Slenczka (2017).

different story of production and reception; the individual copies give information not only about how they were produced, but about who their contemporary audience might have been and how the text was treated as a material object.

Most of the Reformation texts in the Taylorian were acquired in the nineteenth century with the help of its second Professor for Modern European Languages, Max Friedrich Müller (1823–1900). Many of these were procured by the librarian Heinrich Krebs (1844–1921), notably from Heidelberg in 1878.[73] This is most likely the case for all four copies,[74] as reflected in the range of the – obsolete and current – shelf marks and dates noted on the bookplate of the Taylorian Library, which are located on the upper pastedown of the pamphlets and allow the identification of all four acquisition dates.

The first edition by Rhau-Grunenberg shows the date *1878* underneath an *exlibris* and therefore likely belonged to the Heidelberg collection that was purchased by Krebs; above the bookplate, two previous shelf marks are crossed out: *92 b 25* and *Arch II b 36.*

Ill. 1: Taylorian, ARCH.8°.G.1520(25); cf. also the facsimile at the end and online

[73] Cf. chapter 2.2. on the acquisition history of Taylorian copies of the 'Sermon von Ablass und Gnade', https://editions.mml.ox.ac.uk/editions/ablassgnade5/.

[74] Cf. Benzing and Claus (1966), 87–91, nos 734–769, here nos 734, 741, 744, 760. For the online versions of the prints, cf. the VD16, nos VD16 L 7202, L 7201, L 4663, L 7205.

The Speyer version ARCH.8°.G.1519(11/14) was bought in 1877 from a private collection as the date and the entry *W. O. Abel.1835* show.

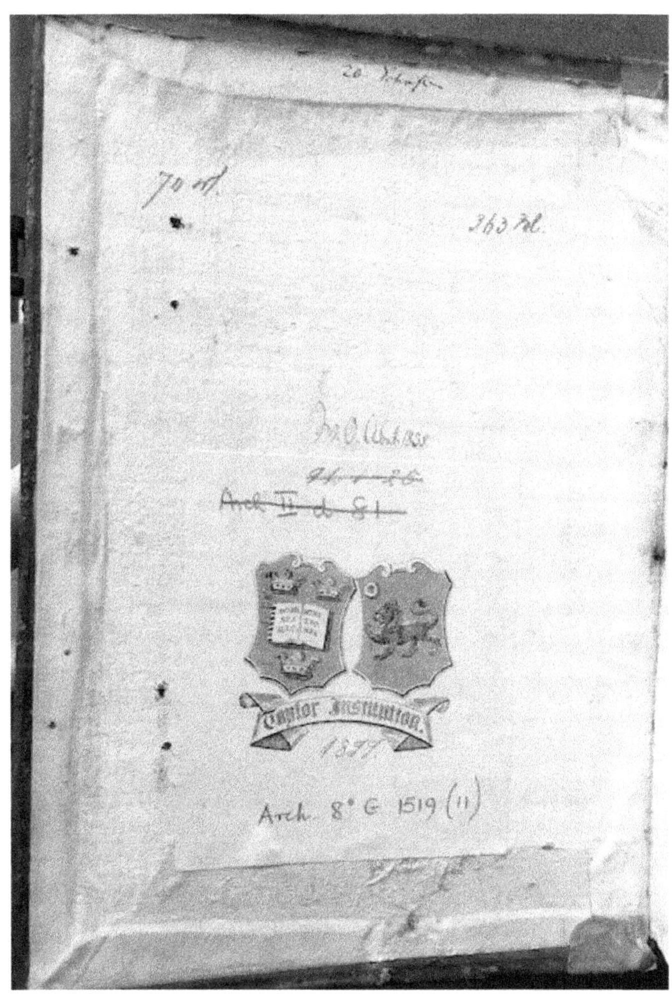

Ill. 2: Taylorian, ARCH.8°.G.1519(11)

The Latin *Freiheitsschrift*, ARCH.8°.G.1521(10) also has the old version of the Taylorian bookplate and two obsolete shelf marks, *91 a 2e* and *Arch II b 47*.

The earliest acquisition by the Taylorian has the newest binding. The German edition by Melchior Lotter the Younger, ARCH.8°.G. 1521(25), displays the modern bookplate of the Taylorian, which was introduced in 1975,[75] and only one old shelf mark on the pastedown, *Arch II b 60*. This was presumably done to give it better protection than the blue paper cover from the 19th century, which is now bound in behind the pamphlet.

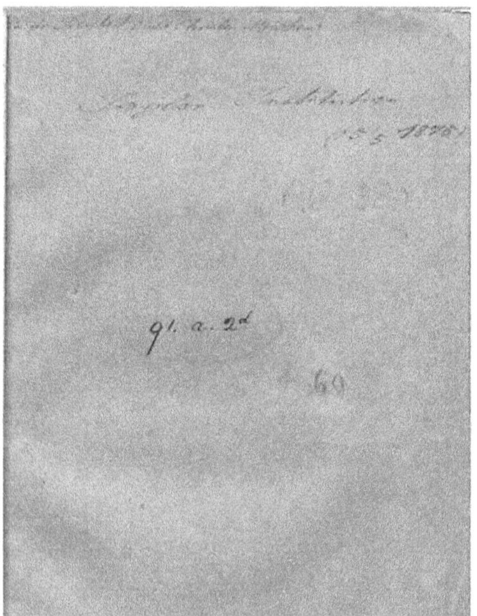

Ill. 3: Taylorian, ARCH.8°.G.1521(25)

On this blue paper of a type used by German booksellers, a modern hand registered the title (*Von dr Freyheit eines Christen Menschen*), the holding library (*Taylor Institution*), and the acquisition date (*15/5/1875*), as well as the original shelf mark (*91.a.2*[d]). On the rear side of the cover we can find yet another owner's mark alongside the date *1856*, testifying to the reuse of the pamphlet over the centuries.

---

[75] Cf. the blog post by Thomas (2019) on the Taylorian editions of *Il Pastor fido*.

1. Johannes Rhau-Grunenberg: Low-quality Printing?

Martin Luther, Von der Freiheit eines Christenmenschen
[Wittenberg, Johannes Rhau-Grunenberg 1520]
Title: Uon der Freyheyt || eynisz Christen || menschen. || Martinus Luther. ||
Imprint: Uittembergae. || Anno Domini || 1520.
12 sheets in 4to. Quire signatures: Aij, Aiij, B, Bij, Biij, C, Cij, Ciij
Taylor Institution Library, ARCH.8°.G.1520(25)
Woodcut by Lucas Cranach the Elder[76]
WA 7, 15, no A; Benzing/Claus (1966: 87), no 734; Benzing (1963: 465); VD16 L 7202

Unlike trade hubs such as Augsburg, Cologne, or Nuremberg, Wittenberg only began to emerge as a centre for printing during the Reformation.[77] Apart from two academic in-house print shops established by two professors of the recently founded University at Wittenberg, Johannes Rhau-Grunenberg was the only printer in town when he set up his workshop in 1508, the same year Luther was appointed to a professorship there.[78] For some time, Rhau-Grunenberg, who also published other reformatory pamphlets e.g. by Andreas Bodenstein and Heinrich von Kettenbach,[79] remained the only printer to issue Luther's writings.

Although Luther later described Rhau-Grunenberg as a pious and commendable man (*Erat pius homo et benedicebatur*)[80] and continued to commission books at his workshop throughout his life, he was dissatisfied with the quality of some of his output. In a letter addressed to Georg Spalatin, we find Luther complaining about Rhau-Grunenberg's *editio princeps* of his sermon *Von der Beicht* (1521):

---

[76] Rhau-Grunenberg used the woodcut again for other editions, e.g. VD16 L 7031.
[77] Cf. the number of printers in the respective cities at the time in Benzing (1963).
[78] Cf. ibid., 465; cf. also Reske (2015: 35–69).
[79] Cf. e.g. VD16 B 6121 (Bodenstein) and VD16 K 808 (Kettenbach).
[80] WA.Tr 2, 58 (*Tischrede* 1532).

> Sed mirum est, quam me peniteat & pigeat eius excusionis. vtinam nihil vernaculi misissem! ita sordide, ita negligenter, ita confuse excuduntur, vt typorum & papyri dissimulem sordes. Iohannes Calcographus est Iohannes in eodem tempore.[81]
> [I can't tell you how much I regret and resent this print. I should never have sent a German manuscript! So dirty, so careless, so disorderly is the print, not to mention the dirt of the types and the paper. The printer Johannes always stays the same, he is incorrigible.]

What exactly was the reason for the apparently poor quality of Rhau-Grunenberg's work? One problem that he was facing might have been the growing demand for his relatively small workshop in the wake of the Reformation, especially after 1518.[82] Additionally, the *typorum & papyri* [...] *sordes*, which Luther complains about, were a result of the increasingly worn-out typeset Rhau-Grunenberg was using, and which he had inherited from his predecessor, Nikolaus Marschalk, when he settled in Wittenberg.[83] If so, it is possible that his edition of the *Freiheitsschrift* from November 1520 – a few months before Luther sent his disgruntled letter to Spalatin – already shows some of the defects that the reformer complained about later.

Indeed, a quick look at the text of Rhau-Grunenberg's first edition of the German *Freiheitsschrift* already reveals some of the flaws which Luther bemoaned: compared to the crisply defined imprint by Melchior Lotter, the edges of Rhau-Grunenberg's letters seem blurry and smudged, testifying to the poor quality of the types he was using. Additionally, the text block is not well aligned with the paper, so the text appears to be on a slant. The title-page conveys a similarly disorderly impression.

---

[81] WA.Br 2, 380.

[82] Weber (2017: 107).

[83] Cf. Benzing (1963: 465).

Dem furſichtigen vñ weyßen herrn
Hieronymo Mulphordt/Stadvogt zu Zwick-
aw meynem beßondernn gunſtigen freund vñ
Patron/Empiete ich genant D. Martinus
Luther Auguſt. meyne willige dienſt/vñ
allis guttis.

Ill. 4: Taylorian, ARCH.8°.G.1521(25), A1v

Dem furſichtigen vñ weyßen herrn
Hieronymo Mülphordt Stadvogt zu Zwyckaw mey-
nen beſondern günſtigen freund vnd Patron
Empiete ich genant D. Martinus Lu-
ther Auguſt. meyne willige dienſt
vnnd allis guttis.

Ill. 5: Taylorian, ARCH.8°.G.1520(25), A2r, cf. facsimile at the end

Even though the edition by Rhau-Grunenberg is the only one of the four Taylorian copies to include a woodcut, its quality is likewise evidence of the printer's hasty execution: the bottom part of the woodcut title frame seems to have been sawn off and not fully aligned when reattached, and there is a fold in the paper which now runs as a diagonal white line through the bottom left-hand corner; this might have contributed to Luther's frustration with Rhau-Grunenberg, especially when he became acquainted with the quality of other printers such as Melchior Lotter in 1519.

Von der Freyheyt eynisz Christen menschen.

Martinus Luther.

Vuittembergae. Anno Domini 1520.

Ill. 6: Taylorian, ARCH.8°.G.1520(25) , cf. facsimile at the end

The original woodcut for the border came from the workshop of Lucas Cranach, a cachet for Luther's Wittenberg production in general.[84] Rhau-Grunenberg continued to use the border, e.g. in an edition of Luther's pamphlet on marriage *Uom Eelichen Leben*.[85] In both cases, the typeset imprint comprises the title (*Uon der Freyheyt* || *eynisz Christen* || *menschen.*), author (*Martinus Luther.*), place and date (*Uittembergae.* || *Anno Domini* || *1520.*), centred in large Gothic font. The border itself includes three coats of arms of the city of Wittenberg: at the centre of the top two crossed swords (*Kur-Schwerter*); at the centre of the bottom the city as a fortified place with two towers on either side, flanking a third, decidedly smaller coat of arms including a crancelin.

The rest of the border shows three sets of figures: at the top two semi-nude hybrid creatures; their figures emerge from a grapevine and flank the upper coat of arms. On the left border of the woodcut is an old, bearded man wearing a hat and holding a rosary, while a squirrel is sitting on his right shoulder, his feet hidden by an ornamental basin which is part of the architectural framing. Opposite him, likewise emerging from a basin, Amor as honey-thief is shown reaching out for a hive; his naked body is surrounded by several bees. At the bottom border, two large hybrid sea-creatures flank the coat of arms.

The verso side of the title-page is left empty, followed by the dedication to the Zwickau mayor, Hermann Mühlpfordt, on a separate page; this text is only present in the German version of the *Freiheitsschrift*. The address to Mühlpfordt is centred in the middle of the page, with the first line printed in larger font size (*Dem fursichtigen vnd weyszen hern*) than the rest.

The actual treatise follows on A2v and was used for the Weimar edition.[86] Again, the first line – as well as the centred invocatio *Jhesus* (A2v) – is presented in large font. After this, Luther begins to present his reform programme, each of the 30 passages being introduced by

---

[84] Kaufmann (2017: 56).

[85] Cf. VD16 L 7031, https://opacplus.bsb-muenchen.de/title/BV023482612.

[86] Cf. WA 7, 15, no A.

a new paragraph indicated by a pilcrow. The text finishes with the – once again centred – word *AMEN* (C4v) in capital letters and spaces in between each letter.

Rhau-Grunenberg's *editio princeps* presents itself as a typical Reformation print from Wittenberg, which includes an ostentatious woodcut on the title-page. However, despite being free of spelling mistakes, the execution of the print is comparatively poor. Perhaps it was the long acquaintance with Luther and the fact that for some time Rhau-Grunenberg remained the only printer to issue his works that led the reformer to continue commissioning books at his workshop until at least 1527, two years before Rhau-Grunenberg's death.[87]

2. Melchior Lotter the Younger: The Better Printer?

Martin Luther, Von der Freiheit eines Christenmenschen
[Wittenberg, Melchior Lotter the Younger 1521]
Title: Uon der Freyheyt eynis || Christen menschen. || Martinus Luther. ||
Imprint: Uittembergae. M.D.Xxi
14 sheets in 4to. Quire signatures: aij, aiij, b, bij, biij, c, cij, ciij, ciiij
Taylor Institution Library, ARCH.8°.G.1521(25)
WA 7, 17, no L; Benzing/Claus, 88, no 744; Benzing (1963: 466); VD16 L 7201

In the same letter addressed to Spalatin from August 1521, in which Luther complains about Rhau-Grunenberg's slovenly print, he praises three sheets of paper in quarto form sent to him by Philip Melanchthon. They contain his pamphlet against Jacobus Latomus *Rationis Latomiæ* (1521), produced by another printer in Wittenberg;[88] Luther declares himself delighted and remarks that the sample sheets 'please him greatly' (*qui valde placet*)[89].

---

[87] Cf. Weber (2017: 107).
[88] WA 7, 41, no A.
[89] WA.Br 2, 380.

The printer Luther is referring to here is Melchior Lotter the Younger (ca 1490–1542). His father was Melchior Lotter the Elder, who established himself as one of the most influential printers of humanist and reformatory texts in Leipzig.[90] In a letter to Spalatin dating from 1519, Luther mentions a visit of the old Melchior Lotter to Wittenberg and praises his excellent Frobenian typeset.[91] The quality of his prints must have left an impression on the reformer, since shortly afterwards he and four other professors at the university, who expressed displeasure at the quality of Rhau-Grunenberg's results, asked Lotter to settle in Wittenberg.[92] Even though Lotter the Elder did not relocate, he sent his son to establish a second printing press in Wittenberg in the same year.[93]

The *Freiheitsschrift* by Lotter the Younger preserved in the Taylorian is listed as edition L in the *Weimarer Ausgabe* (WA 7: 16). It was printed the following year in 1521, which is indicated on the title-page (*Uittembergae. M.D.Xxi*). Looking at the text, it is clearly visible that Lotter was using a better typeset.

Dem fursichtigen vñ weyßzen herrn
Hieronymo Mulphordt/Stadvogt zu Zwick⸗
aw meynem beßondernn gunstigen freund vñ
Patron/Empiete ich genant D. Martinus
Luther August. meyne willige dienst/vñ
allis guttis.

Ill. 7: Taylorian, ARCH.8°.G.1521(25), A1v

Compared to Rhau-Grunenberg (cf. Ill. 5), the positioning of the frame on the sheet is good and creates an elegant, easily legible text. Additionally, Lotter reserves two more leaves for the treatise, as a consequence of which he is able to present the text more lavishly,

[90] Cf. Benzing (1963: 261).
[91] Cf. WA.Br 1, 381.
[92] Cf. Kaufmann (2017: 55–56).
[93] Benzing (1963: 466).

even though he does not leave the back of the title-page empty as Rhau-Grunenberg does, but rather leaves C6v blank, which – along with the title-page – was used as protection of the text from external grime. It therefore comes as no surprise that both the title-page and C6v are besmeared with printing ink. A contributing factor might have been the fact that the print at one point was part of a larger collection, which the numbering of the sheets by a modern hand indicates (51r-64v); Lotter's *Freiheitsschrift* seems to have been the third in the former *Sammelband*, cf. the number "3" on A1r in old ink; later the page number "51" was added, showing that the previous two pamphlets must have been longer treatises.

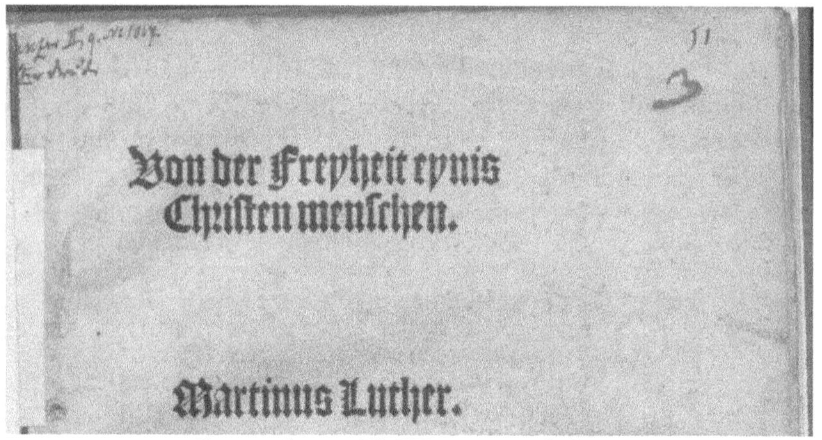

Ill. 8: Taylorian, ARCH.8°.G.1521(25), A1r
with the number "3" in the top right corner and the page number "51".

What sets apart his *Freiheitsschrift* from Rhau-Grunenberg's most clearly, however, is the fact that Lotter's does not include a woodcut on the title-page, but simply gives the title, author, and imprint in large Gothic font. This clearly renders edition L less ostentatious than Rhau-Grunenberg's. Lotter had issued a previous edition of the *Freiheitsschrift* the year before which did include a woodcut by Cranach. However, this earlier version – listed as B (WA 7: 16) – reveals a greater deviation from the original text issued by Rhau-Grunenberg. Therefore, it might come as a surprise that – apart from the non-existent woodcut – in most other aspects Lotter's later edition L is more indebted to Rhau-Grunenberg's *editio princeps* than his earlier version B.

Both A and L use a quarto form as well as Gothic font. Even the font size of the two prints is identical for the corresponding text passages: thus, both printers present the first lines of the address to Mühlpfordt (*Dem fursichtigen v] weyszen hern*) as well as the first lines of the treatise (*Jhesus* || *Zum ersten. Das wyr grundlich*) in the same large font centred in the middle of the page (cf. A1v, A1r in L). Interestingly though, Lotter interprets the date of the address to Mühlpfordt as an imprint. Instead of putting 'Wittenberg 1520' (as do Rhau-Grunenberg and Jacob Eckhart), he prints: *Zu Wytten/* || *berg. M D Xxi.* (A1v). Additionally, both editions make use of pilcrows to indicate the beginning of a new passage. At the end, both A and L centre the last sentence of passage 30 as well as the last, capitalised word *AMEN* with spaces in between each letter (cf. C6r in L).

Despite the use of the same type face and the overall indebtedness of L's to A's text, the two versions show minor differences, such as the use of Roman numerals instead of Arabic ones for quoting Bible passages, the tendency towards longer sentences with subordinate clauses, as well as a more thorough use of punctuation marks in Lotter's edition. There are, however, other noticeable differences in L as well. One is the singular and perhaps accidental replacement of the noun *reych* in §14 with *recht* in L: *Darumb ist er ein kunig vnd priester / doch geystlich / denn sein recht ist nit yrdnisch noch in yrdnischen / szondernn ynn geistlichen guttern* [...] (B2v); another is the accidentally printed syllable *te*: [...] *das alte te testament* (A4v).

Despite the overall better typeset, the better alignment and legibility of the text, Lotter's later edition L of the *Freiheitsschrift* is not the best evidence to justify Luther's praise for Lotter's craftsmanship, since it does include at least some spelling mistakes and lacks the decorative woodcuts of his other versions B from 1520 (WA 7: 16) and O from 1523 (WA 7: 17).

3. Melchior Lotter the Younger: An Edition Revised by Luther

> Martin Luther, Epistola Lutheriana ad Leonem decimum summum pontificem. Tractatus de libertate christiana
> [Wittenberg, Melchior Lotter the Younger 1521]
> Title: EPISTOLA || LVTHERIANA AD LEONEM || DECIMVM SVMMUM || PONTIFICEM. || LIBER DE CHRISTIANA LIBER= || tate, continens summam Christianæ doctri= || næ,quo ad formandam mentem, & ad in || telligendam Euāgelii vim, nihil absolu||tius, nihil cōducibilius neq a veteri= || bus neq a recentiori- bus scriptori || bus perditum est. Tu Christiane || lector, relege iterum atq || iterum, & Christum || imbibe. ❧ || RECOGNITVS WITTEMBERGAE.
> Imprint: ANNO DOMINI || M. D. XXI.
> 22 sheets in 4to, last page empty. Quire signatures: Aii, Aiii, B, Bii, Biii, C, Cii, Ciii, D, Dii, Diii, E, Eii, Eiii
> Taylor Institution Library, ARCH.8°.G.1521(10)
> edited as https://editions.mml.ox.ac.uk/editions/libertate1521/
> Woodcuts: letter F
> WA 7, 41, no E; Benzing/Claus, 90, no 760; Benzing (1963: 466); VD16 L 4663

In the same year that Lotter published his German version of the *Freiheitsschrift* he also issued a Latin one; a colophon can be found at the end of the tract: *ANNO DOMINI* || *M. D. XXI* (E4v). Compared to the relatively similar format of A and L, the Latin version stands in stark contrast to the two German editions. Perhaps most striking is the fact that Luther's Latin version is conceived as a textual unit with the *Epistola Lutheriana ad Leonem*. This is indicated clearly on the title-page.

Lotter prints the word *EPISTOLA* in large Roman font and the title of the *Freiheitsschrift* (*LIBER DE CHRISTIANA LIBER=* || *tate*) in capital letters. Unlike the German title and unlike earlier Latin versions by other printers, Lotter's Latin edition also includes a summary of the treatise on the title-page (*continens summam Christianæ doctri=* || *næ* [...]).

EPISTOLA
LVTHERIANA AD LEONEM
DECIMVM SVMMVM
PONTIFICEM.

LIBER DE CHRISTIANA LIBER-
tate, continens ſummam Chriſtianæ doctri-
næ, quo ad formandam mentem, & ad in-
telligendam Euāgelii vim, nihil abſolu-
tius, nihil cōducibilius neq; a veteri-
bus, neq; a recentioribus ſcriptori
bus ꝑditū eſt. Tu Chriſtiane
lector, relege iterum atq;
iterum, & Chriſtum
imbibe.

RECOGNITVS VVITTEMBERGAE.

Ill. 9: Taylorian, ARCH.8°.G.1521(10)

Whereas Rhau-Grunenberg integrates a Cranach woodcut in order to make his product more appealing and consequently increase sales, Lotter resorts to verbal advertising in his Latin edition, proclaiming that 'nothing is more beneficial from either the old or the more recent authors' (*nihil cōducibilius neq a veteri= || bus neq a recentioribus scriptori || bus*). He then adds: 'You, Christian reader, should reread it time and time again and absorb Christ' (*Tu Christiane || lector, relege iterum atq || iterum, & Christum || imbibe*).[94]

The title-page is then followed by the Latin version of the *Epistola*, which takes up sheets A1v–B1v. The treatise itself begins on B2r and is introduced with a woodcut initial 'F' in Roman font, which includes floral elements and spans the first seven lines of the text. What is most striking when looking at the text is that Lotter includes printed marginalia throughout the treatise, which enable the reader a quick overview of a section's content by giving the most important information in a poignant statement. Thus, the first two entries on B2r say *Fides tribula || tionibus disci || tur* ('Faith is learned in troubled times') and *Themata* ('Topics'), the latter of which refers to Luther's definition of man as master and servant.

What is perhaps most interesting about this is not so much the fact that Lotter includes explanatory notes in the margin, which was customary in many Latin prints at the time, but rather that Rhau-Grunenberg, who issued both the first German and Latin version, does not. Indeed, an attentive reader comparing both versions will quickly find that Rhau-Grunenberg's edition differs from Lotter's in many cases. A few examples can illustrate the case: already on the first page of the treatise we find several alterations: these include frequent changes in punctuation, such as the change from *consecutum posseque* (B1r) in Rhau-Grunenberg's edition, listed as A in the WA, to *consecutum, posseque* (B2r) in Lotter's version, listed as E.[95] There are also more prominent interventions, such as the replacement of individual words, e.g. *nunquam gustauerunt* (B1r) in A with *unquam gustauerunt* (B2r) in E or *nimirum* (B1r) in A with *nimio* (B2r) in E. On D3v in Rhau-Grunenberg's edition it says: *Sunt quam plurimi, qui hanc libertatem fidei audientes, mox eam in occasionem libertatis vertant.*

---

[94] The metaphorical use of 'imbibing' for 'drinking' the word of Christ is reminiscent of I Corinthians 10,4 in the Vulgate version: *et omnes eundem potum spiritalem biberunt bibebant autem de spiritali consequenti eos petra petra autem erat Christus.*

[95] Cf. WA 7, 15–16.

But Lotter omits the second use of the word *libertas* and instead inserts *carnis* (E3r)[96]:

> Sunt quam plurimi, qui hanc libertatem fidei audientes, mox eam in occasionem carnis vertant, ...
> [They are the overwhelming majority of those who, when they hear about this freedom obtained by faith, will then want to transform it into a pretext to indulge in the flesh.]

This passage of the *Freiheitsschrift* is only part of the Latin text, in which Luther attacks those who deliberately use Christian freedom as a pretext for indulging in licentiousness. By replacing the genitive *libertatis* with *carnis*, Lotter's version specifies the word 'freedom' and narrows its meaning down to 'carnal desire'.[97] This alteration is not grammatical or stylistic in nature; it substantially changes the meaning of the text.

Who was responsible for these changes? James Hirstein has recently cut the Gordian knot.[98] After coming across a personal pamphlet of Rhau-Grunenberg's *editio princeps* in the Humanist Library of Sélestat (K 809o), which was formerly in the possession of Beatus Rhenanus, he was able to identify the hands of both Rhenanus himself and Luther as well as at least two other hands in the marginalia. According to Hirstein, the text exhibits at least 135 significant changes that were made to Rhau-Grunenberg's version; 47 of these can be attributed to Luther himself, including the interpolation of *carnis*.[99] Hirstein asserts that the text in Sélestat served as a basis for the Basel print by Adam Petri that was produced in March 1521, listed as D (WA 7: 40). In turn, the Basel print then served as a basis for Lotter's edition in Wittenberg, which must have been produced some time between March and September that

---

[96] Text taken from the edition of the Taylorian copy prepared by Madeleine Ahern, https://editions.mml.ox.ac.uk/editions/libertate1521/#e3r.

[97] Cf. Hirstein (2015: 141).

[98] Cf. also Hirstein (2017a: 385–422) and Hirstein (2017b: 60–65).

[99] Hirstein (2017a: 411–12).

year.[100] Except for a few changes that can be attributed to Lotter's own workshop, both the Basel and the Wittenberg print display the same text. The fact that Luther reworked his Latin *Freiheitsschrift* also accounts for the note on Lotter's title-page: *RECOGNITUS WITTENBERGAE* ('Reviewed in Wittenberg'). However, unlike Adam Petri, Lotter does not add *PER AU* || *TOREM*; perhaps this can be taken as evidence that 'Wittenberg' had already become a cachet that was sufficiently associated with the increasingly popular reformer.[101] In any case, it displays the close communication that existed between the author, Luther, and his printers.

4. Johann Eckhart: A Personal Luther Collection

Martin Luther, Von der Freiheit eines Christenmenschen
[Speyer, Johann Eckhart 1522?]
Title: Uon der Freiheyt Eyns || Christen menschen || Martinus Luther ||
12 sheets in 40. Quire signatures: aii, aiii, b, bii, biii, c, cii, ciii, ciiii
Taylor Institution Library, ARCH.8°.G.1519(11/14)[102]
Marginalia in red ink from one hand
WA 7, 16, no H; Benzing/Claus, 88, no 741; Benzing (1963: 398); VD16 L 7205

The pamphlets in the Taylorian Library, however, do not only display the differences in the production of the prints; what makes the print from Speyer stand out from the other three Taylorian versions is not so much the edition itself, but the readership and ownership history revealed by the print. Unlike the three versions from Wittenberg, the Speyer one, likely produced in 1522, is not preserved as a single print, but is part of a larger, historic collection that includes nineteen German Luther texts, produced between 1519 and 1522. This is indicated by a modern hand on the spine of the

[100] Cf. Hirstein (2015: 133).
[101] Cf. Kaufmann (2017: 59).
[102] An edition of this copy is currently being prepared by Kiara Hart, to be published as https://editions.mml.ox.ac.uk/editions/freiheit-1522.

book: *19 Luther- || Pamphlets. || 1519 u.* The cover still has the original brown calfskin binding with two metal clasps on the front cover and the corresponding catch-plates on the back. Both front and back cover exhibit decorative elements, including a rectangular region created by four borders.

Ill. 10: Taylorian, ARCH.8°.G.1519(11)

These were produced by using a hot metal roll that was pressed onto the surface of the leather.[103] The design shows floral ornaments and faces as well as three coats of arms, including a lion, a double-headed eagle, as well as the coat of arms of Cologne, which figures three trident crowns over flames.[104] Inside the rectangle created by the borders, several blind stamps are visible, which illustrate a budding shrub with leaves extending to either side of its stem.

Consulting the Einbanddatenbank (EBDB) reveals that the identical design was also used for another book whose otherwise unknown workshop is listed as 'w007634'. It contains a print of Sebastian Brant's historiographic work *De origine et conversatione bonorum regum et de laude civitatis Hierosolymae* (1495).[105] Even though the

---

[103] Cf. Gaskell (2015: 149).

[104] Cf. Heiles (2016) for a description of the collective volume ARCH.8°.G.1519 (11).

[105] The book (Stadt- und Landesbibliothek Dortmund) is not digitised; cf. EBDB, https://www.hist-einband.de/de/kulturobjektdoku-mente/?v=210658b&h=false&ex=false&faces-redirect=true.

workshop cannot be identified, the coats of arms suggest that both books were bound in or close to Cologne.

Ill. 11: Taylorian, ARCH.8°.G.1519(11)

Opening up the *Sammelband* reveals annotations by several hands. On the pastedown, we find the bookplate of the Taylorian with the two old shelf marks and the current one as well as the acquisition date noted down by three hands in pencil; above the bookplate, another hand has registered an owner's mark: *W. O. Abel.1835.*[106] Both on the front and back of the fly leaf, a fourth, modern hand has noted down an entry from a sales catalogue, which advertises the collection:

> Von N. 1 sagt A. Strauß (s. dessen opera rariora quae latitant in Biblioth. Can. Reg. Colleg. eccles. ad S. Joh. Bapt. in Rebdorf), p. 136. "das Werkchen ist mit Lotherischen Schriften gedruckt, und wird vielfaeltig als die größste Seltenheit beschrieben. S. Fabricii Gentifol. P II.p.534.

The quote is taken from Andreas Strauß' *Opera Rariora*, which was published in 1790 and provides a list of rare works from the library of Austin canons in Rebdorf.[107] 'N. 1' refers to the first print in the collection, Luther's tract *Augustiners unterricht auff etlich artickell die im von seynen abgunnern auffgelegt und zu gewessen werden* (1519).[108] The entry might already have led W. O. Abel to buy the collection in 1835, before it was resold to the Taylorian in 1877.

On the back of the fly leaf, the same hand started to register the contents of the collection; and on the back pastedown, yet another modern hand registered the titles of all the prints. These include eighteen German texts by Luther as well as one letter in defence of him (no 12). Many of the works are pamphlets against his antagonists Hieronymus Emser (nos 6, 7, 9, 13) and Johannes Eck (nos 8, 16); but the collection also includes Luther's address *An den christlichen Adel* (no 19) as well as the German version of his *Sendbrief an Papst Leo X* (no 11).

---

[106] Probably Wilhelm Otto Abel (also publishing as Otto Abel), *23 January 1802 in Tübingen, +7 February 1886 in Leonberg. He studied theology and worked as deacon in Leonberg 1829 to 1873. Part of his library are catalogued at the University Library in Tübingen. With thanks to Ulrich Bubenheimer for the information.

[107] Cf. Andreas Strauß, Opera Rariora, Quae Latitant in Bibliotheca Canon. Reg. Collegiatae Ecclesiae Ad S. Ioannem Baptistam in Rebdorf (Eichstädt: Mathiae Caietani Schmid, 1790), 136, listed as VD18 12185299.

[108] Cf. WA 2, 67, no E.

The pamphlets come from six different cities, namely Augsburg, Basel, Erfurt, Strasbourg, Wittenberg, and Worms. Five of the editions were produced by the *Wanderdrucker* Hans von Erfurt (nos 3, 8, 10, 16, 19),[109] three by Adam Petri in Basel (nos 4, 17, 18),[110] two by Rhau-Grunenberg (nos 2, 9), Johann Schott (nos 6, 13),[111] and Johann Knobloch the Elder (nos 7, 15)[112] respectively; one each from Melchior Lotter (no 5), Johann Prüß the Younger (no 12)[113] and Johann Eckhart's *Freiheitsschrift* from Speyer (no 14).

Who was the owner of this exclusively vernacular collection, which shows such an avid interest in Luther's oeuvre? One possible hint might be a contemporary ownership mark by *Bernhard Spiegel*. This can be found on four of the nineteen title-pages (nos 1, 2, 8, 9).

Ill. 12: Taylorian, ARCH.8°.G.1519(11/2)

He seems to have received at least one of the pamphlets as a present, since another hand on the title-page of the eighth pamphlet notes down *.pro. d]o. Bernardo Spigel.*

The first pamphlet likewise has two entries on its title-page: one is the ownership mark by Spiegel; the second one says: *Reinhardt Graff zu Leinningen, her zu westerburg vnd schaummburgk vnd* [one word illegible] *in liebe* [two words illegible].[114]

---

[109] Cf. Benzing (1963: 15–16).
[110] Cf. Benzing (1963: 31).
[111] Cf. Benzing (1963: 412).
[112] Cf. Benzing (1963: 411).
[113] Cf. Benzing (1963: 413).
[114] Cf. Heiles (2016: 2).

Von den newen
Eckischñ Bul-
len vñ lůgen.
D. Martini
Luther.

Wittenberg.

Ill. 13: Taylorian, ARCH.8°.G.1519(11/8)

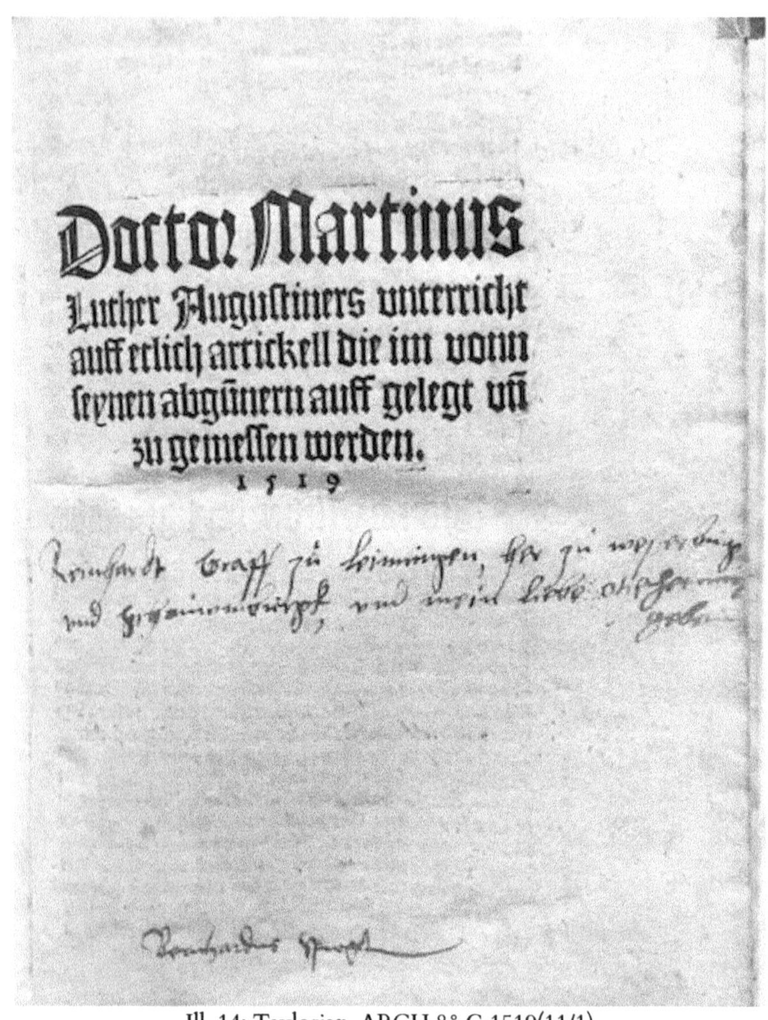
Doctor Martinus
Luther Augustiners vnterricht
auff etlich artickell die im vonn
seynen abgunern auff gelegt vñ
zu gemessen werden.
1519

Ill. 14: Taylorian, ARCH.8°.G.1519(11/1)

Whether Earl Reinhard I von Leiningen-Westerburg (1453–1522) donated the print to Bernhard Spiegel is not clear. Unfortunately, the fact that the prints Spiegel signed were produced in three different cities makes it difficult to locate him.[115] At the same time, this provides evidence for the ample circulation and reuse of prints within the Empire, which helped disseminate reformatory ideas.

Certainly, one of the more interesting pamphlets in the collection is Johann Eckhart's edition of Luther's *Freiheitsschrift*. As in most of his prints, Eckhart, who is described by Benzing as a reprinter, did not include a colophon or imprint;[116] instead, the title-page only gives the author and title in Gothic font (cf. A1r). Other than Rhau-Grunenberg's and Lotter's objective, Eckhart's seems to have been to provide a compact and economical presentation of the text: he neither includes a costly woodcut nor leaves the verso side of the title-page empty; instead, he prints the text of the treatise on the same page as the address to Mühlpfordt.

He separates the two by simply indenting the first four lines, but then forgets to insert the woodcut initial 'Z' at the beginning of the treatise: *[Z]Vm ersten* [...] (A1v). What is more, he frequently refrains from inserting spaces in between individual words (e.g. *vndarff* (B2r) instead of *vn darff*) in order to save space and overall shows less concern for punctuation than Rhau-Grunenberg and Lotter do (e.g. *vnrecht Dan ein* (C3r) or *werck Daher* (C3r). This gives the general impression that Eckhart was less careful in his presentation of the print.

Although Knaake asserts that '[a]us B stammen C, H', the Speyer print exhibits several instances which cannot be found in B (or A and L) and therefore might be attributed to Eckhart himself.

---

[115] A pro-Lutheran priest called Bernhard Spiegel from Speyer is mentioned in a letter from Franz von Sickingen to Wolfgang Capito, cf. Molhuysen (1905: 93–95). He might be identical to one 'Bernhardus Spiegel de Spira, ibidem vicarius maioris ecclesiae, dioc. eiusdem' who matriculated in Heidelberg on 4 February 1515 (Die Matrikel der Universität Heidelberg, ed. Toepke, T. 1: 499); with thanks to Ulrich Bubenheimer for the information.

[116] The following examples from Benzing (1956: 184–92).

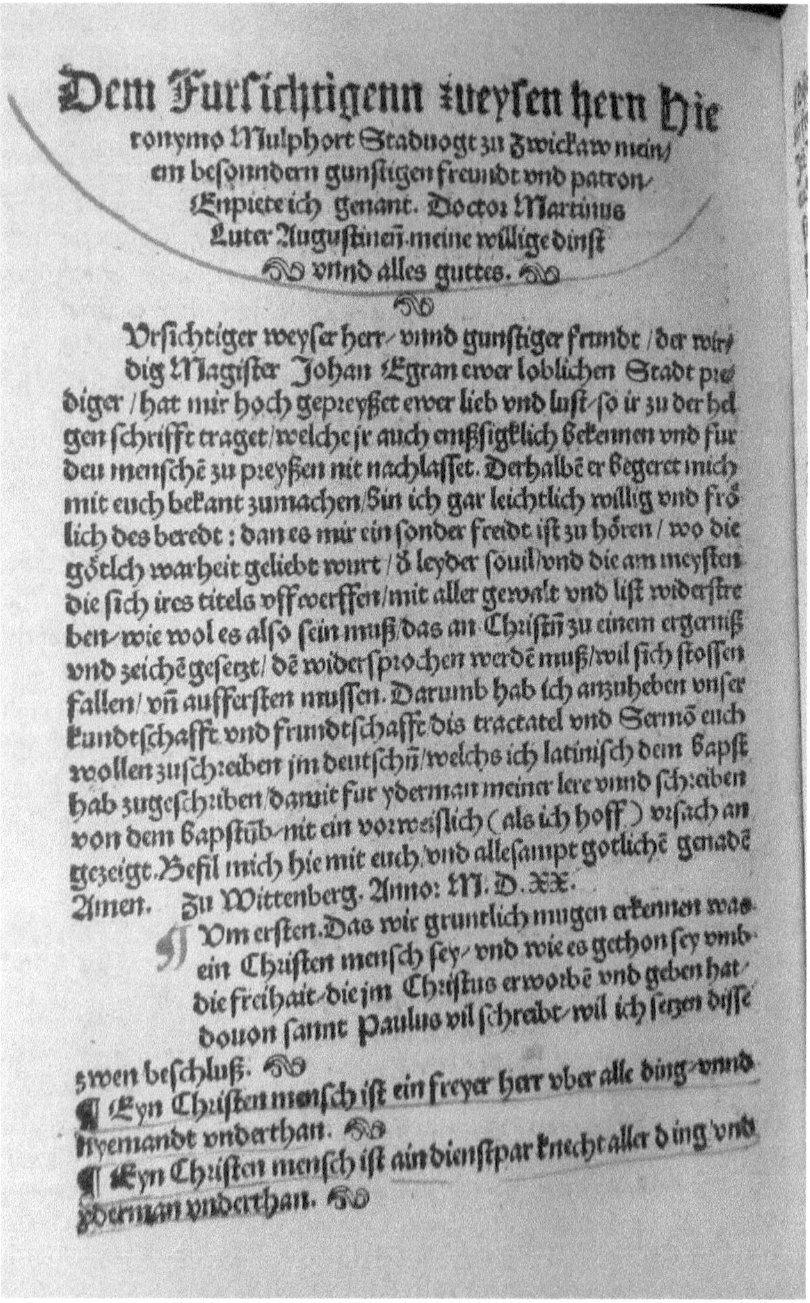

Dem Furſichtigenn weyſen hern Hie ronymo Mulphort Stadvogt zu Zwickaw mein/ en beſonndern gunſtigen freundt vnd patron/ Enpiete ich genant. Doctor Martinus Luter Auguſtiner. meine willige dinſt vnnd alles guttes.

Vrſichtiger weyſer herr/ vnnd gunſtiger frundt/ der wir/ dig Magiſter Johan Egran ewer loblichen Stadt pre/ diger/ hat mir hoch gepreyſſet ewer lieb vnd luſt/ ſo ir zu der hel gen ſchrifft traget/ welche ir auch emßſigklich bekennen vnd fur den menſchē zu preyſſen nit nachlaſſet. Derhalbē er begeret mich mit euch bekant zumachen/ bin ich gar leichtlich willig vnd frö lich des beredt: dan es mir ein ſonder freidt iſt zu hören/ wo die götlch warheit geliebt wurt/ d leyder ſouil/ vnd die am meyſten die ſich ires titels vffwerffen/ mit aller gewalt vnd liſt widerſtre ben/ wie wol es alſo ſein muß/ das an Chriſtū zu einem ergerniß vnd zeichē geſezt/ dē widerſprochen werdē muß/ vil ſich ſtoſſen fallen/ vñ aufferſten muſſen. Darumb hab ich anzuheben vnſer kundtſchafft vnd frundtſchafft dis tractatel vnd Sermō euch wollen zuſchreiben im deutſchē/ welchs ich latiniſch dem bapſt hab zugeſchriben/ damit fur ydermann meiner lere vnnd ſchreiben von dem bapſtūb/ nit ein vorweiſlich (als ich hoff) vrſach an gezeigt. Befil mich hie mit euch/ vnd alleſampt gotlichē genadē Amen. Zu Wittenberg. Anno: M. D. XX.

¶ Vm erſten. Das wir gruntlich mugen erkennen was ein Chriſten menſch ſey/ vnd wie es gethon ſey vmb die freihait/ die im Chriſtus erworbē vnd geben hat/ douon ſannt Paulus vil ſchreibt/ wil ich ſetzen diſſe zwen beſchluß.

¶ Eyn Chriſten menſch iſt ein freyer herr vber alle ding/ vnnd nyemandt vnderthan.

¶ Eyn Chriſten menſch iſt ain dienſtpar knecht aller ding/ vnd yderman vnderthan.

Ill. 15: Taylorian, ARCH.8°.G.1519(11/14), A1v

Thus, he changes the order of words from *gut und frum* to *frH vnd gut* (B4r); and he also – probably mistakenly – prints *noch dem scheinen im wasser schnapt* (B2r) instead of *schemen*, which in a Gothic font looks similar since it has the same number of strokes.

Despite the fact that Eckhart's print seems to be the one produced with the least care among the four Taylorian editions of the *Freiheitsschrift*, it also proves to be the most interesting one, since it includes marginalia by a contemporary hand.

This reader, who writes in red ink, exhibits an active engagement with Luther's text, at least for the first thirteen passages (cf. A1r–B1r). Not only do they number each of the thirteen passages, but they also add pilcrows (cf. A1r, A4v) and try to structure sentences where Eckhart refrained from doing so (e.g. on A2r: *genennet [.] nach* [...]).

Furthermore, they underline all the Bible passages for the first thirteen passages, which once again hints at an active engagement with the work. Important passages in the treatise are likewise underscored; sometimes the hand additionally adds a manicule (cf. A2r, A4v) or writes *Merck* (A4v) in the margin. (S)he also marks Luther's central definition of man as master and servant: *Eyn Christen mensch ist ein freyer herr* [...] (A1v), after which (s)he notes down in the margin of A2r: *Zweyerlei naturen ein mensch* and adds *Verbum Dei & evangelii* (A2v) on the following page.

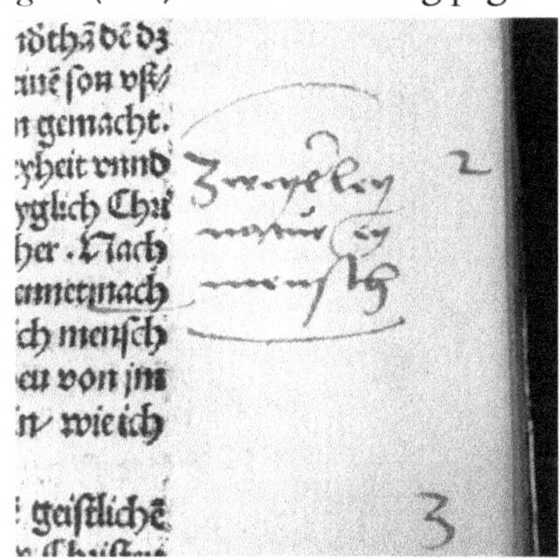

Ill. 14: Taylorian, ARCH.8°.G.1519(11/14), A2r

Eckhart's print from Speyer, which is included in a contemporary collection of Luther texts, thus provides an interesting history of reader- and ownership. It shows that there was an active readership engaging with the text and provides evidence for the reuse, circulation, and collection of Reformation pamphlets in the early modern period.

All four of the Taylorian copies together show the spectrum of publishing at the time of the Reformation: different graphic designs (woodcut versus no woodcut in Rhau-Grunenberg's and Lotter's edition), advertising strategies (Lotter's praise of Luther's treatise in the Latin edition), and a multi-layered history of readership and ownership (Eckhart's print). At the same time, even though the text of the *Freiheitsschrift* proves to be relatively stable, it could still be altered or revised – either by the author or the printer – and therefore displays at least some degree of *mouvance*.[117]

In a *Tischrede* from 1532, Luther shows that he is aware of the enormous influence that the printing revolution had on the Reformation, identifying it ('Calcographia') as a divine gift ('summum et postremum donum') from God, which helps spread His flame-like word: 'Calcographia est summum et postremum donum, durch welche Gott die Sache [des Evangeliums] treibet. Es ist die letzte flame vor dem ausleschen der welt'.[118] [Printing is the most excellent and last gift [from God], through which he helps to spread the word of God. It is the last flame before the extinction of the world].

---

[117] Zumthor (1972) uses the term for the ability of premodern texts to shapeshift constantly.

[118] WA.Tr 2, 650. Cf. also Wenzel (2005: 270).

3. How to Read Reformation Pamphlets

Henrike Lähnemann

Reformation pamphlets are the fast food of early printing. They were produced in haste and as cheaply as possibly, and they were meant to be consumed on the go, passed around, and binned or recycled when the next sensational publication took off. Printers cut corners – sometimes literally, as the broken frame of the first edition shows – and rarely proofread the text. Modern readers must familiarise themselves with standard abbreviation practices and correct typos if they are to take in this fast-paced text, which was designed for maximum impact and intended for curious minds and eager contemporaries, not for bibliophiles.

The following short guide is therefore meant to help 21st century readers understand the system (or not) behind punctuation, spelling, and structuring.

1. Punctuation
   Early modern printers mainly use the '/' (virgule or forward slash) to help users punctuate their speech, not as a grammatical mark-up. Virgules stand for both commas and semicolons, acting as breathing markers, and help to pace performance. Only in one instance (B1r, cf. image) is the virgule replaced by a stop, since otherwise it would have been impossible to squeeze the last word on the line.

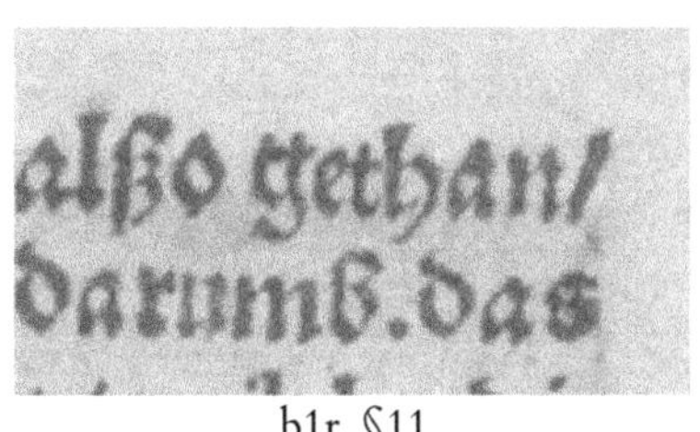

b1r, §11

Full stops are normally combined with a capital letter to mark sentence breaks but, if there is a line break before a new sentence, the full stop can be left out, e.g. in §23 where there is no full stop between 'werck' and the sentence starting 'Bőße werk'.

¶ Czū drey vnd zwentzigsten/ Drumb seyn die zwen sprüch war. Gutte frum werck machen nymmer mehr ein gutten fru= men man/ sondern eyn gutt frum man/ macht gutte frum werck Bőße werck machen nymmer mehr eynen bőßen man/ sondern ein bőßer man macht bőße werck/ alßo/ das allweg/ die person

c1r, §23

The only other punctuation marks are brackets for parentheses and question marks, both used sparingly. Parentheses are used only twice in this text, once characteristically for an explanation that underlines Luther's key point about grace, combined with 'das ist' (i.e.): §24 'durch gottis wort (das ist / durch seyne vorheyschung der gnadenn)'. Question marks come up where Luther uses the didactic structure of an imagined pupil asking for clarification: 'Fragistu aber / wilchs ist denn das wort das solch grosse gnad gibt. Vnd wie sol ichs gebrauchen?' (§6) and for rhetorical questions 'Wer mag nu außdencken / die ehre vnd hőhe eyniß Christen menschen?' (§16).

2. Spacing and Hyphenation

Particularly in the last quire it is clear that the printer tried to avoid half-empty lines, so instead of a paragraph, he often just used a larger space (a so-called 'm space' since it is as wide as the letter *m*) to mark a wider space between full stop and initial. This can also be used to signal a contrast, not necessarily at the start of a new sentence, but quite often before 'Widderumb', e.g. in §5 'Widderumb keyn grősser gnade'. On the other hand a space may be inserted seemingly to concentrate all the spacing of a line in one handy slot, e.g. in §4 after 'heuchler' even though the next part continues the argument with 'Auch'. The normal hyphenation mark is a double line (cf. the image from c1r) which is used fairly consistently; overall the word division is more in line with modern German usage than it is, e.g. in the 'Sermon von Ablass und Gnade'.[119]

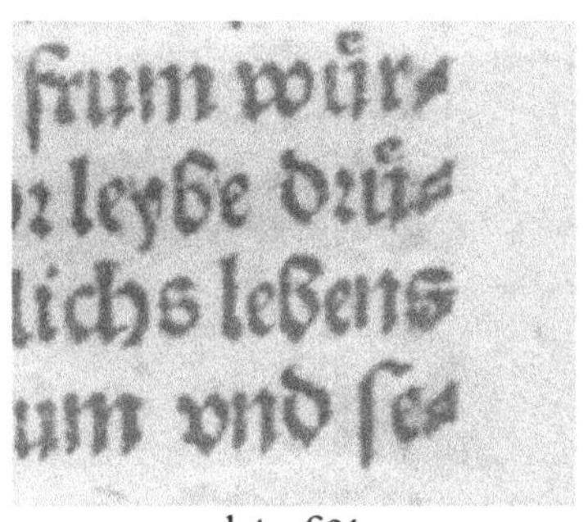
frum wür-
r leybe drü-
lichs lebens
um vnd se-

b4v, §21

3. Abbreviations
   The main abbreviation mark is '-', a bar above a letter, mostly above the last typeset character, to indicate that there would be a further character following, usually an *n* as in 'dē' = *den* or (for Latin case endings) an *m* such as 'Christū' = *Christum*, but also for a missing *e* in 'zurnñ' for *zürnen*; the most frequent use is in 'vñ' for *und*, and just occasionally it occurs above *p* for the Latin prefix 'pre–' in 'p̄digen' = *predigen*. There are also a number of established abbreviations for frequent words, notably 'dz' = *das*, 'd͛' = *der*, and an '-us' abbreviation in the shape of a small elevated nine as in 'Paul^{9}' for *Paulus*. Of the old Roman abbreviation marks, *et* in the form of a 7 (or in this font more like a lower-case *2*) is retained, and is exclusively used for '2c' as *etc*.

4. *u/v/w – v/f – i/j/y*, and different *s*- and *r*-forms
   u/v/w are interchangeable, e.g. *und* is regularly spelled as 'vnd', *reuen* as 'rewen'. Similarly, *i/j/y* are mainly distributed according to word position, with 'j' and 'y' as the more distinctive often employed in first position like an initial, e.g. 'jhn' or 'yhn' for *ihn*.

[119] Cf. the chapter in the second volume of the Taylor Editions Series: Reformation Pamphlets, open access https://editions.mml.ox.ac.uk/editions/ablassgnade5/

v/f are both used for *f*, e.g. 'vleissig' = *fleißig*. There is no phonetic difference in *u/v/w/f/i/j/y* from modern German. The two typographically different forms for *s* (long-*ſ* versus round-*s*) and for *r* (*r* versus *2*, cf. the image for the spelling of *narren* as 'nar2ñ') which are distributed according to different positions in the word, have not been distinguished in this edition.

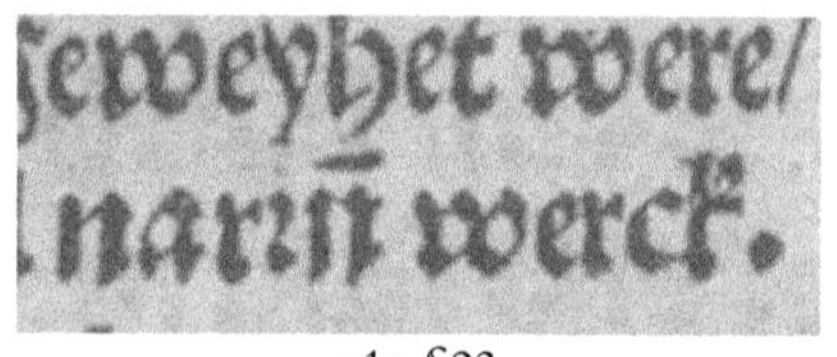
eweyhet were/
narꝛñ werck.

c1r, §23

5. Umlaut and superscript *e*
The umlaut sound would have been in the same position as in modern German but there is no strict rule for writing it; modern *ä* is mostly spelt as *e*, e.g. 'messiger' = *mäßiger*; modern *ü* and *ö* are usually spelt with a superscript *e* as in 'boͤßen luͤsten' for *bösen Lüsten.* Sometimes umlaut is not indicated but implied, e.g. 'furet' for *führet*, or 'gottlich' which could stand for *gottlich* or *göttlich* since the umlaut is variable in Early New High German. In most cases, an umlaut can be assumed whenever there is one in modern German.

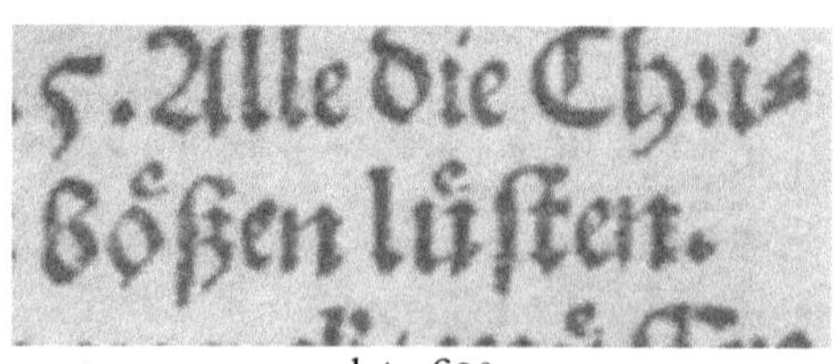
5. Alle die Chꝛi-
boͤßen luͤſten.

b4r, §20

6. Double versus single consonants and *s/ß, k/gk/ck, z/tz/cz*
There is no consistency in writing single and double consonants such as *f/ff* or *n/nn*, nor is there a difference in pronunciation. This also applies to *s* and *ß*, to *k*, *gk* and *ck* (e.g. 'dingk' for *Ding*), and to *z* and *tz*, e.g. 'tzinß' for *Zins*. The capital *Z* which would

be needed for all paragraph openings is in the normal type consistently replaced by *Cz*, e.g. 'Czum eilften'. The frequent spelling of initial *s* as 'ß' indicates that *s* would have been unvoiced throughout (a dialect feature which is not found e.g. in the Speyer edition, cf. chapter 2.4) but overall most consonants are equivalent to their modern counterparts.

7. Double consonants and 'h'
   In the same way that the printer uses 'ß' or even 'sß' for *s* and 'tz' for *z*, he also habitually uses double consonants where they would not be used in modern German, e.g. 'erbeytten' for *arbeiten*, and particularly 'nn' at the end of words, e.g. 'ynn' for *in* or 'andernn' for *andern*. 'h' is occasionally used to indicate vowel length as ('yhn' for *ihn*) but in variable positions, as in 'yhenes' for *jenes*.

8. Capital letters
   Capital letters are used as in English to indicate the beginning of new sentences and for proper names and titles, e.g. 'S. Paul Gal.', 'Bapst' and for all forms related to Christ e.g. 'Christlich'. Occasionally, it seems to have been used for emphasis e.g. 'den leyp zu Casteyen'.

9. Dialect markers
   The main differences between the language of the first edition, which reflects the Central German dialect spoken in Wittenberg, and modern German are some full forms where modern German has an unstressed vowel, as in 'hirschafft' for *Herrschaft*, 'gottis' for *Gottes*, 'wilchs' for *welchs*, 'vor-' for *ver* (e.g. 'vorpflichtet' for *verpflichtet*), and some vowels that have not yet been lowered e.g. 'frum' for *fromm*, 'vormuͤgen' for *vermögen*.

4. The German and Latin Versions

Howard Jones

The *Freiheitsschrift* and the letter to the Pope which introduces it were written by Luther in both German and Latin, and the German versions were published first.[120] Like his other vernacular writings around this time, the German version was intended for a general audience, while the Latin version was intended for the Pope and other highly educated readers (see chapter 1 of this introduction). It is widely accepted that the Latin version of the letter was written first and then put into German,[121] but the order of composition of the two versions of the *Freiheit* itself is a matter of debate.[122] Some scholars, notably Maurer (1949) and Gasse (1984), argue for the priority of the German version, while others, notably Stolt (1969), argue for that of the Latin version.[123] It is also possible that Luther worked on both versions at the same time, and that the German version had priority in some parts and the Latin version in others.

A number of comparisons will be made below between the German and Latin versions and on the way some new, linguistic arguments will be put forward for the priority of the German version, at least for certain parts of the work. These arguments may serve as hypotheses for a more thoroughgoing analysis which would go beyond the scope of this discussion.

---

[120] I thank the following for their generous and valuable help with this piece of work: Ulrich Bubenheimer, John Flood, Martin Jones, Martin Keßler, Henrike Lähnemann, Ralf Plate, Jonathan Reinert, Reinhold Rieger, and William Thurlwell.

[121] See Rieger (2007: 2), Jürgens (2014: 133), and Stolt (1969: 8).

[122] When the German and Latin versions are not distinguished, the work is referred to as the *Freiheit*; otherwise, this will be made clear in context.

[123] Maurer (1949) and Stolt (1969) allow for the existence of a plan or outline which preceded both versions. Their arguments are summarised in Rieger (2007: 5–12), who comes out in favour of Maurer.

1. Length and structure

The Latin version of the work is, by word-count, around 8% longer than the German version. However German, as the more analytic language, generally has a higher word-count than Latin. To illustrate this, the German and Latin word-counts were compared in three paragraphs (§7, §21, and §24)[124] in which the two versions are as close as any in the work. Here the German word-count is around 25% greater than the Latin, so 1.25 : 1.00 may be taken as the neutral ratio of German to Latin for this work, that is, the ratio we should expect if the two versions were close equivalents throughout. Normalizing for this, the Latin version is some 35% longer than the German.[125] The greater length of the Latin partly reflects a short introduction and long end section in the Latin (preceding §1 and following §30)[126] which have no counterpart in the German; these are partly offset by a dedication in the German version before §1 which has no equivalent in the Latin.

If we confine ourselves to §§1–30 in both versions, the Latin is some 25% longer than the German on the normalised basis just explained. This ratio masks considerable variation; for example, §27 in the Latin is some 75% longer than in the German, while §4 in the Latin is around 30% shorter (again on a normalised basis). The greater overall length of §§1–30 reflects three main differences: first, the Latin includes arguments which go beyond those in the German; secondly, the same arguments are developed more in the Latin than in the

---

[124] Although only the German version is divided into numbered paragraphs, these numbers will be used also to refer to the Latin text corresponding to them. For convenience, the numbers have been marked against the Latin transcription in the online edition.

[125] Thus, if the two versions were close equivalents throughout, 125 German words would correspond to 100 Latin words on average. In fact, 125 German words correspond to 125 × 108% = 135 Latin words on average throughout the two versions.

[126] The end section in the Latin begins 'In fine'.

German; and, thirdly, there are 50% more Bible quotations in the Latin. These differences will be illustrated below.

Although only the German version is divided into numbered paragraphs,[127] both versions have the same broad thematic divisions, as follows (my numbering): I introduction; II the inner person; III the outer person; IV conclusion,[128] and these divisions and their subdivisions are signposted in the text in both versions.[129] Stolt (1969: 91–3) maps these sections onto a tripartite structure advocated in Classical rhetoric, in which II and III should be taken together (as 'antitheses'), to give the following structure: I, (II + III), IV. Stolt also shows (ibid) that the two parts of the antithetical middle section are of almost exactly equal length as each other in both the German and Latin versions, again as recommended in the rules of Classical rhetoric.[130]

---

[127] Luther often used numbering in his German works (e.g. *Sermon von Ablass und Gnade* 1518, *Von den guten Werken* 1520, *An den christlichen Adel deutscher Nation* 1520) as well as in those of his Latin works which were set out in the form of 'theses' (e.g. '95 Theses' 1517, 'Heidelberg Disputation' 1518).

[128] I: §§1–2; II: §§3–18; III: §§19–29; IV: §30 (as well as the extra end section of the Latin).

[129] For a more detailed breakdown, see Rieger (2007: 12–15). The signposting of the arguments is somewhat clearer in the Latin version; for example, in the Latin §11 opens, 'Haec prima fidei virtus esto. Alteram quoque videamus', and §12 starts, 'Tertia fidei gratia incomparabilis est haec …'. The corresponding German paragraphs do not make the tripartite virtue of faith so explicit. For further details of the way in which arguments are connected in the two versions, see Gasse (1984: 41–4).

[130] For divisions of the work based on medieval rhetoric, see the introduction to the English translation of the Latin version in Wengert (2015: 470–3). In the Latin version of the present volume, the marginal glosses which summarise the text are those used in editions from that of Adam Petri in 1521 (Basel) onwards. Hirstein (2015) shows that these glosses were added, not by Luther, but by Beatus Rhenanus.

2. Detailed comparisons of the two versions

To illustrate the relationship between the German and Latin versions, we analyse two extracts which show opposite extremes. In the first, from the beginning of §21, the two versions are as close as we find anywhere in the work, while in the second, corresponding to the whole of §6, the two versions are as far apart as in any part of the work which is composed in both languages.[131]

2a. An example of a close match between the German and Latin versions

We start with an extract from the beginning of §21. To show how similar the two versions are, the extract has been divided up into 17 linguistic units, with the German (marked 'a') set out above the equivalent Latin (marked 'b'). Most of these units are clauses and separated in the German by virgulae ('/', probably added by the printer).

1a Aber die selben werck muͤssen nit geschehn ynn der meynung /
1b Verum ea opera oportet, non ea fieri opinione,

2a das da durch der mensch frum werd fur gott /
2b quo per ipsa coram deo iustificetur quisquam,

3a deñ die falsch meynung kan der glaub nit leydē /
3b hanc enim falsam opinionem fides non feret,

4a der alleyn ist uñ sein muß die frumkeyt fur gott /
4b quae sola est iustitia coram deo,

5a sonderñ nur yn der meynung /
5b sed solum ea opinione,

6a das der leyp gehorsam werde /
6b ut corpus in servitutem redigatur

7a und gereynigt von seynen bosen luͤsten /
7b & purificetur a concupiscentiis suis malis,

---

[131] A translation of the Latin version of this extract can be found in this volume as a footnote to the translation of the German version.

8a uñ dz aug nur sehe / auff die bosen luͤsten /
8b ita ut oculum non nisi vertat ad concupiscentias

9a sie auß zu treyben /
9b expurgandas.

10a Deñ die weyl die seel durch den glauben reyn ist /
10b Cum enim anima per fidem purgata sit

11a uñ gott liebet /
11b & amans dei facta,

12a wolt sie gern das auch also alle ding reyn weren zuvor yhr eygen leyp /
12b vellet omnia pariter purgari, praecipue corpus proprium,

13a und yderman gott / mit yhr liebt und lobt /
13b ut omnia secum amarent & laudarent deum.

14a So geschichts /
14b Ita fit,

15a das der mensch seyns eygen leyps halben nit kan muͤßsig gehen /
15b ut homo exigente corporis sui causa ociari non possit,

16a uñ muß vil gutter werck drober uben /
16b cogaturque ob id, multa bona operari,

17a das er yhn zwinge /
17b ut in servitutem redigat.

The comparison of the German and the Latin shows that, in each pair, there is a close match between the two. With very few exceptions, the two members of each pair are semantic equivalents, conveying the same sense and no more.[132] They are also close matches syntactically, as illustrated by the fact that the passage in both versions can be set out into corresponding clauses of very similar length in exactly the same order. Even within clauses the order of sentence constituents is, for the most part, the same.[133] This is

[132] Main semantic differences between the two versions: 'der mensch' (2a) *vs* 'quisquam' (2b), 'ist uñ sein muß' (4a) *vs* 'est' (4b), 'yderman' (13a) *vs* 'omnia' (13b).
[133] A sentence constituent is defined as a group of words which can be taken together as a syntactic unit.

illustrated by an analysis of units 5–7, copied below. Here there is an exact match in sense, construction type, and the order of sentence constituents between the German and the Latin.

Sentence constituent count in 5a–7b above

	1	2	3
5a	sondern̄	nur	yn der meynung /
5b	sed	solum	ea opinione,
6a	das	der leyp	gehorsam werde /
6b	ut	corpus	in servitutem redigatur
7a	und	gereynigt	von seynen bosen luͤsten /
7b	&	purificetur	a concupiscentiis suis malis,

Overall, the German and Latin versions here are so close that it seems likely that Luther translated one from the other, rather than basing both versions merely on notes or an outline. As to which version came first, there is one general linguistic difference between German and Latin which suggests that it was the German version: the more flexible word order of Latin. If the German was composed first, the Latin, with its relatively adaptable word order, could more easily follow the German word order than the German could follow the Latin if the latter was composed first. It could be argued that Luther's Latin word order might have been generally similar to his German word order, in which case either version could have been composed first. However, a comparison with Luther's letter to the Pope, of which the Latin version is considered to have come first and then to have been translated into German, is instructive.

If we compare the two versions of this letter where they are closest to each other, we find a semantic match between them, but far less of a syntactic match than in the passage from the *Freiheit* we have just analysed. To illustrate this, here is an extract from the letter where the two versions are as close as they come:[134]

> German:
> Ich hab wol scharff angriffen, doch yn der gemeyn hyn, ettlich unchristlich lere, und auff meyne widdersacher peyssig geweßen, nit umb yhres boßen lebens, ßondern umb yhrer unchristlichen lere und schutzs willen, wilchs mych ßo gar nichts berewet, das ich myrß auch ynn synn genummen hab, ynn solcher emßickeyt und scherpff zu bleyben, unangesehen, wie myr dasselb etlich außlegen…

> Latin:
> Communiter quidem in impias doctrinas invectus sum acriter, et adversarios non ob malos mores sed ob impietatem non segniter momordi, cuius me adeo non poenitet, ut animum induxerim, contempto hominum iuditio, in ea vehementia zeli perseverare …

It would not be possible to set out these German and Latin extracts above one another as we did with the extract from §21 of the *Freiheit* because the syntactic mismatches between the German and the Latin are too great. For example:

- In the German, 'ettlich unchristlich lere' comes after 'Ich hab … angriffen', while in Latin 'in impias doctrinas' comes before 'invectus sum acriter';
- In the German, 'nit umb yhres … willen' comes after 'peyssig geweßen', while in the Latin 'non ob malos … impietatem' comes before 'non segniter momordi';
- In the German, 'unangesehen, wie myr dasselb etlich außlegen' comes after 'das ich myrß auch … bleyben', while in the Latin the equivalent (but differently constructed) 'contempto hominum iuditio' comes before 'in ea vehementia zeli perseverare'.

[134] WA 7, 4, 17–21 and WA 7, 43, 20–23.

The different relationships between the German and Latin in the letter and the *Freiheit* are therefore explicable if we assume that, in contrast to the letter to the Pope, the German version of the *Freiheit* was written first. This is far from proof, but constitutes a plausible hypothesis, which could be tested by a comprehensive linguistic comparison of the German-Latin relationship in the *Freiheit* with that in the letter to the Pope. A further test would involve a linguistic comparison between the Latin of the *Freiheit* where it is close to the German and the Latin of Luther's original Latin compositions at around the time the *Freiheit* was composed; this might reveal distinctive features of the Latin in the *Freiheit* which could be attributed to its being a translation from German.

2b. An example of a loose relationship between the German and Latin versions

At the other extreme is §6. Apart from the opening words ('Fragistu aber / wilchs ist denn das wort …' and 'Quaeres autem, Quod nam est verbum hoc …') and two quotations from Romans, there are no close verbal similarities like those discussed above. However, the German and Latin deal with a similar topic and make similar arguments, and a comparison between them illustrates the sort of differences we find throughout the two versions of the *Freiheit*.[135]

Both versions open with the questions 'What is the "word" and how is it to be used?' and restate the point made in §5 that the word is the Gospel of God about Christ. Thereafter, however, the two versions differ on a number of levels.

First, some of the arguments in the Latin version go beyond those in the German. Thus (i) in the Latin we are told that faith is the use of the word ('Fides enim sola est salutaris & efficax usus verbi dei') but

[135] A translation of the Latin version of this paragraph can be found in this volume as a footnote to the translation of the German version.

not in the German; (ii) in the Latin it is stated explicitly that 'faith alone' means 'without works' (e.g. 'sola fide et nullis operibus iustificatur'), but not in the German; (iii) in the Latin the interactions between human beings and Christ are spelt out ('Hoc enim cognito … Christi solius'), while in the German they are not; and (iv) in the Latin the contrast between faith and works is paralleled by the difference between the inner and outward person ('Cum ergo haec fides … peccato vel opere') in a way that has no equivalent in the German.

Other differences between the two versions have to do with the order in which the arguments are made and the emphasis they are given. In the German version the argument that God's word leads to a recognition of sinfulness ('ßo du recht glaubst / wie du schuldig bist') precedes the claim that justification is by faith alone ('Ein rechtfertiger Christen / lebt nur von seynem glauben' – a translation from Romans 1,17), while in the Latin the order is the opposite, with the argument that justification is by faith alone ('Fides enim sola …') introduced before the argument that God's word leads to a recognition of sinfulness ('discis, omnia quae in te sunt … damnanda'). The difference in order means that the German starts on the more negative note than the Latin (see Rieger 2007: 128). As an example of a difference in emphasis between the two versions, in the German the argument that justification is by faith alone is confined to the translation from Romans 1,17 at the end of the paragraph, while in the Latin the equivalent Latin quotation comes near the beginning and the point is then restated emphatically.

The tone in which the arguments are presented is also different in the two versions. Overall, the German is more personal and the Latin more academic – which is to be expected since the former was intended for a general audience and the latter for the Pope and other highly-educated readers. The German version includes many more personal references to the reader/listener. Thus (i) the first-personal question at the beginning of the German ('wie sol ichs gebrauchen?')

corresponds to an impersonal phrase in the Latin ('qua arte utendum est eo ...?'); (ii) there is no equivalent of 'du hörist deynen gott zu dir reden' in the Latin; and (iii), while the German version includes direct instructions to the reader/listener ('so mustu an dir selber vortzweyffelnñ', 'Du solt ynn den selben mit festem glauben dich ergeben'), the Latin arguments are framed in logical language (e.g. 'Si confitearis ore tuo ... salvus eris') or are made more abstractly by reference to the soul (e.g. 'Ideo clarum est ... nullis operibus iustificatur').

Finally, the German relies less on Biblical authority than the Latin: the German has one quotation from Hosea and two from Romans, while the Latin has six quotations from, and one reference to, Romans as well as one reference to Job.

3. Bible quotations

In the German version of the *Freiheit* there are 36 Bible quotations and in the Latin there are 64. If we confine the comparison to §§1–30, the numbers are 36 and 54, respectively, making 50% more quotations in the Latin than the German. This reflects both the greater length of the Latin (see section 1 above) and the greater density of Bible quotations in the Latin (see section 2b above).[136]

While there are many Bible quotations in the Latin which have no equivalent in the German, there is only one quotation in the German which has no equivalent in the Latin: in §5 of the German we have 'Ich byn der weg / die warheyt / und das leben' (John 14,6), while in the Latin corresponding to it we have 'Si filius vos liberaverit, vere

---

[136] A Bible quotation is defined here as any text which Luther presents as such in one or both versions of the *Freiheit*. Three of the Bible quotations in the Latin version (from Romans 10,10, Galatians 2,20, and 1 Timothy 1,9) appear twice. In addition to Bible quotations, there are numerous biblical allusions and echoes in both versions. For a discussion of other differences between the German and Latin Bible references in the *Freiheit*, see Gasse (1984: 44–51).

liberi eritis' (John 8,36) instead. The quotation in the Latin has been seen as an improvement on that in the German, given that the part of the work in which this section appears is about the freedom of the inner person, which is brought out more explicitly by the Latin (see Rieger 2007: 101, referencing Maurer 1949: 66).

Turning to the language of the Bible quotations, the Latin seems to be based on the Vulgate – with the edition printed in Basel in 1509 serving as a reasonable proxy for the version which Luther might have used.[137] The relationship between the Latin Bible quotations in the *Freiheit* and the text of the Vulgate is variable. In some cases they match almost word-for-word; one example among many is the quotation from John 1,51 in §30. In other cases the Vulgate is quoted accurately, but parts are edited out; an example is in §24, where 2 Timothy 3, vv. 5 and 7 are quoted almost exactly from the Vulgate, but v. 6 is left out. Elsewhere there is a loose relationship between the Latin quotations and the Vulgate, as in a quotation from Matthew 7,18 in §23, where Luther refers to the good and bad trees in the opposite order to that in the Vulgate.

In cases where the Latin departs significantly from the wording of the Vulgate, the German and Latin are often close to each other.

---

[137] It is not claimed here that this was the edition, or even one of the editions, of the Vulgate used by Luther. Ulrich Bubenheimer (p.c.) has established that editions of the Vulgate printed in the following locations were in use at Wittenberg by Luther's contemporaries (named in parentheses): Lyon 1513 (Heinrich Stackmann); Lyon 1514 (Andreas Karlstadt); Basel 1514 (Johannes Lang). Comparing the Latin quotations in this work with the Latin (and Greek) of Erasmus's 1516 and 1519 versions of the New Testament, I find no strong evidence that Luther's Bible quotations were influenced by these (for one example of possible influence, see the footnote on Luther's use of the future tense in the Latin quotation from Romans 1,17 below). For a study of some of Luther's Bible translations before his 1522 *Septembertestament* (his first translation of the New Testament), see Bluhm (1969).

Here are three examples:

Reference	German	Latin	Vulgate
Isaiah 10,22f	Gott wirt eyn kurtz summa machen auff erden / und die kurtz summa wirt / wie ein syndflut eynfliessen die gerechtickeit (§7)	Verbum abbreviatum & consumans faciet dominus super terram: Et consummata abbreviatio inundabit iustitiam (§7)	(v. 22) … consummatio abbreviata inundabit iustitiam (v. 23) Consummationem enim et abbreviationem dominus deus exercituum, faciet in medio omnis terrae
Genesis 2,15	Das gott den geschaffenen menschen / setzt ynß paradiß / das er dasselb erbeytten und hutten solt (§22)	Posuit deus hominem, quem formaverat in paradisum, ut operaretur & custodiret illum (§22)	posuit eum in paradisum voluptatis, ut operaretur et custodiret illum
1 Peter 2,9	Ihr seyt ein priesterlich kuͤnigreych / un̄ ein kuͤniglich priesterthū (§15)	Vos genus electum, populus acquisitionis, sacerdotium regale, & regnum sacerdotale (§15)	Vos autem genus electum, regale sacerdotium, gens sancta, populus in acquisitionem

In the first of these examples, the German and the Latin both involve a reordering and reduction of the Vulgate. In the second example, both the German and the Latin refer to man being created ('geschaffenen', 'quem formaverat') but this reference has no equivalent in the Vulgate (nor, for that matter, in the Hebrew Old Testament). In the third example, the chiastic wordplay which occurs in both the German and the Latin versions ('priesterlich kuͤnigreych … kuͤniglich priesterthū', 'sacerdotium regale … regnum sacerdotale') does not occur in the Vulgate.

When the German diverges from the Latin, it often resembles a paraphrase rather than a translation, as in the following examples (in which the Latin is close to the Vulgate):[138]

Reference	German	Latin	Vulgate
Psalm 107,20	Er hat seyn wort auß gesandt / damit er yhn hatt geholffen (§5)	Misit verbum suum & sanavit eos, & eripuit eos de interitionibus eorum (§5)	Misit verbum suum et sanavit eos et eripuit eos de interitionibus eorum
Hosea 13,9	O Israel yn dir ist nichts / denn deyn vorterben / alleyn aber yn mir steht deyn hulff (§6)	Perditio tua Israel, tantum in me auxilium tuum (§8)	Perditio tua, Israel, tantummodo in me auxilium tuum

In the first example, the words 'damit er yhn hatt geholffen' in the German are an abbreviated paraphrase of 'sanavit eos, & eripuit eos de interitionibus eorum'. In the second example, the words 'yn dir ist nichts / denn deyn vorterben' are an expanded paraphrase of 'Perditio tua'.

In certain quotations the German departs from the Latin in ways which contribute to Luther's message in the work, as in these three examples:

[138] Comparing the German quotations in this work with the text of the 1466 Mentel Bible, I found no evidence that Luther's translations in the *Freiheit* were influenced by it.

Reference	German	Latin	Vulgate
Rom. 1,17	Ein rechtfertiger Christen/lebt nur von seynem glauben (§6)	Iustus ex fide sua vivet[139] (§6)	Iustus autem ex fide vivit
John 6,29	Das ist das eynige got-liche werck/das yhr glaubt yn denen/den gott gesandt hatt (§7)	Hoc est opus dei, ut credatis in eum, quem misit ille (§7)	Hoc est opus dei, ut credatis in eum, quem misit ille
I Cor. 4,1	Wir wollen nichts mehr von den leuthen gehalten seyn/denn Christ' diener/und schaffner des Evangelii (§17)	Sic nos existimet homo, sicut ministros Christi & dispensatores mysteriorum dei (§17)	Sic nos existimet homo ut ministros christi et dispensatores mysteriorum dei

In the first two of these examples, Luther introduces into the German a notion of exclusiveness with 'nur' and 'eynige' that is absent from the Latin (and from the Vulgate), reinforcing the notion of *sola fide* which is central to Luther's argument in the work.[140] In the third case, Luther uses 'mysteriorum' in the Latin, in line with the Vulgate, but 'Evangelii' in the German, underlining the importance of the Gospel as God's word (see section 2b). An examination of Luther's quotations from these verses elsewhere, both in his Bible translations and in his other works, reveals that his additions here are unusual, and may have been motivated by the particular needs of this work.[141]

[139] In his use of the future 'vivet' against the Vulgate's 'vivit', it is possible that Luther was following Erasmus's 1516/1519 Greek/Latin edition of the New Testament here: Erasmus has the Greek future 'ζησεται' (translated by the Latin periphrastic future 'victurus est').

[140] The introduction of 'nur' foreshadows Luther's famous addition of 'allein' in 'allein durch den glauben' in his rendering of Romans 3: 28 (Vulgate: 'ex fide') in his New Testament translations; see Jones (2017: xix-xx) for details.

[141] The closest I can find to any of these three additions are two references which parallel Romans 1,17. In a sermon from 1521 Luther cites Habakkuk 2,4 (of which

At this time Luther was familiar with the Bible primarily through the Vulgate, so we might assume that the Latin quotations came first and that Luther translated them into German. This would certainly explain why, in most cases, the quotations in the two versions correspond closely. On the other hand there are a number of instances, illustrated above, in which the German and Latin do not match up, including cases in which the German is more of a paraphrase than a translation. Maurer (1949: 66), in arguing that Luther wrote the German version first, suggests that he might have checked some of the Bible quotations against the Vulgate when he came to write the Latin version; this would explain the greater accuracy of the Latin in the quotations from Psalm 107,20 and Hosea 13,9 above. In other cases, like the quotations from Isaiah 10,22–23, Genesis 2,15, and 1 Peter 2,9 above, in which the German and Latin match each other but not the Vulgate, Luther could have started with the German and rendered it into Latin without checking the Vulgate. An examination of Latin quotations in the work which are not matched by a German quotation, including in the end section of the Latin which has no German equivalent, does not show the same degree of lexical independence from the Vulgate as when the Latin is closely matched by the German.[142] This lends support to the case that the German version was written first, but would have to be confirmed by a comprehensive analysis of all Bible quotations in the *Freiheit*, as well as a comparison with Luther's quotations of the same passages in his other works.

Paul's words in Romans 1,17 are an echo) as follows: 'der gerecht lebt allain in seinem glauben' (WA 7, 240, 14), and in a 1530 letter from Luther to Justus Jonas he writes, 'Discimus nunc re ipsa, quid sit iustum ex fide vivere et fide sola' (WA.Br 5, 500, 3).

[142] By 'lexical independence' is meant a departure from the wording in the Vulgate. The Latin-only quotations in the *Freiheit* include cases in which the Luther combines, reorders, or selects from different verses, but in such cases the wording is still close to that of the Vulgate.

4. Righteousness vocabulary

Our final comparison between the two versions of the work concerns the language of righteousness, in particular the way in which the German *gerecht* and *frum* (and their derivatives) and the Latin *iustus* (and its derivatives) correspond.[143] In Jones (2018b) it was argued that, in his 1522 New Testament translation, Luther imposed a separation of function on *gerecht* and *frum* when they were used to translate the Greek δίκαιος (which in most cases corresponds to the Latin *iustus*); accordingly, *gerecht* was used to refer to righteousness in Luther's conception of it at the time, while *frum* was used to refer to worldly goodness. However outside his Bible translations, it was argued, Luther used both *gerecht* and *frum* to refer to righteousness according to his own theology, while also using *frum* for worldly goodness. The explanation put forward was that, in his Bible translations, where Luther could not spell out for the reader when he was referring to righteousness and when he was referring to worldly goodness, he encoded this distinction in the lexical choice of *gerecht* and *frum*, respectively. By contrast, in his other works, Luther could make it clear in context when he was referring to which, and therefore did not have to be so strict in his lexical choice.

The two versions of the *Freiheit* provide an opportunity to examine the distribution of *frum, gerecht,* and *iustus* in this light. The table below shows which Latin words *gerecht* and *frum* (and their derivatives) correspond to and which German words *iustus* (together with its derivatives) corresponds to. Where two words are shown (e.g. *frum* + *gerecht*), both of them (or their derivatives) occur in the German and correspond to only one word in the Latin.[144]

---

[143] The main derivatives of *frum* are *frumkeit, frum machen/werden*; those of *gerecht* are *gerechtigkeit, gerecht machen/werden*; and those of *iustus* are *iustitia, iustificare, iustum facere*.

[144] In such cases the German words may be in either order, e.g. *frum und gerecht* or *gerecht und frum*.

Latin v. German lexemes (incl. derivatives)							
	gerecht	frum	frum + gerecht	frum + gutt	recht-fertig	recht	Total
iustus	11	49	4		5	3	72
bonus		4		6			10
verax		1					1
pius		2					2
Total	11	56	4	6	5	3	85

As the breakdown shows, *gerecht* corresponds only to *iustus*, while *frum* corresponds to *iustus* as well as to Latin words which are not equated with righteousness in Luther's theology.[145] Moreover, when *frum* and *gerecht* are paired (in the column *frum* + *gerecht*), they correspond to *iustus*, but when *frum* and *gutt* are paired, they correspond to *bonus*. This is consistent with the general finding in Jones (2018b) that, outside Luther's Bible translations, *gerecht* is used to refer to righteousness, while *frum* is used to refer to both righteousness and worldly goodness.

The choice of *gerecht*, *frum*, and *iustus* in the German and Latin versions of the work is not revealing in itself about the order of composition of the two versions. After all, their distribution is consistent with that in Luther's non-Bible works in general. However, there is one feature of the context in which these words occur that is easier to explain by assuming that the German was written first. As the following examples show, Luther sometimes includes words about righteousness in lists of several related terms (underlined here):

[145] Note that, when translating *iustus*, Luther uses *frum* many more times than he uses *gerecht*. As Luther explains in his 1522 *Weihnachtspostille*, he finds *frum*, etc. more natural in German than *gerecht*, etc. (WA 10, I, 2, 36, 4–8).

German	Latin
Und alßo durch den glauben / die seele von dem gottis wort / heylig / gerecht / warhafftig / fridsam / frey / und aller guͤtte voll / eyn warhafftig kind gottis wirt (§10)	Hoc igitur modo anima per fidem solam, sine operibus e verbo dei iustificatur, sanctificatur, verificatur, pacificatur, liberatur, & omni bono repletur, vereque filia dei efficitur (§10)
Und wo er ßo toͤricht were und meynet / durch ein gutt werck / frum / frey / selig odder Christen werden / ßo vorluͤr er den glauben mit allen dingen (§16)	Quod si sic desiperet, ut per ullum opus bonum praesumeret, iustus, liber, salvus, Christianus fieri, statim amitteret fidem cum omnibus bonis (§16)

Such lists are an abiding feature of Luther's vernacular writing.[146] In the examples above, and on numerous occasions elsewhere in §§1–30, lists containing words associated with righteousness occur in both German and Latin. However, in the end section of the Latin version, which has no German counterpart, such lists are absent, even though that section continues to deal with righteousness and includes *iustus* and its derivatives many times.[147] This would be consistent with the German version having been written first if it could be demonstrated that such lists were as a rule not a feature of Luther's original Latin compositions, because those in the Latin version of the *Freiheit* could then be explained as having been carried over from the German. To verify this interpretation, an analysis of Luther's other Latin works written around the time of the *Freiheit* would reveal whether such stylistic mannerisms were as absent from his original Latin compositions in general as they are from the Latin at the end of the *Freiheit*.

---

[146] See Jones (2018a: lxxvi).

[147] There is a similar pattern with doublets (pairings of near-synonyms or related words) involving righteousness vocabulary. As Gasse (1984: 53–54) points out, doublets in the German version of the *Freiheit* generally correspond to a single word in the Latin. In the language of righteousness, such doublets, typically of *iustus/verax* or *iustus/salvus* (and their derivatives), occur in both the German and Latin versions of §§1–30 but do not occur in the extra end section in the Latin version.

Conclusion

Some of the differences between the German and Latin versions identified above can be explained by their different target audiences: general readers/listeners on the one hand and the Pope and other highly educated readers on the other. Thus the German version is simpler, shorter, more personal, and less academic than the Latin.

In some ways, however, differences between the two versions are consistent with the German version, or at least some parts of it, having been written first. These relate to the syntactic relationship between the two versions when they are close, to the relationship between German and Latin Bible quotations, and to the inclusion in the Latin version of lists which may have been taken over from the German. These differences, which are discussed above at the end of sections 2a, 3, and 4, respectively, provide us with hypotheses to be tested in a more comprehensive comparison between the two versions of the *Freiheit.*

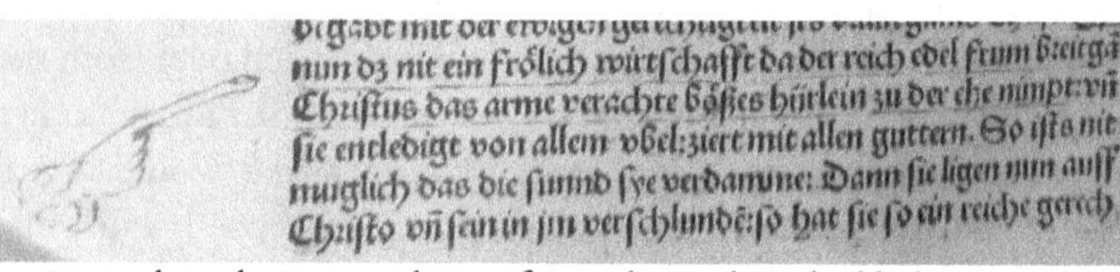
nun dz nit ein frölich wirtſchafft da der reich edel frum breitgã
Chriſtus das arme verachte böſſes hürlein zu der ehe nimpt: vñ
ſie entledigt von allem übel: ziert mit allen guttern. So iſts nit
muglich das die ſünd ſye verdamme: Dann ſie ligen nun auff
Chriſto vñ ſein in jm verſchlunden: ſo hat ſie ſo ein reiche gerech

Manicule in the Speyer edition of 'Von der Freiheit', highlighting article 12. ARCH.8°.G.1519 (11/2), fol. Aiiijv

Bibliography

Anderas, Philip (2017): 'Augustine and Augustinianism' in Derek R. Nelson and Paul R. Hinlicky (eds) *The Oxford Encyclopedia of Martin Luther*, Oxford: Oxford University Press.

Benzing, Josef and Helmut Claus (1966): *Lutherbibliographie. Verzeichnis der gedruckten Schriften Martin Luthers bis zu dessen Tod*, Baden-Baden: Librairie Heitz.

Benzing, Josef (1956): 'Josef Eckhart. Ein Nachdrucker zu Speyer (1521?–1526)' in *Gutenberg-Jahrbuch 1956*, 184–192.

Benzing, Josef (1963): *Die Buchdrucker des 16. und 17. Jahrhunderts im deutschen Sprachgebiet*, Wiesbaden: Harrassowitz.

Blickle, Peter (1981): *The Revolution of 1525. The German Peasants War from a new perspective*, Baltimore: Johns Hopkins University Press.

Bluhm, Heinz (1969): 'An "Unknown" Luther Translation of the Bible', *PMLA* 84(6), 1537–44.

Böcking, Eduard (1854): *Epistolae Ulrich Hutteni* (= vol. 1), Leipzig: Teubner.

Brower, Jeffrey E. and Susan Brower-Toland, (2008): 'Aquinas on Mental Representation. Concepts and Intentionality' in *The Philosophical Review* 117.2, 193–243.

CSEL = *Corpus Scriptorum Ecclesiasticorum Latinorum*, Vindobonae: Gerold u.a., (1866–)

Dieter, Theodor (2014): 'Luther as Late Medieval Theologian: His Positive and Negative Use of Nominalism and Realism', in Robert Kolb et al. (eds) *The Oxford Handbook of Martin Luther's theology*, Oxford: Oxford University Press, 31–48.

Dingel, Irene (2014): 'Von der Freiheit eines Christenmenschen (1520) – Historische und theologische Aspekte' in Irene Dingel and Henning P. Jürgens (eds) *Meilensteine der Reformation. Schlüsseldokumente der frühen Wirksamkeit Martin Luthers*, Gütersloh: Gütersloher Verlagshaus, 122–31.

Zu Dohna, Lothar et al. (eds) (2012): *Johann von Staupitz, Libellus de Executione Aeternae Praedestinationis. Lateinische Schriften* II (= Spätmittelalter und Reformation), Meuchen: De Gruyter.

Ebeling, Gerhard (1980): *Luther. An introduction to his thought*, Minneapolis.

Edwards, Mark U. (1995): 'The Reception of Luther's Understanding of Freedom in the early modern period' in *Lutherjahrbuch* 62, 104–120.

Gaskell, Philip (2015): *A New Introduction to Bibliography*. 2nd revised and reprinted ed. New Castle: Oak Knoll Press.

Gasse, Jean-Louis (1984): *Le traité de la liberté du chrétien de Martin Luther: Étude comparative des deux versions, allemande et latine*, Paris: Presses Universitaires de France. (Publications de l'Université de Poitiers Lettres et Sciences Humaines, XXI).

Gerhardt, Volker (2018): 'Freiheit in der Reformation. Erasmus und Luther im paradigmatischen Streit' in Jörg Noller and Georg Sans (eds) *Luther und Erasmus über Freiheit. Rezeption und Relevanz eines gelehrten Streits*, Freiburg im Breisgau: Verlag Karl Alber, 13–36.

Gerleman, Gillis (2011): *Ruth Das Hohelied. Biblischer Kommentar Altes Testament,* Neukirchen-Vluyn: Neukirchener Verlag.

Gilmont, Jean-François (2016): *The Reformation and the Book*, Abingdon: Routledge. (transl. by Karin Maag)

Habenicht, Georg (2020): *Ablass. Wertpapiere der Gnade. Wie es zur Reformation kommen musste*, Petersberg: Michael Imhof Verlag.

Hamm, Berndt (2014): ,7. Freedom from the Pope and Pastoral Care to the Pope: The Compositional Unity of The Freedom of a Christian and Its Dedication Letter to Pope Leo X.' in *The Early Luther. Stages in a Reformation Reorientation* (English translation of *Der frühe Luther. Etappen reformatorischer Neuorientierung*, Tübingen: Mohr Siebeck 2010), Cambridge: Eerdmans Publishing Company, 172–89.

Hauschild, Wolf-Dieter (2001): *Lehrbuch der Kirchen- und Dogmengeschichte. Volume 2: Reformation und Neuzeit,* Gütersloh: Gütersloher Verlagshaus.

Heiles, Maco (2016): *Beschreibung des Sammelbandes Arch. 8°.G.1519 (11) der Taylor Institution Library, Oxford,* https://www.academia.edu/10742571/Beschreibung_des_Sammelbandes_Arch_8o_G_1519_11_der_Taylor_Institution_Library_Oxford.

Hirstein, James (2015): 'Corrections autographes de Martin Luther. Le "Tractatus de libertate christiana" d'après les éditions de 1520 et de 1521:

des suggestions d'émendation', *Revue d'histoire et de philosophie religieuses* 95(2), 129–63.

Hirstein, James(2017a): 'Des modes d'expression sublimes dans l'Epistola ad Leonem decimum et le Tractatus de libertate christiana corrigés par Martin Luther, par Beatus Rhenanus et par l'officine d'Adam Petri en vue de l'édition de 1521' in *Revue d'Histoire et de Philosophie Religieuses*, 97.3, 385–422.

Hirstein, James (2017b): 'Publizistische Netzwerke der Reformation. Die Schlettstädter Druckvorlage von Luthers Freiheitsschrift' in Ruth Slenczka (ed.) *Reformation und Freiheit. Luther und die Folgen für Preußen und Brandenburg*, Potsdam: Michael Imhof, 60–65.

Iserloh, Erwin (1981): *Johannes Eck (1486–1543). Scholastiker, Humanist, Kontroverstheologe*, Münster Westfalen: Aschendorffsche Buchdruckerei.

Jones, Howard (2017): *Martin Luther: Ein Sendbrief vom Dolmetschen, translation and introduction*, Oxford: Taylor Institution Library.

Jones, Howard (2018a): 'Language and Style' in Howard Jones, Martin Keßler, Henrike Lähnemann, and Christina Ostermann (eds) *Martin Luther: Sermon von Ablass und Gnade & 95 Theses*, Oxford: Taylor Institution Library.

Jones, Howard (2018b): 'The vocabulary of righteousness in Martin Luther's New Testament translations', *Oxford German Studies* 47(4), 381–416.

Jürgens, Henning P. (2014): 'Von der Freiheit eines Christenmenschen (1520) – Zur Druckgeschichte' in Irene Dingel and Henning P. Jürgens (eds) *Meilensteine der Reformation: Schlüsseldokumente der frühen Wirksamkeit Martin Luthers*, Gütersloh: Gütersloher Verlagshaus.

Kant, Immanuel, *Kritik der Praktischen Vernunft*, Akademie-Ausgabe.

Kaufmann, Thomas (2017), 'Luthers Traktat über die christliche Freiheit als publizistisches Phänomen und theologisches Programm', in Ruth Slenczka (ed.) *Reformation und Freiheit. Luther und die Folgen für Preußen und Brandenburg*, Potsdam: Michael Imhof, 43–59.

Kingreen, Jan (2017): *Martin Luther, Von der Freiheit eines Christenmenschen – kommentiert und herausgegeben* (= Uni-Taschenbücher, Vol. 4884),

Tübingen: Uni-Taschenbücher.

Köhler, Hans-Joachim (1986): 'Erste Schritte zu einem Meinungsprofil der frühen Reformationszeit' in Volker Press et al. (eds) *Martin Luther: Probleme seiner Zeit*. Stuttgart, 244–281 (256).

Leppin, Volker (2014): 'Luther's Roots in Monastic-Mystical Piety' in Robert Kolb et al. (ed.) *The Oxford Handbook of Martin Luther's theology*, Oxford: Oxford University Press.

Maurer, Wilhelm (1949): *Von der Freiheit eines Christenmenschen. Zwei Untersuchungen zu Luthers Reformationsschriften 1520/21*, Göttingen: Vandenhoeck & Ruprecht.

McDougall, Sara (2013): 'Women and Gender in Canon Law' in Judith Bennett and Ruth Karras (eds) *The Oxford Handbook of Women and Gender in Medieval Europe*, Oxford: Oxford University Press, 164–176.

McKenna, Michael and D. Justin Coates (2020): 'Compatibilism' in Edward N. Zalta (ed.) *The Stanford Encyclopedia of Philosophy*. URL = <https://plato.stanford.edu/archives/sum2020/entries/compatibilism/>.

Merker, Paul (1918): 'Thomas Murner, Von dem großen lutherischen Narren' in *Volume 9: Thomas Murners Deutsche Schriften*, Straßburg: Verlag von Karl J. Trübner.

Moeller, Bernd (1991): 'Die deutschen Humanisten und die Anfänge der Reformation' in Bernd Moeller and Johannes Schilling (eds) *Die Reformation und das Mittelalter. Kirchenhistorische Aufsätze*, Göttingen: Vandenhoeck & Ruprecht, 98–110.

Molhuysen, P.C., 'Een onuitgegeven brief von Frans von Sickingen', in *NAKG* 3 (1905), 93–95.

Nieden, Marcel (2012): 'Die Reformation als Medienereignis', in *Europäische Geschichte Online*, http://ieg-ego.eu/de/threads/europaeische-medien/europaeische-medienereignisse/marcel-nieden-die-wittenberger-reformation-als-medienereignis.

Reske, Christoph (2015): 'Die Anfänge des Buchdrucks im vorreformatorischen Wittenberg' in Stefan Oehmig (ed.) *Buchdruck und Buchkultur im Wittenberg der Reformationszeit*, Leipzig: Evangelischer Verlag-Anst., 35–69.

Rieger, Reinhold (2007): *Von der Freiheit eines Christenmenschen/De libertate christiana*, Tübingen: Mohr Siebeck.

Roper, Lyndal (2016) *Martin Luther. Renegade and Prophet*, London: Bodley Head.

Sammel, Rebecca (1996): 'The Passio Lutheri' in *Journal of English and Germanic Philology* 95(2), 157–74.

Scheible, Heinz (1996): 'Die Gravamina, Luther und der Wormser Reichstag 1521' in Heinz Scheible and Gerhard May (eds) *Melanchthon und die Reformation. Forschungsbeiträge*, Mainz: Verlag Philipp von Zabern, 393–409.

Schmidt, Georg (2010): 'Luthers Freiheitsvorstellungen in ihrem sozialen und rhetorischen Kontext (1517–1521)' in Dietrich Korsch and Volker Leppin (eds) *Volume 53: Martin Luther – Biographie und Theologie (= Spätmittelalter, Humanismus, Reformation)*, Tübingen: Mohr Siebeck, 9–29.

Schneider-Lastin, Wolfram (1990): *Johann von Staupitz, Salzburger Predigten 1512: eine textkritische Edition*, Tübingen.

Slenczka, Ruth (ed.) (2017): *Reformation und Freiheit. Luther und die Folgen für Preußen und Brandenburg*, Potsdam: Michael Imhof.

Slenczka, Notger (2017): 'Luthers Freiheitsverständnis', in Ruth Slenczka (ed.) *Reformation und Freiheit. Luther und die Folgen für Preußen und Brandenburg*, Potsdam: Michael Imhof, 26–41.

Stolt, Birgit (1969): *Studien zu Luthers Freiheitstraktat mit besonderer Rücksicht auf das Verhältnis der lateinischen und der deutschen Fassung zu einander und die Stilmittel der Rhetorik*, Stockholm: Almqvist & Wiksell.

Stupperich, Robert (ed.) (1960): *Martin Bucer, Deutsche Schriften. Band 1: Frühschriften 1520–1524*, Gütersloh: Verlagshaus Gerd Mohn.

Taylor Editions Online, https://editions.mml.ox.ac.uk/topics/reformation.shtml.

Thomas, David (2019): *The Faithful Shephard and me. A Personal Odyssey. The Taylor Institution Library's editions of II Pastor fido, by G.B. Guarini (1538–1612). Part II. The Once and Future Guarinian*, https://blogs.bodleian.ox.ac.uk/taylorian/2019/03/15/the-faithful-shepherd-and-me-a-personal-odyssey-part-ii/.

Tomlin, Graham (2017): *Luther then and now*, New York.

WA = *D. Martin Luthers Werke, Kritische Gesamtausgabe*, 120 vols (Weimar, 1883–2009) with WA.TR = *Tischreden* and WA.Br = *Briefe*.

Wallmann, Johannes (2012): *Kirchengeschichte Deutschlands seit der Reformation*, Tübingen: Mohr Siebeck.

Weber, Hanna-Christina (2017), 'Buchdrucker', in Helga Schnabel-Schüle (ed.) *Reformation. Historisch-Kulturwissenschaftliches Handbuch*, Stuttgart: Metzler, 93–108 (107).

Wengert, Timothy J. (2015): 'The Freedom of a Christian' in Timothy J. Wengert. (ed) *The Annotated Luther. Volume 1: The Roots of Reform*, Minneapolis: Fortress.

Wenzel, Horst (2005), 'Botschaften und Briefe. Die Spur des Körpers in der Schrift', in Gisela Fehrmann, Erika Linz, and Cornelia Epping-Jäger (eds) *Spuren, Lektüren. Praktiken des Symbolischen*, München: Fink, 259–76.

Wolf, Susan (1990): *Freedom within Reason*, Oxford: Oxford University Press.

Zimmerling, Peter (2017): *Martin Luther: Vater der evangelischen Mystik?* Akademie der Diözese Rottenburg Stuttgart.

Zumthor, Paul (1972): *Essai de poétique médiévale*, Paris: Seuil.

Martin Luther, 'Von der Freiheit eines Christenmenschen'

Preliminary remark on the translation and the two sets of footnotes: The translation keeps close to the original German to allow the reader to compare and contrast it with existing English translations of the Latin text and to check passages discussed in chapter 4.

The footnotes to the German transcription (on the left-hand side) are intended to aid comprehension of the German and should be taken together with the translation. The footnotes to the translation (on the right-hand side) mainly provide biblical references and additional factual information. They are to be read in conjunction with the historical and philosophical introduction (chapter 1) since factual information provided there is not repeated in this section.

As the internal structuring of each numbered article is based on layout constraints of the original page and quire structure (cf. chapter 2), we have taken early modern printers as a model in pragmatic typesetting, structuring the translation in paragraphs where possible, but not following all the spacing in Rhau-Gruneberg.

(A1r)
Von der Freyheyt eynisz[1] Christen menschen.[2]
Martinus Luther. Vuittembergae.
Anno Domini 1520.[3]

(A1v) (A2r)
Dem fursichtigen[4] vn̄[5] weyszen hern Hieronymo[6] Muͤlphordt Stadtuogt zu Zwyckaw meynem besondern guͤnstigen[7] freund vnd Patron Empiete[8] ich genantt D. Martinus Luther August.[9] meyne willige dienst vnnd allis guttis.[10]

---

[1] = New High German (NHG) *eines*. The final *ß* is here typeset as a combination of two characters, long *s* and *z*. This is only the case in the larger font on the title page and in the header on fol. Aijr. On the use of *ß* for *s* and *y* for *i*, and on the use of full vowels in unstressed syllables, such as *i* for *e* here, cf. chapter 3.

[2] = NHG *Christenmenschen*; the compound with 'mensch' is used to indicate the universal application of the address; on the use of spaces, cf. chapter 3.

[3] The 'A ij' following after the date in the bottom right-hand corner of the page is the quire mark, indicating that this is the second folio (ij) of the first quire (A). The quire marks have not been included in the transcription but rather transformed into hyperlinks in the digital version, allowing the alignment of translation, transcription, and facsimile.

[4] Early New High German (ENHG) *für-/vorsichtig* as an honorific is a loan-translation of Latin *prudens*, a common adjective of address.

[5] = *und*. On the exchangable use of *u* and *v* and on the bar above final characters, cf. chapter 3.

[6] Latin dative singular ending for Hieronymus.

[7] NHG *günstig* is generally not used to describe people.

[8] = NHG *entbiete*. On the use of capitalisation for emphasis or as the start of a phrase, cf. chapter 3.

[9] The full stop after 'D.' and 'August.' is an abbreviation marker; the full forms would be 'Doctor' and 'Augustiner'. On the use of abbreviations, cf. chapter 3. The phrase 'genantt ... Augustiner' is in apposition to 'ich'.

[10] = NHG *meine willigen Dienste* (plural) *und alles Gute*.

On the Freedom of a Christian.
Martin Luther. Wittenberg.
AD 1520.

To my judicious and wise lord Jerome Mühlpfort,[11] Town Magistrate of Zwickau, my right honourable friend and patron, I, by name Dr Martin Luther, Augustinian,[12] offer my willing service and best wishes.

---

[11] The correct name of the dedicatee would have been Hermann Mühlpfort (1486–1534). Luther replaced it – either deliberately or by mistake – with the name of the church father Jerome, which in the German form Hieronymus was a popular name among humanists. For more information on the historical context, cf. chapter 1 in this edition. The following footnotes include biblical references given in the form of the King James Version (KJV) and occasionally in the version of the Luther Bible of 1545 (L45), which is taken from the online resource biblija.net; for more on Luther's use of biblical language, cf. chapter 4 on the German and Latin versions.
[12] Luther had joined the Augustinian Order in 1505.

¶ Fursichtiger weyßer Herr / vnd Guͤnstiger freund / der wirdig Magister Johan Egran / ewr loͤblichen stat Prediger[13] / hat mir hoch gepreysset ewr lieb vnd lust / ßo yhr zu der heyligen schrifft traget / wilch[14] yhr auch emßlich bekennen vnd fur den menschen zu preyßen nit[15] nachlasset. Derhalben[16] er begeret / mich mit euch bekennet zu machen / byn ich gar leychtlich willig vnd froͤlich des beredt[17] / denn es mir eyn sondere freudt ist / tzu hoͤren / wo die gottlich warheyt geliebt wirt / der leyder ßo vill / vnd die am meysten / die sich yhres titels auffwerffen[18] / mit aller gewalt vnd list widderstreben / wie wol es alßo seyn muß / das an Christum[19] / zu eynem ergernis vnd tzeychen[20] gesetzt / dem widdersprochen werden muß / vill sich stossen / fallen / vnd aufferstahen mussen. Darūb[21] hab ich an zu heben vnßer kundschafft vnd freuntschafft / diß tractatell[22] vnnd Sermon euch wollen zuschreyben / ym deutschē / wilchs ich latinisch dem Bapst hab zu geschrieben[23] / damit fur yderman[24] / meyner lere vnd schreyben / von dem Bapstum / nit eyn vorweyßlich / als ich hoff / vrsach angetzeygt.[25] Befill mich hie mit / euch / vnd allsampt / gottlichen gnaden.[26] AMEN.

Zu Wittembergk. 1520.

---

[13] = NHG *Prediger eurer löblichen Stadt.*

[14] = NHG *welche.*

[15] = NHG *nicht.*

[16] = NHG *weshalb.*

[17] = *des beredet* 'convinced about this'.

[18] *sich auffwerffen* + gen = 'to appeal to, invoke'.

[19] Latin accusative singular ending.

[20] = NHG *Ärgernis und Zeichen.*

[21] = NHG *darum.* The syntax of this clause is not clear from the punctuation: 'an zu heben ... freuntschafft' is a purpose clause interpolated within the clause 'hab ich … wollen zuschreyben'.

[22] Diminutive corresponding to NHG *Traktat.*

[23] 'zu geschrieben' should be read as one word; it governs 'dem Bapst' = NHG *Papst.*

[24] = NHG *jedermann.*

[25] Also governed by 'hab'.

[26] = NHG *Befehle mich hier mit euch und allesamt der göttlichen Gnade.*

My judicious wise lord and generous friend: the Reverend John Egranus,[27] preacher in your esteemed town, has highly commended to me the love and enthusiasm that you have for Holy Scripture, which you never tire of proclaiming and praising eagerly to all people.[28] In light of his desire to introduce me to you, I was very readily and happily convinced, because it is a special joy for me to hear about love for divine truth, which regrettably so many, and in particular those who pull rank because of their titles,[29] resist with all their might and cunning, even though it must be the case that Christ, placed as a stumbling-block and a sign to be contradicted,[30] will cause many to stumble, fall, and rise again.

Therefore, to start off our acquaintance and friendship, I wanted to dedicate to you the German version of this little treatise and sermon, which I wrote in Latin for the Pope, to show to everyone the reason for this teaching and writing about the Papacy, which I hope is unobjectionable. Herewith I commend myself, you, and everybody to divine grace. Amen

At Wittenberg. 1520.

---

[27] Johannes Sylvius Egranus was the humanist name of Johannes Wildenauer (1480–1535), minister in Zwickau since 1517.

[28] Resonances of biblical languages, here KJV Matthew 7,32: 'Whosoever therefore shall confess me before men, him will I confess also before my Father which is in heaven.'

[29] Reference to the papal court.

[30] For Christ as stumbling block, cf. KJV I Corinthians 1,23: 'But we preach Christ crucified, unto the Jews a stumblingblock, and unto the Greeks foolishness'; KJV Isaiah 8,14–15: 'And he shall be for a sanctuary; but for a stone of stumbling and for a rock of offence to both the houses of Israel, for a gin and for a snare to the inhabitants of Jerusalem. And many among them shall stumble, and fall, and be broken, and be snared, and be taken.'

(A2v)

Ihesus.

Zum ersten. Das wir grundlich muͤgen[31] erkennen / was eyn Christen mensch sey[32] / vñ wie es gethā sey / vmb die freyheyt / die yhm Christus erworben vñ geben[33] hatt / dauon[34] S. Paulus viel schreybt / will ich setzen[35] / dyße zween beschluß.[36]

Eyn Christen mensch ist eyn freyer herr / uͤber alle ding[37] / vnd niemandt vnterthan.

Eyn Christen mensch ist eyn dienstpar knecht aller ding vnd yderman vnterthan.

Diße zween beschluͤß seynd klerlich[38] sanct Paulus 1. Cor.[39] 9. Ich byn frey yn allen dingen / vñ hab mich eynß ydermā knecht gemacht. Itē[40] Ro. 13. Ihr solt niemand ettws vorpflichtet seyn / den dz[41] yr euch vnternāder liebet. Lieb aber / die[42] ist / dienstpar / vñ vnterthan dem das sie lieb hatt. Alßo auch von Christo Gal. 4. Gott hatt seynen ßon außgesandt / von eynem weyb[43] geporen vnd dem gesetz vnterthan gemacht.

---

[31] = NHG *können.*

[32] The subjunctive, against NHG usage, can be explained by the fact that it is in a clause of indirect question; it does not indicate doubt.

[33] = NHG *gegeben.*

[34] = NHG *wovon.*

[35] Here 'set down, propose'.

[36] = NHG *Beschlüsse*; 'propositions'.

[37] = NHG *Dinge.*

[38] = NHG *sind klar / deutlich.*

[39] The full stop after all biblical references is an abbreviation mark, mostly after the Latin title for the biblical books, e.g. here short for 'Epistula I ad Corinthios' = NHG *Erster Korinther(brief).* For the English full form and the quotation referenced, cf. the footnotes to the translation on the right-hand side of this edition. The following Pauline letters referenced are those 'Ad Romanos' = NHG *Römerbrief* and 'Ad Galatas' = NHG *Galaterbrief.*

[40] Latin 'likewise'.

[41] On the spelling of 'das' as 'dz', cf. chapter 3. 'den das' = NHG *außer dass.*

[42] A resumptive pronoun, literally 'But love, it is …'.

[43] ENHG *weib* without the pejorative connotations of NHG *Weib.*

Jesus.

1 In order that we may thoroughly recognise what a Christian is and what is meant by their freedom, which Christ has purchased and given them, as St Paul writes at length, I will set down these two propositions:

A Christian is a free lord over all things and subject to no-one.

A Christian is a bound[44] servant of all things and subject to everyone.

These two propositions are evident in St Paul's first letter to the Corinthians, chapter 12: 'I am free in all things, and I have made myself a servant to all'.[45] Likewise, Romans 13: 'Owe no man anything, but to love one another'.[46] But love is bound and subject to what it loves. The same applies to Christ in Galatians 4: 'God sent forth His Son, born of a woman, subject to the law'.[47]

---

[44] Luther uses 'dienstbar' to mean 'enslaved' and elsewhere he uses 'dienstbar sein' to mean 'to serve'. The Latin has 'officiosissimus' 'most/very obedient'. The term 'dienstbar' echoes KJV Acts 7,6: 'And God spake on this wise, That his seed should sojourn in a strange land; and that they should bring them into bondage, and entreat *them* evil four hundred years.'

[45] This is, in fact, KJV I Corinthians 9,19: 'For though I be free from all men, yet have I made myself servant unto all.'

[46] KJV Romans 13,8: 'Owe no man any thing, but to love one another: for he that loveth another hath fulfilled the law.'

[47] KJV Galatians 4,4: 'But when the fulness of the time was come, God sent forth his Son, made of a woman, made under the law.'

¶ Czum andern[48] / Diße zwo widderstendige rede / der freyheyt vnd dienstparkeyt zuuornehmen[49] / sollen wir gedencken / das eyn yglich Christen mensch ist zweyerley natur / geystlicher vñ leyplicher. Nach der seelen[50] wirt er eyn geystlich[51] / new / ynnerlich mensch genennet / nach dem fleysch vnd blut wirt er eyn leyplich allt vnd eußerlich mensch genennet. Vnd vmb dißes vnterschiediß willen / werden von yhm gesagt yn der schrifft / die do[52] stracks widdernander seyn[53] / wie ich itzt[54] gesagt[55] / von der freyheyt vnd dienstparkeit.

---

[48] Each of the paragraphs from number 2 is prefaced by a pilcrow '¶' followed by the number, first spelled out in German, and then from paragraph twenty-four (xxiiij) in Roman numerals. 'Czum andern' = NHG *Zum zweiten, Zweitens*. The use of *Cz* for *Z* at the start of each paragraph is a practice developed when using Latin font sets which did not have an upper-case *Z*. In the larger font set used for the first paragraph ('Zum ersten', A2v), a *Z* from a different font is used, not in keeping with the Gothic character of the rest of the font.

[49] = NHG *zu vernehmen* in the sense of *verstehen*; NHG would place *um* at the beginning of such a purpose clause. Cf. chapter 3 for the missing space between *zu* and *vornehmen*.

[50] Dative singular of *seele*.

[51] The adjectives *geystlich*, *new*, and *ynnerlich* agree with *mensch*; the 'zero inflection' was an alternative for the nominative (and sometimes accusative) singular of strong adjectives in ENHG.

[52] = NHG *da*; it often occurs immediately after a pronoun to indicate that it should be read as a relative; here 'die do' can be translated as 'things which'.

[53] = NHG *sind*.

[54] = NHG *jetzt*.

[55] The finite verb *habe* is understood.

2 In order to understand these two conflicting statements about freedom and bondage, we should remember that each Christian is of a dual nature, spiritual and physical.[56] As to the soul they are called spiritual, new, inner persons; as to flesh and blood they are called physical, old, and outer persons.[57] Owing to this difference, things are said about them in Scripture which flatly contradict each other, as I have just been saying about freedom and bondage.

[56] The contrast references Romans 7/8, e.g. KJV Romans 8,5: 'For they that are after the flesh do mind the things of the flesh; but they that are after the Spirit the things of the Spirit.' In Martin Luther's translation from 1545: 'DEnn die da fleischlich sind / die sind fleischlich gesinnet /Die aber geistlich sind/die sind geistlich gesinnet.'
[57] On this dichotomy 'new /ynnerlich' versus 'allt /eußerlich', cf. chapter 1.

¶ Czum dritten / So nhemen wir fur vns den ynwendigen geystlichen menschen / zusehen was datzu gehoͤre / dz er eyn frum[58] frey / Christen mensch sey vnd heysse. So ists offenbar / das keyn eußerlich ding mag yhn frey / noch[59] frum machen / wie es mag ymmer genennet werden / denn seyn frumkeyt vñ freyheyt / widerumb seyn boͤßheyt vnd gefenckniß[60] / seyn nit leyplich noch eußerlich.[61] Was hilffts die seelen[62] / das der leyp / vngefangen / frisch vnd gesund ist / ysszet[63] / trinckt / lebt / wie er will? Widderūb was schadet das der seelen / das der leyp / gefangen krang[64] vnd matt (A3r) ist / hungert / duͤrstet vnd leydet / wie er[65] nit gerne wolt? Dißer ding reychet keyniß[66] / biß an die seelen / sie zu befreyhen oder fahen[67] / frum oder boͤße zu machen.

---

58 On the meaning of *frum* in this text, cf. chapter 4, section 4.

59 *noch* 'nor' in ENHG can occur on its own without *weder*.

60 = NHG *Gefängnis*.

61 = NHG *äußerlich*.

62 = NHG *hilfft es der Seele*; 'helfen' is constructed here with the accusative singular 'seelen'.

63 = NHG *isst*.

64 = NHG *krank*.

65 Refers to 'der leyp' = NHG *der Leib*.

66 'Dißer ding ... keyniß' = NHG *keines dieser Dinge*, 'none of these things'.

67 = NHG *fangen*.

3 Now let us consider the inner, spiritual person, to see what it meant by their being, and being called, righteous, free Christians. It is then obvious that nothing external can make them either free or righteous, whatever you may call it, since their righteousness and freedom, and conversely their evil-doing and inprisonment, are neither physical nor external. What profit is it for the soul if the body is unshackled, active, and healthy, if it eats, drinks, lives as it will?[68] Conversely, how does it harm the soul if the body is imprisoned, sick and weary, hungers and thirsts and suffers against its will? None of these things can touch the soul, to free it or bind it, to make it righteous or evil.

[68] Reference to KJV Mark 8,36: 'For what shall it profit a man, if he shall gain the whole world, and lose his own soul?' L45 Mark 8,36: 'Was hülfe es dem Menschen, wenn er die ganze Welt gewönne, und nähme an seiner Seele Schaden?'

¶ Czum vierden / Alßo hilfftet es die seele nichts / ob d᷑[69] leyp heylige kleyder anlegt / wie die priester vñ geystlichen thun / auch nit ob er ynn den kirchen vnd heyligen stetten sey. Auch nit ob er mit heyligē dingē vmbgah[70]. Auch nit ob er leyplich bette / faste/ walle[71] / vnd alle gute werck[72] thue / die durch vnd ynn dem leybe geschehen mochten ewiglich. Es muß noch allis etwas anders seyn / das[73] der seelen bringe vnd gebe frumkeyt vnd freyheyt. Denn alle diße obgenanten[74] stuck / werck vnd weyßen / mag auch an sich haben vnd ůben eyn bőßer mensch / eyn gleyßner vnd heuchler. Auch durch solch weßen[75] keyn ander volck / denn[76] eyttell gleyßner werden. Widderumb / schadet es der seelen nichts / ob d᷑ leyp vnheylige kleyder tregt / an vnheyligen őrten ist / yßt / trinckt / wallet / bettet nit / vnd lessit alle die werck onstehen[77] / die die őbgenanten gleyßner thun.

---

[69] On the abbreviation *d᷑* for *der*, cf. chapter 3.

[70] = NHG *umgehe, Umgang habe.*

[71] = NHG *wallfahre*, 'go on pilgrimage'.

[72] 'werck' is plural here, as often in this text.

[73] = NHG *was.*

[74] = NHG *obengenannten.*

[75] = NHG *Wesen*, here 'conduct'.

[76] = NHG *als.*

[77] = NHG *anstehen*; here 'be outstanding, not be done'.

4 Equally, what profit is it for the soul if the body puts on holy garments[78] as priests and clerics do, or if the body is in churches and holy places. Nor if it is engaging in religious matters. Nor physically praying, fasting, going on pilgrimages, or doing any good works, which might be achieved through and in the body forever. There must be something completely different which brings to and bestows upon the soul righteousness and freedom. All the above-named activities, works, and practices are available to and can be performed by an evil person, an imposter, and a hypocrite.[79] Nothing comes from such conduct except simply a people of hypocrites. Conversely, the soul is not harmed if the body wears unholy garments or dwells, eats, drinks, goes on pilgrimages in unholy places, does not pray, and leaves aside all good works, as the aforementioned hypocrites do.

---

[78] Phrase from KJV Exodus 28,4: 'And these *are* the garments which they shall make; a breastplate, and an ephod, and a robe, and a broidered coat, a mitre, and a girdle: and they shall make holy garments for Aaron thy brother, and his sons, that he may minister unto me in the priest's office.'

[79] This seems to be a reference to Matthew 6 where the ostentatious alms-giving, praying, and fasting of the hypocrites is denounced by Christ.

¶ Czum funfften / Hatt die seele keyn ander dinck[80] / widder[81] yn hymel noch auff erden darynnen[82] / sie lebe / frum / frey / vnd Christen sey / den[83] das heylig Euãgelij / das wort gottis von Christo gepredigет. Wie er selb[84] sagt Joh. 11. Ich byn das leben vñ aufferstehung / wer do glaubt yn mich / der lebet ewiglich. Item 14. Ich byn der weg / die warheyt / vnd das leben. Item Matt. 4. Der mensch lebet nit alleyn von dem brot / sondern von allen worten die do gehen von dem mund gottis. So mussen wir nu[85] gewiß seyn / das die seele kan allis dings emperen[86] on[87] des worts gottis / vnd on das wort / ist yhr mit keynem ding beholffen. Wo sie aber das wort hatt / ßo darff[88] sie auch keyneß andern dings mehr / sondern / sie hat in dem wort / gnugde / speiß freud / frid / licht / kunst / gerechtickeyt / warheyt / weyßheyt / freyheit vnd allis gutt[89] ůberschwenglich. Alßo leßen wir ym Psalter sonderlich ym 118. psalm / das der prophet nit mehr schreyet den nach[90] dem gottis wort. Vnd yn d'[91] schrifft die aller hochste plag vnd gottis zorn gehalten wirt / ßo[92] er seyn wort von den menschen nympt /

---

80 = NHG *anderes Ding*.
81 = NHG *weder*.
82 = NHG *in dem, worin*.
83 ENHG 'den' = NHG *außer*.
84 = NHG *selber/selbst*.
85 = NHG *nun*.
86 = NHG *entbehren*, here with genitive 'allis dings'.
87 = NHG *ohne* with genitive *des Worts Gottes*, here in the sense of *außer*.
88 = NHG *bedarf*, with genitive 'keyneß andern dings' = NHG *keines andern Dings*.
89 = NHG *Genüge, Speise, Freude, Friede, Licht, Kunst, Gerechtigkeit, Wahrheit, Weisheit, Freiheit und alles Gut*.
90 'nit mehr ... den nach' literally 'no more than for', i.e. 'only for'.
91 On the abbreviation *d'* for *der*, cf. the chapter 3.
92 = NHG *so*, 'when'.

5 The soul has nothing else, either in Heaven or on earth, in which it may live, be righteous, free, and Christian, than the holy Gospel, the word of God preached by Christ. As he himself says, in John 11: 'I am the life and the resurrection. Whoever believes in me will live eternally'.[93] Likewise in chapter 14: 'I am the way, the truth, and the life'.[94] Likewise in Matthew 4: 'Man shall not live by bread alone, but by every word that proceeds out of the mouth of God'.[95]

So we must now be certain that the soul can forego all things except the word of God, and, except the word, nothing can help it. But when it has the word, then it needs nothing else, but has in the word full sufficiency,[96] sustenance, joy, peace, light, knowledge, righteousness, truth, wisdom, freedom, and all good things in abundance. Thus we read in the Psalter, and particularly in Psalm 118, that the prophet cries out only for the word of God.[97] And Scripture holds the very greatest curse and sign of God's wrath to be when He takes His word from the people.

---

[93] Paraphrase of KJV John 11,25–26: 'I am the resurrection, and the life: he that believeth in me, though he were dead, yet shall he live: And whosever liveth and believeth in me shall never die.'

[94] KJV John 14,6: 'Jesus saith unto him, I am the way, the truth, and the life: no man cometh unto the Father, but by me.'

[95] KJV Matthew 4,4: 'But he answered and said, It is written, Man shall not live by bread alone, but by every word that proceedeth out of the mouth of God.'

[96] KJV Job 20,22: 'In the fulness of his sufficiency he shall be in straits.'

[97] The desire for the word of God is the main topic of Psalm 119 (in the numbering of KJV and L45; Luther here uses still the Vulgate numbering of the Psalms and references it as Psalm 118).

Widderumb keyn groͤsser gnade / wo er seyn wort hyn sendet / wie psalmus 106. stet Er hat seyn wort auß gesandt / damit er yhn[98] hatt geholffen. Vnd Christ vmb keyns (A3v) andern ampts [geholffen][99]/ den zu predigen das wort gottis kummen[100] ist. Auch alle Apostell / Bischoff / priester vñ gantzer geystlicher stand / alleyn vmb des worts willen ist beruffen vnd eyngesetzt / wie woll es nu leyder anders gaht.[101]

---

[98] = NHG *womit er ihnen.*

[99] 'geholffen' is a typographical error, accidentally repeated from the previous sentence instead of 'willen'.

[100] 'u' is smudged in the copy but clear from other copies of the same edition.

[101] = NHG *wiewohl* … *geht* in the sense of 'even though … it goes'.

Conversely, there is no greater grace than when He sends forth His word, as stated in Psalm 104: 'He sent out His word and helped them thereby'.[102] And Christ has come for nothing other than to preach the word of God. And so also all apostles, bishops, priests, and the whole of the clergy are called and appointed solely for the word, although that is now unfortunately not the case.

---

[102] In fact, a paraphrase of KJV Psalm 107,20: 'He sent his word and healed them'. In the Vulgate numbering it would be Psalm 106,20: 'Misit verbum suum, et sanavit eos'.

¶ Czum sechsten[103] / Fragistu[104] aber / wilchs ist denn das wort das solch grosse gnad gibt. Vnd wie sol ichs gebrauchen?

---

[103] For a comparison between the German and Latin versions of §6, cf. chapter 4, section 2b. The Latin text (taken from the digital version of the Taylor Editions https://editions.mml.ox.ac.uk/editions/libertate1521/#d1r) is as follows (marginalia are in square brackets):
'[Verbum dei quod sit.] Quaeres autem, Quod nam est verbum hoc, aut qua arte utendum est eo, cum tam multa sint verba dei? Respondeo, Apostolus Ro. i. id explicat, scilicet Euangelium dei de filio suo incarnato, passo, resuscitato, & glorificato per spiritum sanctificatorem. Praedicasse enim Christum, hoc est, animam pavisse, iustificasse, liberasse, & salvam fecisse, si crediderit praedicationi. Fides enim sola est salutaris & efficax usus verbi dei. Ro. x. Si confitearis ore tuo, IESVM esse dominum, & corde tuo credideris, quod deus illum suscitavit a mortuis, salvus eris. Et iterum. Finis legis Christus ad iustitiam omni credenti. Et Ro. i. Iustus ex fide sua vivet. Neque enim verbum dei, operibus ullis, sed sola fide suscipi & coli potest.
[Sola fides iustificat.] Ideo clarum est, ut solo verbo anima opus habet ad vitam & iustitiam, ita sola fide & nullis operibus iustificatur. Si enim alio quopiam iustificari posset, verbo non haberet opus, ac per hoc nec fide. Verum haec fides subsistere prorsus non potest cum operibus, hoc est, si per opera (quaecunque sunt) simul iustificari praesumas, hoc enim esset in duas partes claudicare, Baal adorare, & manum osculari, quae est iniquitas maxima, ut Iob ait.
[Credenda.] Ideo dum credere incipis, simul discis, omnia quae in te sunt, esse prorsus culpabilia, peccata, damnanda. Iuxta illud Ro. ii. Omnes peccaverunt & egent gloria dei. Et Ro. iii. Non est iustus, non est, qui faciat bonum, omnes declinaverunt, simul inutiles facti sunt. Hoc enim cognito, scies Christum necessarium tibi, qui pro te passus & resuscitatus est, ut in eum credens, alius homo hac fide fieres, donatis omnibus peccatis tuis, & iustificato te alienis meritis, nempe Christi solius.
[Nullo externo opere iustificatur homo.] Cum ergo haec fides non nisi in homine interiore regnare possit. Sicut dicit Ro. x. Corde creditur ad iustitiam: & sola ipsa iustificet, manifestum est, hominem interiorem prorsus nullo externo opere vel negotio posse iustificari, liberum & salvum fieri, & opera quaecunque, ad eum nihil pertinere: sicut econtra, sola impietate & incredulitate cordis, reus fit & servus peccati damnandus, nullo externo peccato vel opere.'

[104] = NHG *Fragst du.*

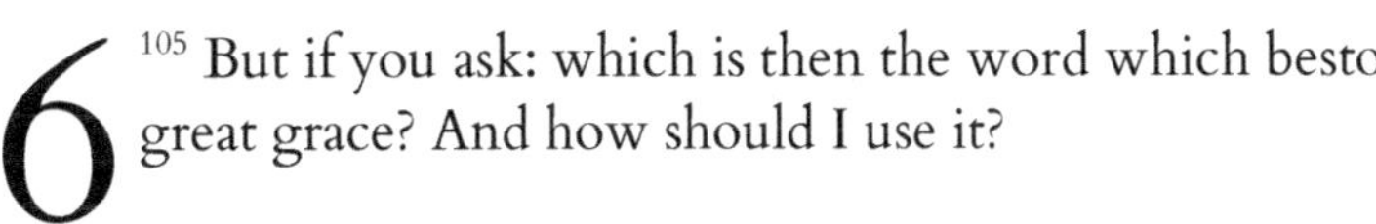

6 [105] But if you ask: which is then the word which bestows such great grace? And how should I use it?

---

[105] Translation of the Latin version:
'[What the word of God is] But you will ask, 'Now what is this word and by what means is it to be used, since there are so many words of God?' I answer, 'The Apostle in Romans 1 explains what it is, namely the Gospel of God about His Son who was made flesh, suffered, was raised up, and glorified through the Spirit which is the sanctifier. For to preach Christ is to nourish the soul, to justify it, to set it free, and to save it, if it believes what is preached. For faith alone is the sanctifying and efficacious use of the word of God. 'If you confess with your mouth that Jesus is Lord and you believe in your heart that God raised him from the dead, you will be saved'. And again, 'Christ is the end of the law for all believers to become righteous'. And Romans 1, 'The righteous will live by faith'. For the word of God cannot be taken up and honoured by any works, but by faith alone.
[Only faith justifies] Hence it is clear that, as the soul needs the word alone for life and justification, so it is justified by faith alone, and not by any works. For if it could be justified by anything else, it would have no need of the word and therefore no need of faith. But this faith cannot coexist at all with works, if, that is, you imagine that you can at the same time be justified by those works, whatever they are. For this would be to limp in two directions, to worship Baal and kiss his hand, which is the greatest iniquity, as Job says.
[What should be believed] Therefore, when you begin to believe, you learn at the same time that everything that is in you is utterly guilty, sinful, damnable according to that passage in Romans 3, 'All have sinned, and come short of the glory of God', and Romans 3, 'There is no-one righteous, no-one who does good, they have all turned aside, they have all at once become useless'. For having realised this you will know that Christ is necessary to you, Christ who suffered for you and was raised up, so that, believing in him, you might become another person through this faith, with all your sins forgiven and yourself justified by the merits of another, namely of Christ alone.
[By no outword work are people justified] Therefore, since this faith can reign only in the inward person, as it is said in Romans 10, 'With the heart one believes and is justified', and since it alone justifies, it is evident that the inward person cannot, by any outward work or activity at all, be justified, made free, and saved, and that no works whatever affect them; and so, conversely, it is only by impiety and unbelief in the heart that they become guilty and a damnable slave of sin, not by any outward sin or work.'

Antwort / Es ist nit anders / deñ die predigt von Christo geschehen[106] / wie das Euangeliũ ynnehelt.[107] Wilche soll seyn / vnd ist alßo gethan / das du hͤorist deynen gott zu dir reden / Wie alle[108] deyn leben vnd werck / nichts seyn fur[109] gott / sondern mͤußsist[110] / mit allen dem das ynn dir ist ewiglich vorterben.[111] Wilchs ßo du recht glaubst / wie du schuldig bist / so mustu an dir selber vortzweyffelnñ[112] / vnd bekennen / das war[113] sey der spruch Osee: O Israel yn dir ist nichts / denn deyn vorterben / alleyn aber yn mir steht deyn hulff.[114] Das du aber auß dir vnd von dir / das ist auß deynem vorterbeñ kōmen mͤugist[115] / ßo setzt er dir fur[116] / seynen lieben ßon Ihesum Christũ / vnd leßsit dir durch seyn lebendigs trostlichs wort sagen: Du solt ynn den selben mit festem glauben dich ergeben / vnd frisch ynn yhn vortrawen.[117] So sollen dir vmb desselben glaubens willen / alle deyne sund vorgeben[118] / alle deyn vorterben vberwunden seyn / vnd du gerecht / warhafftig / befridet / frum vñ alle gebott erfullet seyn / vō allen dingen frey sein. Wie S. Paulus sagt Ro. 1. Ein rechtfertiger[119] Christen / lebt nur von seynem glauben. Vnd Ro. x. Christus ist das ende vnd fͤulle aller gebot / denen / die ynn yhn glauben.

---

[106] = NHG *vollzogen* (DWB s.v. 'geschehen' agreeing with 'die predigt').

[107] ENHG 'innehelt' = NHG *in sich hält / enthält.*

[108] Plural agreeing with the two following nouns.

[109] = NHG *vor.*

[110] = NHG *du müssest* (present subjunctive).

[111] = NHG *verderben.*

[112] = NHG *verzweifeln.*

[113] = NHG *wahr.*

[114] = NHG *deine Hilfe.*

[115] = NHG *aus deinem Verderben kommen könntest.*

[116] 'setzt er dir fur' = NHG *stellt er dir vor Augen.*

[117] = NHG *sollst [dich] demselben … ergeben und frisch auf ihn vertrauen.*

[118] = NHG *Sünden vergeben.*

[119] On *gerecht, frum*, and *rechtfertig* (here a synonym of *gerecht*), cf. chapter 4, section 4.

The answer:[120] It is nothing other than the preaching done by Christ as contained in the Gospel. This should be (and indeed is) done in such a way that you hear your God speaking to you, how all your life and works are nothing before God, but that you must, along with everything that is within you, perish forever. When you truly believe this, how you are sinful, then you must despair of yourself and recognise the truth of the line from Hosea: 'O Israel, in you is nothing than your own destruction, but in me is your help'.[121] In order that you might come out of and away from yourself, i.e. out of your destruction, He put his beloved son Jesus Christ before you and conveys through him His living comforting word: You should give yourself over to him with firm faith and trust in him directly. Then for the sake of this faith all your sins shall be forgiven and all your destruction overcome, and you will be just, true, at peace, righteous, with all commandments fulfilled, and freed from all things. As St Paul says in Romans 1: 'A righteous Christian lives by faith alone'.[122] And in Romans 10: 'Christ is the end and fulfilment of all commandments for those who believe in him'.[123]

---

[120] This question-and-answer structure is reminiscent of a catechism, an outline of doctrine often taking the form of a series of questions and answers designed to be memorised. The format was adopted from the beginning of the Reformation, with Luther himself authoring a number of catechisms.

[121] KJV Hosea 13,9: 'O Israel, thou hast destroyed thyself, but in me is thine help.'

[122] KJV Romans 1,17: 'For therein is the righteousness of God revealed from faith to faith: as it is written, the just shall live by faith.'

[123] KJV Romans 10,4: 'For Christ is the end of the law for righteousness to everyone that believeth.'

¶ Czū siebenden. Drumb solt das billich aller Christen eynigs[124] werck vnd ůbung seyn / das sie das wort vñ Christū wol[125] ynn sich bildeten / solchen glauben stetig vbeten vñ sterckte̅. Deñ keyn ander werck / mag eynen Christen machen. Wie Christus Joh. 6. zu den Juden sagt / da sie yhn fragten / was sie fur werck thun solten / dz sie gottlich vñ Christlich werck thetten.[126] Sprach er: Das ist das eynige gotliche werck / das yhr glaubt yn denen[127] / den gott gesandt hatt. Wilchen gott der vatter allein auch dartzu vorordnet[128] hatt. Darūb ists gar ein vberschwencklich reychtumb / ein rechter glau[d][129] yn Christo / denn er mit sich bringt alle seligkeit / vnd abnympt alle vnseligkeyt. Wie Mar. vlt.[130] Wer do glaubt vnd taufft[131] ist / der wirt selig. Wer nit glaubt / der wirt (A4r) vordampt.
Darumb der prophet Isa. X. Den reychtumb des selben glaubens ansach vnd sprach. Gott wirt eyn kurtz summa[132] machen auff erden / vnd die kurtz summa wirt / wie ein syndflut eynfliessen die gerechtickeit / das ist / der glaub / darynn[133] kurtzlich aller gebot erfullung steht / wirt vberflussig[134] rechtfertige̅ alle die yhn haben / das sie nichts mehr bedurffen / das[135] sie gerecht vnd frum seyn. Alßo sagt S. Pauel Ro. x. Das man von hertzen glaubt / das macht eynen gerecht vnd frum.

---

[124] = NHG *sollte das rechtmäßig aller Christen einziges*; 'billig' as in NHG *recht und billig*.

[125] 'truly'; stronger than NHG *wohl*.

[126] = NHG *täten* in the sense 'would do'.

[127] = NHG *denjenigen*.

[128] = NHG *dazu verordnet* in the sense of 'ordained for that'.

[129] Typographical error of 'd' instead of 'b'; it should read 'glaub'.

[130] 'Mar. ult.' is an abbreviation of Latin *Marci ultimo*, meaning 'in the last [chapter] of [the Gospel according to] Mark'.

[131] = NHG *getauft*.

[132] The Latin *summa* means the summing up of a calculation or process; 'eyn kurtz summa machen' = NHG *einen kurzen Prozess machen*. Here used to describe the Last Judgement.

[133] = NHG *worin*.

[134] ENHG 'überflüssig' = 'abundantly', not 'redundantly'.

[135] Introduces a purpose clause.

7 It should therefore rightly be the sole work and practice of all Christians that they truly impress upon themselves this word and Christ, and constantly practise and strengthen this faith. For no other work can make a Christian. As Christ says to the Jews in John 6, when they asked him what sort of works they should do in order to do godly and Christian works. He said: 'This is the only work of God: that you believe in him whom God has sent',[136] whom God the Father has alone ordained for this purpose. Therefore true faith in Christ is indeed abundant riches, for it brings with it all salvation and takes away all damnation. As in Mark chapter 16, 'He who believes and is baptised shall be saved. He who does not believe shall be damned'.[137] Thus the prophet Isaiah, chapter 10, looked upon the riches of this faith and said: 'God will make a short account on earth, and the short account will bring righteousness like a flood',[138] that is, faith which in short contains the fulfilment of all commandments, will abundantly justify all those who possess it, so that they will need nothing more in order to be justified and righteous. Thus Saint Paul says in Romans 10: 'What you believe with your heart makes you justified and righteous'.[139]

[136] The word 'only' is Luther's addition. Paraphrase of KJV John 6,29: 'Jesus answered and said unto them, This is the work of God, that ye believe on Him whom He hath sent.'

[137] KJV Mark 16,16: 'He that believeth and is baptised shall be saved; but he that believeth not shall be damned.'

[138] Paraphrase of KJV Isaiah 10,22–23 (The verse refers to the destruction of the nation of Israel, who have not believed in God. Because of Israel's sin, God would punish the people through foreign invasion by the Assyrians): 'The consumption decreed shall overflow with righteousness. For the Lord God of hosts shall make a consumption, even determined, in the midst of all the land.' The word used for overflow in Hebrew, שֹׁטֵף (shoṭēph), usually refers to a stream breaking its banks and flooding the land. Here is it used figuratively to refer to the judgement which will flow through the land.

[139] Paraphrase of KJV Romans 10,10: 'For with the heart man believeth unto righteousness; and with the mouth confession is made unto salvation.'

¶ Czū achten / Wie gaht es aber zu / das der glaub allein mag frum machen / vnd on alle werck ßo uͤberschwencklich reychtumb geben / ßo doch souill gesetz / gebot / werck / stend vnd weyße vns furgeschrieben seyn[140] / ynn der schrifft. Hie ist fleyßsig zu mercken / vnd yhe mit ernst zubehalten[141] / dz allein der glaub on alle werck frum / frey / vn̄ selig machet / wie wir hernach mehr hoͤren werden Vnd ist zu wissen / das die gantze heylige schrifft / wirt yn zweyerley wort geteyllet / wilche seyn. Gebot oder gesetz gottis / vnd vorheyschen oder zusagunge.[142] Die gebott / leren vnd schreyben vns fur / mancherley gutte werck aber damit seyn sie noch nit geschehen. Sie weyßen wol / sie helffen aber nit / leren was man thun soll / geben aber keyn sterck dartzu.[143] Darūb seyn sie nur datzu geordnet / das der mensch drynnen sehe sein vnuormuͤgen zu dem gutten / vnd lerne an yhm selbs vortzweyffeln.[144] Vnd darumb heyssen sie auch das alte testament / vnd gehoͤren alle ynß alte testament. Als[145] / das gebott / Du solt nit boͤß begird haben / beweysset das wir allesampt sunder seyn / vnd kein mensch vormag / zu sein on boͤße begirde / er thue was er will[146] / Darauß er lernet an yhm selbs vortzagen vnd anderßwo zu suchen hulff / das[147] er on boͤße begird sey / vnnd alßo[148] das gebott erfulle / durch eynen andern / das er auß yhm selb nit vormag[149] / alßo sein auch alle andere gebott / vns vnmuglich.[150]

---

[140] = NHG *wenn doch so viele Gesetze, Gebote, Werke, Stände und Weisen uns vorgeschrieben sind*; all the nouns in this list are plural.

[141] = NHG *Hierdurch ist aufmerksam zu vermerken und dauerhaft mit Ernst zu behalten.*

[142] = NHG *Verheißung oder Zusage.*

[143] = NHG *geben aber nicht die nötige Stärke dafür.*

[144] = NHG *Unvermögen zum Guten und lerne an sich selbst verzweifeln.*

[145] The virgule after the 'Als', which acts like a colon, shows that 'Als' here means 'for example', 'thus'.

[146] Literally 'may he do what he will', i.e. 'whatever he may do'.

[147] Introduces a purpose clause.

[148] = NHG *so*, 'in that way'.

[149] = NHG *aus sich selbst nicht vermag.*

[150] = NHG *für uns unmöglich.*

8 But how is it that faith alone can make you righteous and bring such ample riches without any works, when there are after all so many laws, commandments, works, instructions, and regulations prescribed to us in Scripture? Here it should be carefully noted and always seriously borne in mind, that faith alone without any works makes you righteous, free and saved, as we will hear more later. And it should be noted that all holy Scripture can be divided into two words, which are commandments or God's laws, and promises and pledges. The commandments teach and prescribe to us various good works, but that does not mean that these have occurred yet. They direct but they do not help, they teach what should be done, but do not give the strength to do it. Therefore they are only ordained for people to see their inability to do good and to learn to despair of themselves. And that is why they are called the Old Testament and they all belong in the Old Testament. For example, the commandment 'You shall have no evil desire'[151] proves that all of us are sinners and nobody can be without evil desire, whatever they may do. By this, they learn to despair of themselves and to seek help elsewhere, so that they can be without evil desire and thereby through another person fulfil the commandment which they cannot do by themselves. In the same way all the other commandments are impossible for us.

[151] KJV Exodus 20,17: 'Thou shalt not covet thy neighbour's house, thou shalt not covet thy neighbour's wife, nor his manservant, nor his maidservant, nor his ox, nor his ass, nor any thing that *is* thy neighbour's.'

¶ Czū neunden / Wen nu der mensch auß den gebotten sein vnuormuͤgen gelernet vn̄ empfunden hatt / das[152] yhm nu angst wirt / wie er dem gebott gnug thue. Seyntemal[153] das gebot muß erfullet seyn / oder er muß vordampt seyn. So[154] ist er recht[155] gedemuͤtigt vnd zu nicht worden / ynn seynen augen / findet nichts yn yhm damit[156] er muͤg frum werden. Dan ßo kūpt[157] das ander wort. Die gottlich vorheyschung vnd zusagung / vnd spricht / (A4v) wiltu[158] alle gepott erfullen / deyner boͤßen begirde vnd sund[159] loß werden / wie die gebott zwyngen vnd foddern.[160] Sihe[161] da / glaub in Christū / yn wilchem ich dir zusag / alle gnad / gerechtickeyt / frid vn̄ freyheyt / glaubstu so hastu[162] / glaubstu nit / so hastu nit. Den das[163] dir vnmuglich ist / mit allen wercken dᷣ gebott / der vill vnd doch keyn nutz seyn mussen[164] / das wirt dir leycht vnd kurtz durch / den glauben. Den ich hab kurtzlich[165] / yn den glauben gestellet alle ding / das[166] / wer yhn hat / sol alle ding haben vnd selig seyn / wer yhn nit hatt / soll nichts haben. Alßo geben die zusagung gottis / was die gepott erfoddern / vnd volnbringen / was die gepott heyssen / auff das es allis gottis eygen sey. Gepot vn̄ erfullung / er heysset allein / er erfullet auch alleyn. Darumb seyn die zusagung gottis / wort des newen testaments vnd gehoren auch yns newe testament.

---

[152] Introduces a result clause.
[153] ENHG ‘sintemal’, ‘since’.
[154] ‘then’, picking up from the earlier ‘Wen’ clause.
[155] Adverb modifying ‘gedemuͤtigt’.
[156] = NHG *womit/wodurch*.
[157] = NHG *kommt*.
[158] Contraction of ENHG ‘wilt du’ = NHG *willst du*.
[159] = NHG *deiner bösen Begierden und Sünden*: genitive governed by ‘los’.
[160] = NHG *erzwingen und fordern*.
[161] = NHG *Sieh*. The *e*-ending is a feature of Lutheran publications.
[162] = NHG *glaubst du, dann hast du* (contracted forms reflect spoken German).
[163] = NHG *was*, related to the later ‘das’.
[164] ‘der vill und doch keyn nutz seyn mussen’ ‘of which [there are] many and yet [they] can be of no assistance’.
[165] ‘simply, completely, by way of a shortcut’.
[166] Introduces a purpose clause.

9 Now, when a person has learned of and has come to feel their helplessness through the commandments, so that they are now fearful about how to fulfil the Law – since the Law must be fulfilled or they must be damned –, then they are truly humbled and annihilated in their own eyes, finding nothing within themselves that might make them righteous. Then comes the other word – God's promise and pledge –, and says: 'if you want to fulfil all the commandments, to be rid of your evil desires and sins, as the commandments require and demand, behold, believe in Christ, in whom I pledge to you all grace, righteousness, peace, and freedom. Believe it and you have it; don't believe and you don't. For what is impossible for you with all the works of the commandments, which are many and yet cannot be helpful, will become easy and complete through faith. For I have grounded everything completely in faith, so that whoever has it should have all things and be saved, and whoever does not have it should have nothing.' Thus the pledges of God give that which fulfil the commandments and complete what the commandments demand, so that everything belongs to God – commandments and fulfilment: He alone demands, He alone fulfils. Therefore God's pledges are the word of the New Testament, and also belong in the New Testament.

¶ Czum tzehenden / Nu seyn diße vnd alle gottis wort / heylig / warhafftig / gerecht / fridsam / frey vnd aller guͤtte voll / darrumb wer yhn[167] mit eynem rechten glauben anhangt / des[168] seele wirt mit yhm voreynigt / ßo gantz vnd gar / das alle tugent des worts / auch eygen[169] werden der seelen / Vnd alßo durch den glauben / die seele von dem gottis wort / heylig / gerecht / warhafftig / fridsam / frey / vnd aller guͤtte voll / eyn warhafftig kind gottis wirt / wie Johan. 1. sagt Er hatt yhn[170] geben / das sie mugen kynder gottis werden / alle die ynn seynem namen glauben.

Hierauß leychtlich[171] zu mercken ist / warumb der glaub ßo vill vormag / vnd das keyne gutte werck yhm gleych seyn mugen / Den keyn gut werck / hanget an dem gottlichen wort / wie der glaub / kan auch nit yn der seelen seyn / sondern alleyn das wort vnd glaube regiren[172] / yn der seelen/ Wie dz wort ist / ßo wirt auch die seele vō yhm / gleych[173] / als das eyssen wirt gluttrodt[174] wie das fewr auß der voreynigung mit dem fewr. Alßo sehen wir / das an dem glaubenn eyn Christen mensch gnug hatt / darff keynis wercks / das[175] er frum sey / darff er[176] den keynis wercks mehr / ßo ist er gewißlich empunden[177] von allen gepotten vnd gesetzen / ist er[178] empūden / so ist er gewißlich frey / Das ist die Christlich freiheit / der eynige glaub / der do macht / nit das wir muͤßsig gahn oder uͤbell thun mugen / sondern das wir keynis wercks bedurffen zur frumkeyt vnd seligkeyt zu erlangen / dauon wir mehr hernach sagen wollen. (B1r)

---

[167] = NHG *ihnen* (i.e. the words of God).

[168] = NHG *dessen*, referring back to ‘wer’.

[169] ‘proper to, belonging to’ + dative (here ‘der seelen’).

[170] = NHG *ihnen.*

[171] ‘easily’.

[172] = NHG *regieren.*

[173] = NHG *durch ihn, in gleicher Weise wie.*

[174] = NHG *glutrot*, literally ‘glowing red’.

[175] = NHG *damit.*

[176] ‘darf er’ (= NHG *bedarf er*), beginning a conditional clause.

[177] = NHG *entbunden.*

[178] This is the beginning of another conditional clause.

10 Now these and all of God's words are sacred, true, righteous, peaceful, free, and full of all goodness, so that the soul of all who adhere to them with true faith will be united with Him, so fully and completely, that all the virtues of the word becomes the soul's own property, and thus through faith the soul by the word of God becomes sacred, righteous, truthful, peaceful, free, and full of goodness, a true child of God, as John chapter I says: 'He has granted them to become children of God, all who believe in his name'.[179]

Thus it is easy to recognise how faith can do so much and that no good works can equate with it, since no good work depends on the divine word as faith does, nor can it be within the soul, but only the word and faith reign in the soul. Through the word, the soul becomes like the word, just as iron becomes red-hot by its union with fire. Thus we can see that for Christians their faith is sufficient: they do not need any work to be righteous. If they no longer need any work, they are certainly released from all commandments and laws; if they are released, they are certainly free. That is Christian freedom, the real faith which does not make us idle or able to do evil, but rather makes us not need any work to achieve righteousness and salvation, about which we will say more later.

---

[179] KJV John 1,12: 'But as many as received him, to them gave he power to become the sons of God, even to them that believe on his name.'

¶ Czū eylfften[180] / Weytter ists mit dem glauben alßo gethan / das / wilcher dem andern glaubt / der glaubt / yhm darumb. das[181] er yhn fur eynen frumen warhafftigen man achtet / wilchs die groͤßte ehre ist / die ein mensch dem andern thun kan / als widderumb die groͤßte schmach ist / ßo[182] er yhn fur eynen loßen lugenhafftigen leychtfertigen[183] man achtet.[184] Alßo auch wenn die seele gottis wort festiglich glaubt / ßo helt sie yhn fur warhafftig / frum vn̄ gerecht / da mit[185] sie yhm thut die aller groͤßsiste ehre die sie yhm thun kann / denn da gibt sie yhm recht / da lessit sie yhm recht / da ehret sie seynen namen / vnd lessit mit yhr[186] handeln wie er will / denn̄ sie zweyffelt nit er sey frum / warhafftig ynn allen seynen worten.[187]

---

[180] = NHG *Zum elften*; on the nasal bar above the letter *u*, cf. chapter 3.

[181] = NHG *weil.*

[182] = NHG *wenn.*

[183] 'losen, lügenhaftigen, leichtfertigen', an alliterative combination of ENHG bywords for evil: 'vicious, lying, frivolous'.

[184] ENHG 'achten … für' = NHG *halten … für.*

[185] = NHG *womit.*

[186] = NHG *sich*, referring to the soul.

[187] After this the printer left – as in several other places – a larger space to indicate a new argument without having to waste half a line by having a paragraph break.

11 It is further the case with faith that if someone believes another person, they believe them because they consider them to be a righteous, truthful person, which is the greatest honour that one person can do another; and conversely it is the utmost disgrace, if they consider them immoral, mendacious, unreliable.

Thus when the soul firmly believes God's word, it considers Him truthful, righteous and just, and so it does Him the greatest possible honour, for thereby it accepts Him, acknowledges Him, honours His name, and permits Him to do with it what He wants, for it does not doubt that He is righteous, truthful in all His words.

Widderumb kan man gott keyn grősſere vnehre aufſthun / deñ[188] yhm nit glauben / damit[189] die seel yhn fur eynen vntuchtigen lugenhafftigen leychtfertigen[190] helt / vñ ßouil an yhr ist[191] / yhn vorleugnet mit solchem vnglauben / vnd ein abgott yhres eygens synn[192] / ym hertzen widder gott auffricht[193] / alß wolt sie es[194] besser wissenn deñ er. Wenn denn[195] gott sihet / das yhm die seel / warheit gibt vnd alßo ehret[196] durch yhren glauben / ßo ehret er sie widderumb / vnd helt sie auch fur frum vnd warhafftig / vnd sie ist auch frum vnd warhafftig durch solchen glauben / denn das[197] man gott die warheyt vñ frumkeit gebe / das ist recht vnd warheit / vnnd macht recht vnd warhafftig. Die weyll[198] es war ist vnd recht / das gotte[199] die warheit geben werd. Wilchs die nit thun / die nit glauben / vnd doch sich mit vielen gutten wercken treyben vnd můhen.

[188] = NHG *antun, als.*

[189] = NHG *womit.*

[190] 'Untüchtigen, Lügenhaftigen, Leichtfertigen', a string of deadjectival nouns, meaning 'one who is … '.

[191] 'soviel an ihr ist' = NHG *soweit es an ihr liegt.*

[192] = NHG *ihres eigenen Sinnes / Eigensinns.*

[193] = NHG *statt / gegen Gott aufrichtet.*

[194] This does not have a referent in the text, but refers to things in general.

[195] = NHG *dann.*

[196] The object 'yhn', referring to God, is understood here.

[197] Introduces a subject clause: 'the fact that', correlating with the following 'das'.

[198] 'Die weyll' = NHG *weil*, giving the reason for what is stated in the clause before (NHG would have a comma, not a full stop, between these clauses).

[199] Dative.

Conversely one cannot do God greater dishonour than not to believe Him, whereby the soul regards Him as worthless, mendacious, and unreliable, and as far as it is concerned denies Him by such a lack of faith, and in its heart erects an idol of its own mind against God, as though thinking it knows better than He.

So when God sees that the soul accepts His truth and therefore honours Him by its faith, then He honours it in return, and also considers it righteous and truthful, and it *is* also righteous and truthful through this faith, for to accept God's truth and righteousness is justice and truth, and makes the soul just and truthful. For it is true and right that God's truth be accepted. And this is what they do not do, who do not believe and yet busy and occupy themselves with many good works.

¶ Czum zwoͤlfften / Nit allein gibt der glaub ßouil / das die seel / dem[200] gottlichen wort gleych wirt aller gnaden voll / frey / vñ selig / sondernñ voreynigt[201] auch die seele mit Christo / als eyne brawt mit yhrem breudgam. Auß wilcher ehe folget / wie S. Paulus sagt / das Christus vñ die seel / eyn leyb werden / ßo werden auch beyder gutter[202] / fall / vnfall vnd alle ding gemeyn[203] / das was[204] Christus hatt / das ist eygen / der glaubigen seele / was die seele hatt / wirt eygen Christi. So hatt Christus alle guͤtter vnd seligkeit / die seyn der seelen eygen. So hatt die seel alle vntugent vnd sund auff yhr[205] / die werden Christi eygen. Hie hebt sich nu der froͤlich wechßel vnd streytt / Die weyl Christus ist gott vnd mensch / wilcher noch[206] nie gesundigt hatt / vnd seyne frumkeyt (B1v) vnuͤbirwindlich / ewig vnd almechtig ist / ßo[207] er denn der glaubigen seelen sund / durch yhren braudtring / das ist / dᷣ glaub / ym selbs eygen[208] macht vnd nit anders thut / deñ als hett[209] er sie gethā / ßo mussen die sund ynn yhm vorschlundeñ[210] vñ erseufft werden / Denn sein vnuͤbirwindlich gerechtigkeyt / ist allenn sunden zustarck / also wirt die seele vō allen yhren sunden / lauterlich durch yhrē malschaczts[211] / das ist des glaubens halben[212] / ledig vnd frey / vnd begabt / mit der ewigen gerechtickeit yhrs breuͤdgamß Christi.

---

200 ‘dem göttlichen Wort gleich’: dative, literally ‘similarly to the divine word’.

201 = NHG *vereinigt*; ‘der glaub’ is the subject.

202 = NHG *beider Güter*: ‘the goods of them both’; ‘beyder’ is genitive, ‘gutter’ nominative plural.

203 = NHG *alle Dinge gemeinsam*.

204 ‘das was … ’ ‘so that what … ’.

205 = NHG *sich,* referring to the soul.

206 = NHG *dennoch*. This emphasises that although Christ became flesh, he remained free from sin.

207 ‘if, when’.

208 = NHG *sich selbst zu eigen*, referring to Christ.

209 = NHG *hätte*.

210 ENHG ‘verschlunden’, related to NHG *Schlund* ‘throat, gullet’: ‘swallowed up’.

211 ENHG ‘Mahlschatz’ = NHG *Brautschatz*, ‘dowry’.

212 = ‘das … halben’ is a parenthesis; = NHG *des Glaubens wegen*.

12 Not only does faith give so much, that the soul, like the word of God, becomes full of all grace, free and saved, but it also unites the soul with Christ, as a bride with her bridegroom. From this marriage it follows, as Saint Paul says, that Christ and the soul become one body;[213] therefore also their respective goods, ups, downs, and all other things become shared, so that what Christ has is the property of the believing soul, and what the soul has becomes the property of Christ.

Thus Christ has all goods and salvation: they will be the property of the soul. Thus the soul has all the vices and sins on it: they become the property of Christ. Here the joyous exchange and competition begin. For Christ is God and human, who has never sinned and whose righteousness is unsurpassable, eternal, and almighty; thus if he makes the sins of the believing soul by its wedding ring, i.e. faith, his own and acts no differently than if he had done them himself, then the sins must be swallowed up and drowned.[214]

For his unsurpassable righteousness is too strong for all sins, so that the soul becomes rid of its sins and free purely through its dowry, i.e. due to faith, and endowed with the gift of the eternal righteousness of its bridegroom Christ.

---

[213] KJV Ephesians 5,30: 'For we are members of [Christ's] body, of his flesh, and of his bones.'

[214] KJV I Corinthians 15,54–55: 'So when this corruptible shall have put on incorruption, and this mortal shall have put on immortality, then shall be brought to pass the saying that is written, Death is swallowed up in victory. O death, where is thy sting? O grave, where is thy victory?'

Ist nu das nit ein froͤliche wirtschafft / da[215] der reyche / edle / frummer breuͤdgam Christus / das arm vorachte[216] boͤßes hürlein[217] zur ehe nympt / vnd sie entledigt von allem uͤbell / zieret mit allen guͤtern. So ists nit muglich / das die sund sie vordampne[218] / deñ sie ligen nu auff Christo / vñ sein ynn yhm vorschlunden / so hat sie ßo ein reyche gerechtickeyt ynn yhrem breuͤtgam / das sie abermals / wider alle sund bestahn mag / ob sie schon[219] auff yhr legē. Dauon sagt Paulus 1. Cor. 15. Gott sey[220] lob vnd danck der vns hatt gegeben ein solch uͤbirwindung ynn Christo Ihesu / ynn wilcher vorschlunden ist / der todt mit der sund.

---

215 = ENHG 'wirtschaft', meaning any major undertaking or organised feast; 'da' = NHG *wenn.*

216 = NHG *verachtete.*

217 ENHG 'böse' = 'of a poor quality'. 'hürlein' = diminutive of 'hure' 'whore'.

218 = NHG *verdammen* (a nasal bar is missing).

219 'ob … schon' = NHG *obschon, auch wenn.*

220 A jussive subjunctive, expressing what ought to be done.

Is that not a joyous feast, when the mighty, noble, and righteous bridegroom Christ takes the poor, despised, flawed, little whore in marriage and frees her of all bad things, and adorns her with all goods.

Thus it is not possible for the sins to condemn the soul, for they now lie upon Christ and are swallowed up within him; thus she has such a rich righteousness in her bridegroom that she once again can withstand all sins, even if they lie upon her. About this St Paul says in 1. Corinthians 15: 'God be praised and thanked who gave us such a victory in Jesus Christ, in which death is swallowed up together with sin'.[221]

[221] KJV I Corinthians 15,57: 'But thanks be to God, which giveth us the victory through our Lord Jesus Christ.'

¶ Czū dreytzehenden / Hie sichstu[222] aber / auß wilchem grund dem glauben ßouil billich zugeschrieben wirt / das er alle gepott erfullet / vnd on alle andere werck frum macht. Denn du sihest hie / das er das erste gepott erfullet alleine da gepotten wirt / Du solt eynen gott ehren. Wenn du nu eytell[223] gutt werck werist / biß auff die versenn[224] / ßo weristu[225] dennoch nit frum vnd gebist[226] gott noch keyn ehre / vnd alßo erfullistu[227] das aller erst[228] gepott nicht. Denn gott mag[229] nicht geehret werden / yhm werd dan[230] / warheyt vnd allis gut zu geschrieben / wie er denn warlich[231] ist / Das thun aber keyn gutte werck / sondern allein der glaube des hertzen.

Darumb ist er allein / die gerechtickeit des menschen vnd aller gepott erfullung. Den wer das erste haubt gepott erfullet / der erfullet gewißlich vnd leychtlich auch alle ander gepott. Die werck aber seyn todte ding / kunden[232] nit ehren noch loben gott / wie wol sie mugen geschehen / vnd lassen sich thun gott zu ehren vñ lob / aber wir suchē hie den / dˀ nit gethan wirt / als die werck[233] / sondern den selbthetter vnd werckmeyster / der gott ehret vnd die werck thut.

---

[222] = NHG *siehst du.*

[223] ENHG 'eitel' = 'completely'.

[224] = NHG *bis zu den Fersen*, literally 'down to your ankles'.

[225] = NHG *so wärst du.*

[226] = NHG *gäbst.*

[227] = NHG *erfülltest du.*

[228] = NHG *allererste.*

[229] = NHG *kann / will.*

[230] = NHG *ihm werde denn … zu geschrieben*, 'unless … are ascribed'.

[231] = NHG *wahrlich* 'truly'.

[232] = NHG *könnten.*

[233] = NHG *wie die Werke.*

13 Now here you see the reason why so much is rightly ascribed to faith, that it fulfils all commandments and confers righteousness without any other works. For you see here that it alone fulfils the first commandment, where it is commanded: 'You shall honour one God'.[234] If you were made of nothing but good works from head to toe, you would still not be righteous and would not do honour to God, and so you would not fulfil the very first commandment. For God does not want to be honoured, unless truth and all good are ascribed to Him, as He truly is. But no good works do this, only the faith of the heart.

This is why it alone justifies humankind and fulfils all commandments. For whoever fulfils the first principal commandment, certainly and easily fulfils all other commandments as well. But works are dead things; they could neither honour nor praise God, although they may come about and be done to honour and praise God; but here we are seeking that which is not done as the works are done, but rather the doer and master craftsman, who honours God and performs the works.

---

[234] KJV Exodus 20,2–3: 'I *am* the LORD thy God, which have brought thee out of the land of Egypt, out of the house of bondage. Thou shalt have no other gods before me.'

Das ist niemāt dan der glaub des hertzen / der ist das haubt vnd gantzis weßens[235] der frumkeyt / darumb[236] es eyn (B2r) ferlich[237] finster rede ist.[238] Wenn man leret / die gottis gepott mit wercken zu erfulleñ / ßo[239] die erfullung fur[240] allen wercken / durch den glauben muß geschehen seyn / vnd die werck folgen nach der erfullung / wie wir hörenn werdenn.

[235] 'wesens' is a variant of 'wesen' and is nominative here.

[236] = NHG *weswegen*.

[237] = NHG *gefährlich*.

[238] Here we should expect a comma in NHG, as 'Wenn' begins an explanation of the previous clause.

[239] = NHG *da*.

[240] = NHG *vor und in dem Alten Testament*, meaning before and under the Mosaic Law.

That is none other than the faith of the heart; that is the principal part and whole essence of righteousness, so that it is a dangerous and sinister statement if one teaches that God's commandments are fulfilled by works, for the fulfilment must happen before all works through faith, and the works follow on from this fulfilment, as we shall hear.

¶ Czum viertzehenden / Weytter zusehen[241] / was wir yn Christo haben / vnd wie groß gutt sey / ein rechter glaube. Ist tzu wissenn / das fur[242] vnd ynn dem altenn testament / gott yhm außtzog vnd furbehilt[243] alle erste menliche gepurt / von menschen vñ von thierren / Vnd die erste gepurt war koͤstlich vnd hatt tzwey grosse forteyll fur allen anderñ kindernn / nemlich die hirschafft[244] vnd priesterschafft odder kuͤnigreych vnd priesterthum / alßo[245] das auff erden / das erste geporn kneblin[246] / was[247] eyn herr vbir alle seyne bruͤder vnd ein pfaff[248] odder Babst fur gott Durch wilche figur bedeutt ist Ihesus Christus / der eygentlich die selb erste menlich gepurt ist gottis vatters / von der Junpfrawen Marie. Darumb ist er ein kuͤnig vñ priester / doch geystlich. denn seyn reych ist nit yrdnisch[249] noch yn yrdenischen / sonderñ yn geystlichen guttern / als da seyn / warheyt / weyßheyt / frid / freud / seligkeyt 2c.[250] Damit aber nit außgetzogen[251] ist zeytlich gutt / denn es ist yhm alle ding[252] vnterworffen / ynn hymell / erdenn vnd helle[253] / wie wol man yhn nit sicht / das macht / das[254] er geystlich / vnsichtlich[255] regirt.

---

[241] = NHG *Um weiter zu sehen.*

[242] = NHG *vor* (with a temporal meaning).

[243] = NHG *sich auswählte und vorbehielt*: 'for Himself selected and retained'.

[244] = NHG *Herrschaft.*

[245] = NHG *so.*

[246] = NHG *Knäblein*; diminutive of 'knabe'.

[247] = NHG *war.*

[248] ENHG 'Pfaffe' = 'priest', not pejorative as in NHG.

[249] = NHG *irdisch.*

[250] 2c. = NHG *etcetera.* On the use of a 2-shaped character for the 'et' abbreviation, cf. chapter 3.

[251] = NHG *sich vorbehalten*; cf. above on the phrase 'ausziehen und behalten'.

[252] There is incongruence here between the singular verb and the plural subject.

[253] = NHG *in Himmel, Erde und Hölle.*

[254] The first 'das' is a demonstrative pronoun referring back to the previous clause and the object of 'macht'; the second is a relative pronoun introducing the following clause and the subject of 'macht'.

[255] = NHG *unsichtbar.*

14 Let us look further at what we have in Christ and what a great good true faith is. It must be known that before and in the Old Testament God reserved and kept for himself the male first-born of all humans and animals.[256] And the first-born was precious and had two great advantages over all other children, namely lordship and priesthood or royal and priestly power, so that on earth the first-born boy was a lord over all his brothers and a priest or pope before God.

By which sign Jesus Christ is meant who by nature is the real first male-born of God the Father by the Virgin Mary. Therefore he is a king and priest, but spiritually, for his kingdom is not on earth[257] nor in earthly things, but in spiritual goods such as truth, wisdom, peace, joy, and salvation etc.

But at the same time, temporal possessions are reserved by him, since all things are subject to him, in heaven, on earth, and in hell, although one cannot see him; this is because he reigns spiritually and invisibly.

---

[256] KJV Exodus 13,2: 'Sanctify unto me all the firstborn, whatsoever openeth the womb among the children of Israel, *both* of man and of beast: it *is* mine.'
[257] KJV John 18,36: 'Jesus said: My kingdom is not of this world.'

Alßo[258] auch seyn priesterthum steht[259] nit ynn den eußerlichenn geperdenn[260] / vnd kleydern / wie wir bey den menschen sehen / ßondernn̄ es steht ym geyst vnsichtlich / alßo / das er fur gottis augen on vnterlaß / fur die seynen steht vnd sich selb opffert vnd allis thut / was eyn frum priester thun soll. Er bittet fur vns / Wie S. Paul Ro. 8. sagt. So leret er vns ynnwendig ym hertzen / wilchs sein tzwey eygentliche recht ampt[261] eyniß priesters Denn alßo bitten vnd leren auch eußerlich menschlich tzeytlich priester.

---

[258] Here 'likewise'.

[259] = NHG *besteht.*

[260] = NHG *äußerlichen Gebärden.*

[261] = NHG *Ämter* 'offices'.

In the same way his priesthood does not consist of outward manifestations and garments, such as those we see in people, but it dwells in the spirit invisibly, so that he stands before God's eyes unceasingly for those who belong to him and sacrifices himself and does everything that a righteous priest should do. He intercedes for us, as St Paul says in Romans 8.[262] In this way he teaches us inwardly in our hearts, which are two true and right offices of a priest, for in the same way, human secular priests pray and teach outwardly, too.

[262] KJV Romans 8,34: 'Who is he that condemneth? It is Christ that died, yea rather, that is risen again, who is even at the right hand of God, who also maketh intercession for us.'

¶ Czum funfftzehenden / Wie nu Christus die erste gepurtt hatt / mit yhrer[263] ehre vnd wirdickeit / alßo / teyllet er sie mit allenn seynen Christen / das[264] sie durch den glauben / mussen auch alle kuͤnige vnd priester seyn / mit Christo / Wie S. Petrus sagt 1. Pet. 2. Ihr seyt ein priesterlich kuͤnigreych / vñ ein kuͤniglich priesterthū. (B2v)

Vnd das geht also zu / das ein Christen mensch durch den glauben ßo hoch erhaben wirt vbir alle ding / das er aller eyn herr wirt geystlich / denn es kan yhm kein ding nit[265] schaden zur seligkeit. Ia[266] es muß yhm alles vnterthan seyn vnd helffen zur seligkeyt / Wie S. Paulus leret Ro. 8. Alle ding muͤssen helffenn den außerwelten[267] / zu yhrem besten / es sey leben / sterben / sund / frumkeit / gut vñ boͤßes / wie man es nennen kan. Item 1. Cor. 3. Alle ding seynd ewr / es sey[268] das leben oder dͬ todt / kegenwertig oder zukuͤnfftig 2c.[269]

---

[263] = NHG *ihrer*, referring to ‘gepurtt’.

[264] = NHG *sodass*.

[265] ‘kein … nit’ as negators reinforce each other, rather than cancelling each other out.

[266] = NHG *Ja*.

[267] = NHG *Auserwählten*.

[268] = NHG *sind euer, es sei* (‘all yours, whether it be…’).

[269] = NHG *gegenwärtig oder zukünftig etc.*

15 As Christ is the first-born, with all the honour and rank that entails, so he shares this birthright with all his Christians, so that through faith they must also be kings and priests with Christ, as St Peter says in I Peter 2: 'You are a priestly kingdom and a kingly priesthood'.[270]

And so it is also the case that Christians are exalted by faith so far above all things as to become spiritually lords of all, for nothing can imperil their salvation. Indeed, everything must be subject to them and work towards their salvation, as St Paul teaches in Romans 8: 'All things must work for the best of the elect, whether life, death, sin, righteousness, good and evil, whatever it may be called'.[271] Likewise, I Corinthians 3: 'Whether life or death, present or to come, all things are yours etc.'.[272]

---

[270] Paraphrase of KJV I Peter 2,9: 'But ye are a chosen generation, a royal priesthood.'
[271] Paraphrase of KJV Romans 8,28: 'All things work together for good to them that love God, to them who are the called according to His purpose.'
[272] KJV I Corinthians 3,22: 'Whether Paul, or Apollos, or Cephas, or the world, or life, or death, or things present, or things to come; all are yours.'

Nit das wir aller ding leyplich mechtig seyn / sie zu besitzen oder zu brauchen / wie die menschen auff erdeñ / denn wir muͤssen sterben leyplich vnd mag niemant dem todt entfliehen / ßo muͤssen wir auch viel andern dingen vnterligeñ / wie wir yn Christo vñ seynen heyligen sehen / Denn diß ist ein geystliche hirschafft / die do regiert / yn der leyplichen vnterdruckung / das ist / ich kann mich on[273] allen dingen bessern nach der seelen[274] / das[275] auch der todt vnd leyden / muͤssen mir dienen vnd nuͤtzlich seyn zur seligkeyt / das ist gar ein hohe ehrliche wirdickeit vnd eyn recht almechtige hirschafft / ein geystliche kuͤnigreych / da keyn ding ist ßo gut / ßo boͤße / es muß mir dienen zu gut/ ßo[276] ich glaube / vñ darff[277] seyn doch nit / sondern meyn glaub ist mir gnugsam.

Sihe wie ist das ein koͤstlich freyheyt vnd gewalt der Christen.

---

[273] = NHG *ohne*, but here with the dative.

[274] 'according to the soul'.

[275] = NHG *sodass*.

[276] = NHG *wenn*.

[277] = NHG *bedarf*; it takes the genitive 'seyn' 'it' (referring to 'ding').

Not that we have physical power over all things, to possess or use them, as people do on earth, for we must die physically, and no-one can escape death; likewise we must also submit to many other things, as we see in Christ and his saints.

For this is a spiritual dominion, which reigns in physical suppression, i.e. I can without all things better myself with regard to my soul, so that also death and suffering must serve me and be useful for salvation; that is a truly lofty, noble dignity, and a truly almighty dominion, a spiritual kingdom, where nothing is so good or so bad that it cannot serve me for good, if I believe, and yet I do not need it, but rather my faith is sufficient for me.

Behold, how precious are the freedom and power of Christians.

¶ Czum sechtzehenden / Vbir das[278] seyn wir priester / das ist noch vil mehr / denn kuͤnig sein / darumb / das das priesterthum vns wirdig macht fur gott zu tretten vnd fur andere zu bitten / Denn fur gottis augen zu stehn vnd bitten / gepuͤrt[279] niemāt denn den priestern. Alßo hatt vns Christꝰ erworben / das wir muͤgen geystlich / fur ein ander tretten vñ[280] bitten / wie ein priester fur das volck leyplich tritt vnd bittet. Wer aber nit glaubt yn Christū dem[281] dienet keyn ding zu gut / ist ein knecht aller ding / muß sich aller ding ergern.[282] Datzu ist sein gepett nit angenehm / kumpt auch nit fur gottis augen / Wer mag nu außdencken / die ehre vnd hoͤhe eyniß Christen menschen? durch seyn kuͤnigreych ist er aller ding mechtig[283] / durch sein priesterthū ist er gottis mechtig / denn gott thut was er bittet vnd wil / wie do stet geschrieben im Psalter. Gott thut den willen der / die yhn furchten / vnd erhoͤret / yhr gepett / zu wilchen ehren er nur allein durch den glauben vnd (B3r) durch keyn werck kumpt. Darauß mā clar sihet / wie eyn Christen mensch frey ist von allen dingen vnd vbir alle ding / alßo das er keyner gutter werck / datzu bedarff / das er frum vnd seligk sey[284] / sondern der glaub bringts ym alles vber flußsig[285]. Vnd wo er ßo toͤricht were vnd meynet / durch ein gutt werck / frum / frey / selig odder Christen werden / ßo[286] vorluͤr[287] er den glauben mit allen dingen / Gleych als / d'[288] hund / der ein stuck fleysch ym mund trug vnd nach dem schemen ym wasser schnapt / damit / fleysch vnd schem vorloͤr.

---

278 Literally 'Above that' in the sense 'Over and above that', 'In addition'.

279 = NHG *gebührt.*

280 = NHG *und*; on the abbreviation and use of *v*, cf. chapter 3.

281 Refers to 'Wer' in the previous clause.

282 = NHG *sich ärgern*, but in the sense of 'to take offence at'.

283 'aller ding mechtig' 'having power over all things'.

284 'das er ... sey' 'for him to be ... '.

285 = NHG *bringt es ihm alles überflüssig.*

286 = 'wo … ßo' = NHG *wenn … dann.*

287 = NHG *verlöre.*

288 On the abbreviation 'd'' for 'der', cf. chapter 3.

16 In addition, we are priests, which is far greater than being kings, for priesthood makes us worthy to stand before God and pray for others, since it is appropriate for no-one but priests to stand and pray before the face of God. Therefore Christ has achieved this for us, that we may stand for and pray for one another spiritually, as a priest stands for and prays for his people physically.

But those who do not believe in Christ benefit from nothing; they are servants of all things and must take offence at all things. Besides, their prayers are not welcome and do not come before the face of God. Now who can fathom the honour and exalted status of a Christian? By their kingdom they have power over all things; by their priesthood they have power over God, for God does what a Christian asks for and wants, as it is written in the Psalter, 'God fulfils the desire of those who fear Him and hears their prayer',[289] and to this honour they come only and solely through faith and not through any work.

From this it can be clearly seen how a Christian is free of all things and above all things, so that they do not need any good works to be righteous and saved, but faith brings everything to them in abundance. And if they were so foolish as to think that they become righteous, free, saved, or Christian through a good work, they would then lose their faith along with all things, just like the dog which held a piece of meat in its mouth and snapped at its shadow in the water, thereby losing the meat and the shadow.[290]

---

[289] KJV Psalm 145,19: 'He will fulfil the desire of them that fear him: he also will hear their cry, and will save them.'

[290] Cf. Aesop's Fable No. 133: The Dog and the Shadow.

¶ Czum siebentzenden fragistu / Was ist den fur ein vnterscheydt / zwischen den priestern vnd leyen[291] ynn der Christenheyt / ßo[292] sie alle priester seyn? Antwort / Es ist dem wortlin[293] priester / pfaff / geystlich vnd des gleychen vnrecht geschehen / das sie von dem gemeynen hauffen seyn getzogen / auff den kleynen hauffen / den man itzt nennet geystlichen stand. Die heylige schrifft / gibt keynen andern vnterscheyd[294] / denn das sie / die gelereten odder geweyhetē / nēnet ministros / seruos / oeconomos / das ist / diener / knecht / schaffner[295] / die do sollen / den andern / Christū / glauben / vnd Christliche freyheit predigen / Denn ob wir wol[296] alle gleych priester seyn / ßo kunden wir doch nit alle dienen odder schaffen vnd predigen. Alßo sagt S. Paulus 1. Cor. 4. Wir wollen nichts mehr von den leuthen gehalten seyn[297] / denn Christ⁹ diener[298] / vnd schaffner des Euangelij. Aber nu ist aus der scheffnerey worden eyn solch weltlich / eußerliche / prechtige / forchtsam hirschafft vnd gewalt / das yhr die recht weltlich macht[299] / ynn keynen weg mag gleychen / gerad als weren die leyen etwas anders denn Christenleuth / damit hyngenummen[300] ist der gantz vorstand[301] Christlicher gnad / freyheit / glaubens / vnd allis was wir von Christo habeñ / vnd Christ⁹ selbs / haben dafur vbirkūmen / viel menschen gesetz vnd werck[302] / seyn gantz knecht wordenn / der aller vntůchtigsten leuth[303] auff erden.

---

291 = NHG *Laien.*

292 = NHG *wenn.*

293 = NHG *Wörtlein* in the sense of a 'single word, term'; cf. DWB s.v. 2a.

294 = NHG *macht … Unterschied.*

295 = NHG *Verwalter* (as a translation of 'oeconomos').

296 = NHG *obwohl wir.*

297 'to be considered'; NHG requires *für* with *halten* in this sense.

298 '9' at the end of 'Christ' abbreviates 'us' but should read 'Christi' (Latin genitive).

299 'true secular power'.

300 = NHG *weggenommen*, 'taken away'.

301 = NHG *Verständnis.*

302 = NHG *stattdessen bekommen viele Menschengesetze und -werke*; cf. DWB s.v. 3.

303 = NHG *Knechte der alleruntüchtigsten Leute geworden.*

17 You may ask what difference there is in Christendom between priests and lay-people, if all are priests. Answer: wrong has been done to the term 'priest', 'cleric', 'spiritual', and similar, so that they have been moved from the general group and applied to the small group who are now called the spiritual estate.

Holy Scripture does not recognise any difference other than that it calls the learned or consecrated 'ministros', 'servos', 'oeconomos', i.e. ministers, servants, stewards, who are to preach faith and Christian freedom to other Christians. For although we are all equally priests, we could not all serve or administer and preach. Hence St Paul says in I Corinthians 4: 'We do not want to be held by the people to be anything but Christ's servants and stewards of the gospel'.[304]

But now this stewardship has turned into such a secular, outward, grand, fearsome dominion and power, that true secular power cannot in any way compare with it, just as if lay-people were something other than Christians, so that the whole understanding of Christian grace, freedom, faith, and all that we have from Christ, and Christ himself, have been taken away, and we have received instead many human laws and works, and we have been made complete servants to the most worthless people on earth.

[304] KJV I Corinthians 4,1: 'Let a man so account of us, as of the ministers of Christ, and stewards of the mysteries of God.'

¶ Czum achttzehenden / Auß dem allen lernen wir / das es nit gnug sey gepredigt / Wen man Christus leben vnd werck oben hynn vnd nur als ein histori vnd Cronicken geschicht predigt / schweyg denn[305] / ßo man seyn[306] gar schweygt / vnd das geystlich recht oder ander menschen gesetz vn̄ lere predigt. Er[307] ist auch vill/ die Christū alßo predigen / vnd leßen / das sie ein mit leyden (B3v) vbir yhn habenn / mit den Juden zurnn̄[308] odder sonst mehr kyndisch weyß / drynnen vben. Aber er soll vnd muß alßo predigt[309] sein / dz mir vn̄ dir / der glaub drauß erwachß vn̄ erhalten werd. Wilcher glaub da durch erwechst vnd erhalten wirt. Wen[310] mir gesagt wirt. Warumb[311] Christus kūmen[312] sey / wie man sein[313] brauchen vnd nießen soll / was er mir bracht vnd geben[314] hat / das geschicht[315] / wo man recht außlegt / die Christlich freyheit / die wir von yhm haben / vnd wie wir kuͤnig vnd priester seyn / aller ding mechtig. Vnd[316] allis was wir thun / das fur gottis augen angenehm / vnd erhoͤret[317] sey / wie ich biß her gesagt hab.

---

305 = NHG *geschweige denn.*

306 This is the genitive of *er* referring to Christ, and governed by 'schweygt'.

307 = NHG *Ihrer*. 'Of those who … there are many'.

308 = NHG *Mitleid mit ihm haben, mit den Juden zürnen.*

309 = NHG *gepredigt.*

310 'Wenn' correlates with 'da durch'; the full stop between clauses corresponds to a comma in NHG.

311 This should not be read as a new sentence, despite the full stop, but as an object clause after 'gesagt wird'.

312 = NHG *gekommen.*

313 Genitive (referring to Christ) governed by 'brauchen' and 'nießen' = NHG *gebrauchen und genießen.*

314 = NHG *gebracht und gegeben.*

315 = NHG *geschieht.*

316 'Vnd' starts a new clause, not a new sentence, despite the full stop.

317 *erhören* is used specifically in the context of a prayer being answered.

18 From all this we learn that it is not enough to preach Christ's life and works superficially and merely as a story from history or a chronicle, let alone not to mention him at all, and to preach about spiritual right or other human law and teaching. There are also many who preach and interpret Christ[318] so that they have compassion for him and are angry with the Jews or otherwise deal childishly with the matter. But he shall and must be preached in such a way that for me and for you faith grows and is kept up by it.

This faith grows and is kept up if I am told why Christ has come, how one should use and enjoy him, what he has brought and given me; and that happens when one rightly interprets the Christian freedom which we have from him, and how we are kings and priests with power over all things, and that everything we do is welcome before God's eyes and received well by Him, as I have been saying so far.

[318] KJV II Cor 4,5: 'For we preach not ourselves, but Christ Jesus.'

Dañ[319] wo ein hertz alßo Christū hőret / das muß frőlich werden von gantzem grund / trost empfahen[320] / vnd sůß werden gegen Christo / yhn widderumb lieb zuhaben. Dahyn es nymmer mehr mit gesetzē odder werck kummen mag / Deñ wer wil eynem solchen hertzen schaden thun / oder erschreckenn? felt[321] die sund vnd der todt daher[322] / ßo glaubt es Christ⁹ frumkeit sey sein[323] / vnd sein sund sein[324] nymmer sein / sondern Christi / ßo muß die sund vorschwinden / fur Christus frumkeit / ynn dem glauben / wie droben gesagt ist / vnd lernet / mit dem Apostell dem todt vnd sund trotz bieten / vñ sagen Wo ist nu du todt[325] deyn sig? Wo ist nu todt dein spieß? deyn spieß / ist die sund. Aber gott sey lob vnd danck / der vns hatt geben den sieg / durch Ihesum Christū vnsern herrñ. Vnd der todt ist erseufft ynn seynem sieg 2c.[326]

---

[319] = NHG *denn.*

[320] = NHG *empfangen.*

[321] = NHG *fällt.*

[322] 'on it', referring to the heart.

[323] = NHG *Christi Frömmigkeit sei sein eigen.*

[324] = NHG *seien.*

[325] 'you, death'; death is being apostrophised.

[326] On the use of a 2-shaped character for the 'et' abbreviation in 'etc.', cf. chapter 3.

For whenever a heart hears Christ in this way, it must become completely joyful, take comfort, and begin to feel tender towards Christ, to love him in return. It can never get there with laws or works.

For who will harm or frighten such a heart? If sin and death fall upon it, it believes that Christ's righteousness is its own and that its sins never belong to it, but to Christ, so sin must vanish before Christ's righteousness in faith, as was said above, and it learns, with the apostle, to show defiance to death and sin and to say, 'Death, where is your victory now? Where is your sting now, death? Your sting is sin. But praise and thanks be to God, who has given us victory through Jesus Christ our Lord. And death is drowned in his victory, etc.'.[327]

---

[327] KJV I Corinthians 15,55–57: 'O death, where is thy sting? O grave, where is thy victory? The sting of death is sin; and the strength of sin is the law. But thanks be to God, which giveth us the victory through our Lord Jesus Christ.'

¶ Czum neuntzehenden / Das sey nu gnug gesagt / von dem ynnerlichen menschen / von seyner freyheit / vnd der heubt[328] gerechtickeit / wilch keynis gesetzs noch gutten wercks bedarff / ya yhr[329] schedlich ist / so[330] yemant da durch wolt rechtfertig zu werdē sich vormessenn. Nu kummen wir auffs ander teyll / auff den eußerlichen menschen Hie wollen wir antworten allen denen / die sich ergern auß den vorigen reden vñ pflegen zusprechen Ey so denn[331] der glaub alle ding ist vnd gilt allein gnugsam frum zumachen. Warūb sein denn die gutten werck gepotten? so wollen wir gutter ding sein / vnd nichts thun. Neyn lieber mensch nicht also. Es wer[332] wol / also / wen du allein ein ynnerlich mensch werist / vnd gantz geystlich vnd ynnerlich worden[333] / wilchs nit geschicht biß am Juͤngsten tag. Es ist vñ bleybt auff erdē nur ein anheben vñ zu nehmen[334] / wilchs wirt in yhener welt[335] voln(B4r)bracht. Daher heyssets der Apostell primitias spiritꝰ / das sein die ersten fruͤcht des geysts / drumb gehoͤrt hie her / das[336] droben gesagt ist Ein Christen mensch / ist ein dienstpar knecht / vñ ydermā vnterthan / gleych[337] / wo er frey ist / darff[338] er nichts thun / wo er knecht ist / muß er allerley thun. Wie dz zugahe[339] / wollen wir sehē.

---

[328] = NHG *Haupt-*, 'cardinal, principal', the first part of the compound with *Gerechtigkeit.*

[329] Refers to 'freyheit'/'heupt gerechtickeit'.

[330] = NHG *wenn.*

[331] 'so denn' = NHG *wenn dann.*

[332] = NHG *wäre.*

[333] = NHG *geworden.*

[334] = NHG *ein Anfangen und Zunehmen.*

[335] = NHG *jener Welt* i.e. the next world as opposed to 'auff erden'.

[336] = NHG *was.*

[337] 'gleych' here has the force of English 'equals', 'that is'.

[338] 'needs', like NHG *bedarf.*

[339] = NHG *zugehe.*

19 Now that is enough said about the inward person, about their freedom and the principal righteousness, which needs no law nor good works; indeed, it is damaging to righteousness if anyone would presume to be justified thereby. Now we come to the second part, to the outward person. Here we shall answer all those who take offence at what has been said above, and are used to saying: 'Oh, so if faith is everything and is sufficient for righteousness, why, then, are good works commanded? Let us be merry and do nothing'. No, my dear, it's not like that. It would be like that if you were solely an inward person, and had become wholly spiritual and inward, which will not happen until Judgement Day. There is and remains on earth only a beginning and an increase of what will be completed in that world. This is why the apostle calls them 'primitias spiritus',[340] namely the first fruits of the Spirit. That is why what we said earlier belongs here. A Christian is a bound servant and subject to all, which is the same as saying: insofar as they are free, they need to do nothing; insofar as they are servants, they need to do all kinds of things. Let us see how this comes about.

---

[340] KJV Romans 8,23: 'And not only *they*, but ourselves also, which have the firstfruits of the Spirit, even we ourselves groan within ourselves, waiting for the adoption, *to wit*, the redemption of our body.' VLC (Vulgate, Clementine version): 'Non solum autem illa, sed et nos ipsi primitias spiritus habentes: et ipsi intra nos gemimus adoptionem filiorum Dei exspectantes, redemptionem corporis nostri.'

¶ Czum zwentzigsten / Ob wol der mensch ynwendig nach der seelen / durch den glauben gnugsam rechtfertig ist / vnd alles hatt was er haben soll / on das[341] der selb glaub vñ gnugde / muß ymer zunehmen / biß ynn yhenes leben. So[342] bleybt er doch noch ynn dißem leyplichen lebenn auff erdenn / vnd muß seynen eygen leyp regiern vnd mit leuthen vmbgahen. Da heben sich nu die werck an / hie muß er nit můßsig gehn / da muß furwar der leyb mit fasten / wachen / erbeytten vnd mit aller messiger[343] zucht getrieben / vñ geůbt sein / das er dem[344] ynnerlichen menschen vñ dem glauben gehorsam vnd gleychformig werde / nit hyndere noch widderstreb / wie sein art ist / wo er nit getzwungen wirt / deñ der ynnerliche mensch ist mit gott eyniß[345] / frőlich vnd lustig / vmb Christus willen / der yhm ßovil than hat / vñ stett[346] alle seyn lußt darynn / das er widderumb mocht gott auch vmbsonst dienen ynn freyer lieb / ßo[347] findt er ynn seynem fleysch eynen widerspenstigen willen / der wil der welt dienen vñ suchen was yhn lustet[348]
Das mag der glaub nit leyden / vnd legt sich mit lußt / an seynen halß yhn zu dempfen vñ weren.[349] Wie S. Pauel sagt Ro. 7. Ich hab ein lust / yn gottis willen nach meynem ynnerñ mencheñ / ßo find ich eynen andernn willen ynn meynem fleysch / der wil mich mit sunden gefangē nehmen. Item ich zuchtige meynen leyp vñ treib yhn zu gehorsam / auff das ich nit selbs vorwerfflich werde / der[350] die andern leren soll. Item Gal. 5. Alle die Christū angehőren / creutzigen yhr fleysch mit seynen bőßen lůsten.

---

[341] = NHG *außer dass*; this clause, running until 'ynn yhenes leben', is parenthetical.

[342] This clause correlates with the clause starting 'Ob wol' at the beginning of §20.

[343] = NHG *Arbeiten* (in the sense of *Anstrengung*) *und mit aller mäßiger.*

[344] Dative object of 'gehorsam ... werde'.

[345] = NHG *eins mit Gott.*

[346] = NHG *soviel getan hat und steht.*

[347] = 'so', here with an adversative sense 'but'.

[348] = NHG *gelüstet.* There was no space for a full stop after the sentence and no need for it since the next sentence starts with an upper-case letter on the next line.

[349] = NHG *abwehren.*

[350] = 'der' beginning a relative clause modifying 'ich'.

20 Even if inwardly people are, according to their soul, sufficiently righteous through faith, and have everything they should have – except that that same faith and sufficiency must always grow into the life beyond –, nonetheless in this physical life they still dwell on earth and must govern their own bodies and deal with people.

This is when the works begin; here people must not go idly about, now in fact the body must be driven and trained with fasting, vigils, working, and all reasonable discipline so that it becomes obedient and uniform with the inward person and with faith, and does not obstruct or resist, which is its way when it is not compelled. For the inward person is one with God, joyful and delighted because of Christ, who has done so much for them, and all their delight consists in wanting in return to serve God for no gain with a love freely given, but they find in their flesh a recalcitrant will which tries to serve the world and seek what it pleases.

That is something which faith cannot abide and it seizes it eagerly by the throat to stifle it and fight against it. As St Paul says in Romans 7, 'I take delight in God's will according to my inward person, but I find another will in my flesh, which tries to imprison me with sins'.[351] Likewise, 'I chastise my body and bring it into subjection so that I, who am meant to teach others, should not myself become blameworthy'.[352] Likewise in Galatians 5, 'All those who belong to Christ crucify their flesh with its evil desires'.[353]

---

[351] KJV Romans 7,22–23: 'For I delight in the law of God after the inward man: But I see another law in my members, warring against the law of my mind, and bringing me into captivity to the law of sin which is in my members.'

[352] KJV I Corinthians 9,27: 'But I keep under my body, and bring *it* into subjection: lest that by any means, when I have preached to others, I myself should be a castaway.'

[353] KJV Galatians 5,24: 'And they that are Christ's have crucified the flesh with the affections and lusts.' The KJV translation does not make it clear that it is the 'fleisch', the body of the believers, which has the evil desires. The NIV reads 'Those who belong to Christ Jesus have crucified the flesh with *its* passions and desires.'

¶ Czū eyn vnd zwentzigsten / Aber die selben werck muͤssen[354] nit geschehn ynn der meynung / das da durch der mensch frum werd fur gott / deñ die falsch meynung kan der glaub nit leydē / der alleyn ist vñ sein muß die frumkeyt fur gott / sonderñ nur yn der meynung / das der leyp gehorsam werde / vnd gereynigt von seynen bosen luͤsten / vñ dz aug nur sehe / auff die bosen luͤsten / sie auß zu treyben / Deñ die weyl die seel durch den glauben reyn ist / vñ gott liebet / wolt sie gern das auch also[355] alle ding reyn weren (B4v) zuuor[356] yhr eygen leyp / vnd yderman gott / mit yhr liebt vnd lobt /
So geschichts / das d᷑ mensch seyns eygen leyps halben nit kan muͤßsig gehen / vñ muß vil gutter werck drober vben / das er yhn zwinge / vnd doch die werck nit das rechte gutt seyn / dauon er frum vnd gerecht sey fur gott / ßondern thue[357] sie auß freyer lieb vmbsonst / got zu gefallen / nichts darynn anders gesucht noch angesehen / denn das es gott also gefellet / wilchs willen[358] er gerne thet[359] auffs allerbeste. Darauß denn[360] ein yglicher kan selbs nehmen[361] die maß vnd bescheydenheit den leyp zu Casteyen / Denn / er fastet / wachet / erbeyt / ßoviell er sicht[362] dem leyp nott seyn / seynen muttwillen zu dempffen.[363]

---

[354] = NHG *dürfen.*

[355] = NHG *ebenso.*

[356] = NHG *vor allem.*

[357] The present subjunctive has jussive force: literally 'he must do'.

[358] = NHG *um dessentwillen* 'for the sake of which'.

[359] = NHG *täte* 'would do'.

[360] = NHG *dann.*

[361] = NHG *entnehmen.*

[362] = NHG *sieht* in the sense of 'perceives'.

[363] For a comparison between the German and Latin versions of this paragraph, cf. chapter 4, section 2a. The Latin text (taken from the digital version of the Taylor Editions https://editions.mml.ox.ac.uk/editions/libertate1521/#d1r) is as follows (marginalia are in square brackets): '[Qua opinione opera facienda.] Verum ea opera oportet, non ea fieri opinione, quo per ipsa coram deo iustificetur quisquam, hanc enim falsam opinionem fides non feret, quae sola est iustitia coram deo, sed solum ea opinione, ut corpus in servitutem redigatur & purificetur a concupiscentiis suis malis, ita ut oculum non nisi vertat ad concupiscentias expurgandas.'

21 But these works must not be carried out in the opinion that through them the person may become righteous before God – for faith cannot abide this false opinion, as it alone is and must be righteousness before God – but only in the opinion that the body should become obedient and cleansed of its evil desires, and the eye should only look on evil desires to drive them out. For when the soul is pure through faith and loves God, it would want everything else to be similarly pure, first and foremost its own body, and for everyone also to love and praise God as it does. So it is that case that, because of their own body, people cannot be idle and must, moreover, carry out many good works in order to subdue it; and yet the works are not the true good that makes them righteous and justified in the sight of God, but rather they must do them for no gain, freely out of love in order to please God, not seeking or having regard to anything other than that it may please God; and for that, they will gladly do their very best. From this every person can then infer the degree and precise way in which to chasten the body. For they fast, watch, and work as much as they feel is necessary to subdue the wantonness of the body.[364]

---

[364] Translation of the Latin text (cf. the facing page): '[In which opinion works should be done.] But these works must not be carried out in the opinion that through them anyone can be justified before God – for faith will not tolerate this false notion, as it alone is righteousness before God—but only in the opinion that the body should be brought into subjection and be cleansed of its evil desires, so that the eye should be directed only to purging those desires.'

Die andern aber / die do meynen mit wercken frum zu werden / haben keyn acht auff die casteyung / sondern sehen nur auff die werck / vnd meynen / wenn sie der selben nur viel vnd groß thun / ßo sey es wol than vnd sie frum wuͤrden / zu weyllen zu brechen die koͤpff vnd vorterben yhr leybe druͤber / das ist ein groſse torheyt / vñ vnuorstand[365] Christlichs lebens vnd glaubens / das sie on glauben / durch werck frum vnd selig werden wollen.[366]

[365] = NHG *Unverstand*, 'lack of understanding'.

[366] Latin continued: 'Cum enim anima per fidem purgata sit & amans dei facta, vellet omnia pariter purgari, praecipue corpus proprium, ut omnia secum amarent & laudarent deum. Ita fit, ut homo exigente corporis sui causa ociari non possit, cogaturque ob id, multa bona operari, ut in servitutem redigat.'

But the others, who think they can become righteous through works, do not pay attention to chastening, but only focus on the works, and think that if they only do sufficient and great works, then they have done well and have become righteous, sometimes wracking their brains and destroying their bodies in doing this: that is great folly and a lack of understanding of Christian life and faith to want to become righteous and saved by works without faith.[367]

[367] Translation of the Latin continued: 'For when the soul has been purged by faith and made to love God, it would want all things to be likewise cleansed, and especially its own body, so that all things might love and praise God as it does. So it is the case that, because of the demands of their own body, the person cannot be idle, but is compelled because of it to carry out many good works, in order to bring it into subjection.'

¶ Czum zwey vnd zwentzigsten / Das wir des[368] etlich gleychniß geben. Soll man die werck eynis Christen menschen der durch seynen glaubē / vñ auß lautern gnaden gottis / vmbsonst ist rechtfertig vnd selig worden / nit anders achten / den wie die werck Adam vnd Eue ym paradiß geweßen weren / Dauon Gen. 2. stett geschrieben. Das gott den geschaffenen menschen / setzt ynß paradiß / das er dasselb erbeytten vnd hutten solt.[369]
Nu war Adam von gott frum vnd wol geschaffen / on sund / das[370] er durch seyn erbeytten vnd hutten nit durfft[371] frum vñ rechtfertig werden / doch das er nit mů̈ssig gieng / gab yhm gott zu schaffen / das paradeys zu pflantzen / bawen vnd bewarenn. Wilchs weren eytell frey werck geweßen / vmb keynß dings willen gethan / denn[372] allein gott zu gefallen / vnd nit vmb frumkeyt zu erlangen / die er zuuor hett / wilch vns auch allen naturlich were angeborn geweßenn. Alßo auch eynis glaubigen menschen werck / wilcher durch seynen glauben ist widderumb ynß paradiß gesetzt / vnd von newen geschaffen / darff keyner werck frum zu werden / sondern das er nit mů̈ssig gahe vnd seynen leyb erbeytt[373] vnd beware / seyn yhm solche freye werck zu thun alleyn gott zu gefallenñ befolhen.

---

[368] = NHG *dessen*, 'of this'.

[369] = NHG *setzte … bearbeiten und behüten sollte.*

[370] = NHG *ohne Sünde, so dass.*

[371] = NHG *bedurfte, brauchte.*

[372] = NHG *außer.*

[373] ENHG 'arbeiten' means 'labour', used here in the parallel between Adam's work and human labour.

22 Let us give some examples of this. One should regard the works of Christian people who have without merit become righteous and saved through faith and out of God's pure grace no differently from the works of Adam and Eve in Paradise. Of that it is written in Genesis 2[374] that God placed man, once created, in Paradise so that he should work and look after it.

Now Adam was created by God righteous and good, without sin, so that he did not need to become righteous and just through his work and care; but, so that he did not go about idly, God gave him the task of planting, cultivating, and preserving Paradise. These works would have been entirely voluntary and done for no other purpose than solely to please God and not to achieve righteousness, which he already had and which would also have been naturally inborn in us.

And so it is the same with the works of faithful people, who, likewise placed in Paradise through their faith and created anew, do not need any works to become righteous; but, so that they do not go about idly and so that they exercise and look after their bodies, such works are ordained to be done freely and solely to please God.

---

374 KJV Genesis 2,15: 'And the LORD God took the man, and put him into the garden of Eden to dress it and to keep it.'

(C1r) Item gleych wie eyn geweyheter Bischoff / wen der[375] kirchen weyhet / fermelt[376] od᷑ sonst seynis ampts werck vbet / ßo machen yhn die selben werck nit zu eynem bischoff / Ja wenn er nit zuuor ein Bischoff geweyhet were / ßo tůͤchte der selben werck keyniß[377] vnd were eytell narrñ werck. Alßo eyn Christen / der durch den glauben geweyhet / gutte werck thut / wirt durch die selben nit besser oder mehr geweyhet (wilch nit denn[378] des glauben mehrung thut) zu eynem Christen / Ja wenn er nit zuuor glaubet[379] vñ Christen were / ßo gůͤlten[380] alle seyne werck nichts / sondern weren / eytell nerrisch / strefflich vordamplich sund.

---

375 'when he'.

376 = NHG *firmt* 'confirms'.

377 = NHG *taugte keines der selben Werke.*

378 = NHG *nichts außer.*

379 = NHG *glaubte.*

380 = NHG *gälten.*

Similarly, just as an ordained bishop, if he consecrates the church, confirms, or otherwise performs the works of his office, is not made a bishop by such works – indeed, if he had not already been ordained as a bishop, none of these works would count and would be nothing but the works of a fool, – in just the same way Christians, who, ordained through their faith, do good works, are not better or more ordained as Christians by those works (only an increase in faith does that).

Indeed, if they did not believe or were not already Christians, all their works would be worth nothing, but would just be foolish, punishable, damnable sins.

¶ Czū drey vnd zwentzigsten / Drumb seyn die zween sprůch war. Gutte frum werck machen nymmer mehr ein guten frumen man / sondern eyn gutt frum man / macht gutte frum werck Bőße werck machen nymmer mehr eynen bőßen man / sondern ein bőßer man macht bőße werck / alßo / das allweg[381] / die person zuuor muß gut vñ frum sein vor allen gutten wercken / vñ gutte werck folgen vnd auß-gahn / von der frumen gutten person.
Gleych wie Christus sagt. Ein bőßer bawm tregt keyn gutte frucht. Ein gutter bawm tregt keynn boße frucht. Nu ists offenbar / das die frucht tragen nit den bawm / ßo wachßen auch die bawm nit auff den fruchten / sondern widerumb / die bawm tragen die frucht / vnd die frucht wachßen auff den bawmen. Wie nu die bawm mussen ehe[382] seyn / den[383] die frucht / vnd die frucht machen nit die bawm wid᷑ gutte noch bőse / sondern die bawm machen die frůchte.
Alßo muß der mensch ynn der person zuuor frum oder bőße seyn / ehe er gutte oder bőße werck thut / Vnd seyne werck machen yhn nit gutt odder bőße / sondern er macht gutt odder bőße werck. Des gleychen sehen wir ynn allen handwercken.
Ein gutt oder bőße hauß macht keynen gutten oder bőßen zymmer-man / sondern ein gutter oder boßer tzymmermā / macht ein bőß oder gutt hauß / keyn werck macht eynenn meyster / darnach das werck ist / sondern wie d᷑ meyster ist / darnach ist sein werck auch.
Alßo seyn die werck des menschen auch / wie es mit yhm stett ym glauben od᷑ vnglauben / darnach seind seyne werck gutt oder bőße. Vnd nit widerūb / wie seyne werck stehn darnach sey er frum odder glaubig / die werck / gleych wie sie nit glaubig machen / ßo machen sie auch nit frum.

381 'always'.

382 = NHG *eher*.

383 = NHG *als*.

23 For this reason the two statements are true: good, righteous works can never make a good, righteous person, but rather a good, righteous person does good, righteous works. Evil works never make an evil person, but rather an evil person does evil works. So it is always the case that somebody must first be good and righteous before all good works, and good works follow and proceed from somebody righteous and good.

Just as Christ says, 'a bad tree bears no good fruit',[384] a good tree bears no bad fruit. Now it is obvious that the fruit does not bear the tree, nor do the trees grow on the fruit, but rather the trees bear the fruit, and the fruit grows on the trees. And just as the trees must come before the fruit, and the fruit does not make the trees either good or bad, but the trees make the fruit, so somebody must first be righteous or evil in their person before they do good or evil works. And their works do not make them good or evil, but they do good or evil works.

We see the same principle in all crafts. A good or bad house does not make a good or bad carpenter, but a good or bad carpenter makes a bad or good house. No work makes its craftsman like itself, but as the craftsman is, so too is the work.

And this is also the case with human works: according to the person's faith or lack of faith, their works are good or bad. And it is not the other way around: that they are righteous or faithful according to their works. Just as the works do not make them faithful, so they also do not make them righteous.

---

[384] KJV Matthew 7,17–18: 'Even so every good tree bringeth forth good fruit; but a corrupt tree bringeth forth evil fruit. A good tree cannot bring forth evil fruit, neither can a corrupt tree bring forth good fruit.'

(C1v) Aber der glaub gleych wie er frum macht / ßo macht er auch gutte werck. So dañ die werck niemant frum machen / vnd der mensch zuuor muß frum sein / ehe er wirckt[385] / so ists offenbar / das allein der glaub auß lauttern gnaden / durch Christū vnd seyn wort / die person gnugsam frum vnd selig machet.[386] Vnd das keyn werck / keyn gepott / eynem Christen nott[387] sey zur seligkeit / sondern er frey ist von allen gepotten / vñ auß lauterer freyheit / vmb sonst thut / alls was er thut / nichts damit gesucht[388] seyneß nutzs oder selickeyt / Denn er schon satt vnd selig ist / durch seynenn glaubenn / vnd gottis gnaden / sondernñ nur gott darynnen gefallen.

385 = NHG *Werke ausführt*, 'performs works'.

386 The following sentence is dependent on 'ists offenbar' despite the full stop followed in the original by a larger space and an upper-case letter, which normally indicate a new paragraph.

387 = NHG *nötig*.

388 Present tense of 'gesuchen' (meaning the same as 'suchen').

But just as faith makes righteous, so it also produces good works. So, as works make no-one righteous, and somebody must first be righteous before performing works, it is obvious that only faith makes somebody sufficiently righteous and saved by pure grace through Christ and his word; and that no work, no commandment is necessary to a Christian for salvation, but rather they are free from all commandments, and they do everything for no reward, out of pure freedom, not thereby seeking their own benefit or salvation, for they are already satisfied and saved by their faith and the grace of God, but only to please God in what they do.

¶ Czum .xxiiij.[389] Widderumb dem / der on glauben ist / ist kein gutt werck furderlich[390] zur frumkeyt vnd seligkeit / Widderumb keyn boße werck yhn boße vnd vordampt machen / sondern̄ der vnglaub / der die person vnd den bawm boͤß macht der[391] thutt boße vnd vordampte werck.

Darumb wen man frum odder boße wirt / hebet sichs nit an den wercken an[392] / sondern an dem glauben / Wie der Weyße man sagt. Anfang aller sund / ist von gotte weychen vnd yhm nit trawen.

Also leret auch Christꝰ / wie man nit an den wercken muß anheben vñ sagt Entweder macht den bawm gutt vnd seyne fruchte gutt / oder macht den bawm bose / vnd seyne fruͤchte boͤße / als solt[393] er sagen / wer gutte fruͤcht haben wil / muß zuuor an dem bawm anheben / vnd den selben gutt setzen.

Alßo wer do wil gutte werck thun / muß nit an den wercken an heben / sondern an der person / die die werck thun soll. Die person aber macht niemant gut / denn[394] allein der glaub / vnd niemand macht sie boße denn allein der vnglaub. Das ist wol war / die werck machen eynen frum odder boße fur den menschen / das ist / sie zeygen eußerlich an / wer frum od᷑ bose sey. Wie Christus sagt. Matt. 7. Auß yhren fruͤchten sollet yhr sie erkennen.

---

[389] The printer switches to Roman numerals (enclosed in full stops to mark them as numbers) to save space, using the additive form ‘iiij’ for 4, but subtractive ‘ix’ for 9.

[390] = NHG *förderlich*.

[391] A resumptive pronoun, correlating with ‘der’ in the previous clause.

[392] = NHG *fängt es nicht bei den Werken an*.

[393] = NHG *würde* or *wollte*.

[394] = NHG *sondern*.

24 Similarly, for those without faith, no good work moves them closer to righteousness and salvation. Similarly, no bad works make them evil and damned, but the lack of faith that makes the person and the tree evil does evil and damnable works.

Therefore, becoming righteous or evil does not start with works, but with faith. As the wise man says: 'The beginning of all sins is departing from God and not trusting Him'.[395] Christ, too, teaches in the same way how one must not start with works and says: 'Either make the tree good and its fruit good or make the tree evil and its fruit evil' – as if he were saying: 'Whoever wants to have good fruit, must first begin with the tree and set it up well'.

Therefore, whoever wants to do good works, must not start with works, but with the person who is supposed to do the works. No-one makes the person good but faith alone, and no-one makes them evil but lack of faith alone. That is indeed true: works make someone righteous or evil before other people, i.e. they show outwardly who may be righteous or evil. As Christ says in Matthew 7: 'You shall know them by their fruits'.[396]

---

[395] KJV Ecclesiasticus 10,12: 'The beginning of pride is when one departeth from God, and his heart is turned away from his Maker.'

[396] KJV Matthew 7,20: 'Wherefore by their fruits ye shall know them.'

Aber das ist alles / ym scheyn vnd eußerlich. Wilchs an sehenn[397] yrre macht viel leuth / die do schreyben vnd leren / wie man gutte werck thun soll vnd frum werdenn. ßo sie doch[398] / des glaubens nymmer gedenckenn / gahn dahynn / vnd furet ymmer ein blind den anderñ / marterñ[399] sich mit vielen wercken vnd kūmen doch nymmer zu der rechten frumkeit / von wilchen Sanct Pauel sagt. 2. Timo. 3. Sie haben eynen scheyn der frumkeyt / (C2r) aber der grund ist nit da / gehn hynn vnd lernen ym̄er vñ ymmer vnd kummen doch nymmer zur erkentniß der waren frumkeit. Wer nu mit den selben blinden nit wil yrren / muß weytter sehen / den ynn die werck / gepott / odder lere der werck[400]. Er muß ynn die person sehen fur allen dingen / wie die frum werd. Die wirt aber nit durch gepott vnd werck / sondernn durch gottis wort (das ist / durch seyne vorheyschung[401] der gnadenn) vnd den glaubenn / frum vnd selig / auff das[402] bestehe seyn gottliche ehre / das er vns nit durch vnser werck / sondern durch seyn gnedigs wort vmbsonst vnd lauter barmhertzickeit[403] selig mache.

---

397 = NHG *Welches Ansehen* 'Which (i.e. this) appearance'.

398 'ßo ... doch' 'although'.

399 = NHG *gehen dahin und führt jeweils ein Blinder den andern, quälen.*

400 = NHG *als an die Werke, Gebote oder Lehre der Werke.*

401 = NHG *Verheißung* 'promise'.

402 'auff das' introduces a purpose clause.

403 A genitive of cause: 'out of pure compassion'.

But that is all in appearance and outwardly. This appearance misleads many people who write and teach how one should do good works and become righteous. But they never think of the faith, and walk around, and the blind always lead the blind,[404] tormenting themselves with many works and never coming to proper righteousness, about whom St Paul says in II Timothy 3: 'They have an appearance of righteousness, but the foundation is not there, walking around, forever learning but never coming to the recognition of true righteousness'.[405]

Anyone who does not want to go astray with those blind people must look beyond works, commandments, or the teaching of works. They need above all to look into the person, how they become righteous. But they will not become righteous and saved by commandments and works, but by God's word (i.e. by his promise of grace) and by faith, in order to rest His divine honour on this, so that He saves us not by our works, but by His gracious word, freely and out of pure compassion.

[404] Saying based on KJV Matthew 15,14: 'Let them alone: they be blind leaders of the blind. And if the blind lead the blind, both shall fall into the ditch.' And KJV Luke 6,39: 'And he spake a parable unto them, Can the blind lead the blind? shall they not both fall into the ditch?'

[405] KJV II Timothy 3,5/7: 'Having a form of godliness but denying the power thereof: from such turn away. ... Ever learning, and never able to come to the knowledge of the truth.'

¶ Czū .xxv. Auß dißem allen ist leychtlich zuuorstehen / wie gutte werck zu vorwerffen vñ nit zuuorwerffen seyn. Vnd wie man alle lere vorstahn[406] soll / die do gutte werck leren / dann[407] wo der falsch anhang[408] / vñ die vorkerete meynūg dryn ist / das durch die werck / wir frum vnd selig werden wollen / seyn sie schon nit gutt / vnd gantz vordamlich / deñ sie seyn nit frey / vnd schmehen[409] die gnad gottis / die allein durch den glauben frum vnd seligk macht / wilchs die werck nit vormůgen / vñ nehmē es yhn[410] doch fur[411] zu thun / vnd damit der gnaden / ynn yhr werck vnd ehre greyffenn.[412] Drumb vorwerffen wir die gutte werck / nit vmb yhren willen / ßondernn / vmb des selben boßen zusatzs vnd falscher vorkerter meynung willen. Wilche macht / das sie nur gutt scheynen / vnd seyn doch nit gutt / betriegen[413] sich vnd yderman damit / gleych wie die reyssend wolff / ynn schaffs kleydernñ.[414]

Aber der selb boße zusatz vnd vorkerete meynung / ynn den werckenn / ist vnůbirwindlich / wo der glaub nit ist. Er muß sein / ynn dem selben wirckheyligenn / biß der glaub kum vnd vorstőre yhn / die natur vormag yhn / von yhr selb nit auß treybenñ.[415] Ja auch nit erkennen / sondernn sie helt yhn fur eyn kőstlich / selig dingk / drumb werden yhr auch ßo viel da durch vorfuret.[416]

---

406 = NHG *verstehen.*

407 = NHG *denn.*

408 = NHG *Zusatz*, 'addition, addendum'.

409 = either NHG *verschmähen* ('disregard') or *schmähen* ('blasphemously insult').

410 = NHG *sich* (dative), referring to works.

411 = NHG *vor*, a separable prefix going with the preceding *nehmen.*

412 = NHG *und damit das Werk und die Ehre der Gnade angreifen.*

413 = NHG *betrügen.*

414 = NHG *reißende Wölfe in Schafskleidern.*

415 = NHG *von sich aus nicht austreiben.*

416 = NHG *darum werden auch so viele von ihnen dadurch verführt.*

25 From all this it is easy to understand how good works are to be rejected or not rejected, and how all teachings should be understood which preach good works, for if they contain the false addendum and wayward opinion that by works we are made righteous and saved, then they are not good, but wholly damnable. For they are not free, and they scorn God's grace, which alone makes us righteous and saves us by faith, which works cannot do, but which they nonetheless undertake to do, thereby trespassing onto the work and honour of grace. For this reason we reject good works, not in themselves, but because of this evil addition and false, wayward opinion, which makes them only appear good, but they are not in fact good, and so deceive themselves and everyone, just like the ravening wolves in sheep's clothing.[417]

But this same evil addition and wayward opinion about works is insurmountable if faith is not present. It must be so in the works-righteous person[418] until faith should come and break in on them: nature cannot drive it out by itself. Indeed, it cannot even recognise it, but rather considers it to be a precious, holy thing. This is why so many are led astray by it.

---

[417] KJV Matthew 7,15: 'Beware of false prophets, which come to you in sheep's clothing, but inwardly they are ravening wolves.'

[418] *Werkheilige* is a term coined by Luther for those who believe that through good works they will reach salvation.

Derhalben / obs woll[419] gutt ist / von rewen / beychten / gnugthun[420] / schreyben vnd predigenn / ßo[421] man aber nit weytter feret[422] biß zum glauben[423] / sein es gewißlich / eitel teuffelische / vorfurische lere. Mā muß nit eynerley allein p̄digen / sondern̄ alle beyde[424] wort gottis / Die gepot / sol mā predigen / die sunder zurschrecken̄[425] vn̄ yhr sund zu offenbarnn / das[426] sie rewe haben vnd sich bekeren. Aber da soll es nit bleyben / mā muß / das ander wort / Die zusagūg der gna(C2v)den / auch predigen / den glauben zu leren / on wilchenn die gepott rew vnd allis ander vorgebenß geschicht. Es sein wol noch blieben[427] prediger / die rew der sund vn̄ gnad p̄digen / aber sie streychen die gepott vnd zusagung gottis nit auß[428] / das mā lere[429] / woher vnd wie die rew / vnd gnad kumme. Denn die rew / fleust[430] auß den gepotten / der glaub / auß den zusagung gottis / vnd alßo wirt d᷑ mensch / durch den glauben gotlicher wort gerechtfertiget vnd erhaben / der durch die furcht gottis gepottis gedemůtiget vnd ynn seyn erkentniß kummen ist.

[419] = NHG *Deshalb, obwohl es.*

[420] = NHG *Bereuen, Beichten, Genügetun.* Three deverbal nouns.

[421] = NHG *wenn.*

[422] = NHG *fährt.*

[423] A smudge above the letter 'u' in the copy, not a diacritical mark.

[424] = NHG *nicht eins allein predigen, sondern alle beide* (i.e. the 'wort gottis' which are explained in the following as 'gebot' and 'zusagung der gnaden').

[425] = NHG *zu erschrecken.*

[426] Introduces a purpose clause.

[427] = NHG *ge- or verblieben.*

[428] ENHG 'ausstreichen' is a translation of Latin 'explicare', referring literally to 'uncreasing' or 'unfolding'; see DWB s.v. 1.

[429] = NHG *damit man lerne*, 'so that one might learn'.

[430] = NHG *Reue fließt.*

For this reason, although it is good to write and preach about penitence, confession, and satisfaction, if it is not carried through to include faith, then it is certainly nothing but devilish, seductive teaching. One must not preach one thing alone, but rather both words of God. The commandments should be preached in order to alarm sinners and reveal their sins so that they might repent and change their ways.[431] But it should not stop there. The other word must also be preached, namely the promise of grace, which teaches faith, without which the commandments, repentance, and everything else are done in vain. There are indeed still preachers who preach repentance for sin, and also grace, but they do not emphasise God's commandments and promises so that one might learn whence and why repentance and grace come. For repentance flows from the commandments, and faith from the promises of God, and so somebody is justified and raised up through faith in divine words who has been humbled by the fear of God's commandment and has come to realise this fact.

---

[431] KJV Psalm 51,13: '*Then* will I teach transgressors thy ways; and sinners shall be converted unto thee.'

Czum .xxvi. Das sey von den wercken gesagt ynn gemeyn[432] vnd die ein Christen mensch gegen seynem eygen leybe ůben sol. Nu wollen wir von mehr wercken sagen / die er gegen andere menschen thut. Denn der mensch lebt nit allein / ynn seynem leybe / sondern auch vnter andernn menschen auff erdenñ. Darumb kan er nit on werck sein gegen die selbenn / er muß yhe mit yhn[433] zu reden vnd zu schaffen habenñ / wie wol yhm der selben werck keyns nodt[434] ist zur frumkeit vnd seligkeyt. Drumb soll seyne meynung ynn allen werckenn frey vnd nur dahynn gericht seyn / das er anderñ leutten damit diene vnd nůtz sey[435]. Nichts anders yhm furbilde[436] / denn was deñ anderñ nott ist / das heyssit denn ein warhafftig Christen leben / vnd da geht der glaub mit lust vnd lieb ynß werck / als S. Paulus leret die Galatas.

Denn zu den Philippeñ / do[437] er sie geleret hatte / wie sie alle gnad vnd gnugde hettenn durch yhren glauben yn Christo / leret er sie weytter vnd sagt.

---

[432] = NHG *insgemein.*

[433] = NHG *je mit ihnen.*

[434] = NHG *derselben Werke keines nötig*, 'none of those same works necessary'

[435] = NHG *nützlich sei.*

[436] ENHG 'ihm fürbilden' = NHG *sich vorstellen*, DWB s.v. 2; the subject is 'der mensch'.

[437] = NHG *Denn (im Brief) zu den Philippern, als.*

26 That is enough said about works in general and about those that Christians should practise with regard to their own body. Now we will talk about further works which they should do with regard to other people. For nobody lives alone in their body, but among other people on earth. Therefore nobody can be without works with regard to others; one always has to talk to them and deal with them, even though none of these works is necessary for righteousness and salvation. Therefore their judgement about all works should be free and aimed only at serving and being useful to other people through them, and have in mind nothing but what is necessary for others; now that is what is called a true Christian life, and here faith goes to work with passion and love, as St Paul teaches the Galatians.[438]

Then, after he had taught the Philippians how they had complete grace and sufficiency through their faith in Christ,[439] he continues teaching them and says:

---

[438] KJV Galatians 5,6: 'For in Jesus Christ neither circumcision availeth anything, nor uncircumcision; but faith which worketh by love.'

[439] KJV Philippians 1,9–11: 'And this I pray, that your love may abound yet more and more in knowledge and in all judgment; That ye may approve things that are excellent; that ye may be sincere and without offence till the day of Christ. Being filled with the fruits of righteousness, which are by Jesus Christ, unto the glory and praise of God.'

Ich vorman[440] euch allis trosts / den yhr ynn Christo habt / vnd allis trosts / den yhr habt von vnßer liebe zu euch / vn̄ aller gemeinschafft / die yhr habt mit allen geystlichen frumen Christen / yhr wolt meyn hertz erfrewen volkoͤmlich / vn̄ das damit / das yhr hynfurt / wollet eyniß synnes seyn / eyner gegen dem andern̄ lieb ertzeygen / eyner dem andern̄ dienen / vnd ein yglicher acht haben / nit auff sich noch auff das seyne / sondern̄ auff den andern̄ / vnd was dem selben nott sey.
Sihe da hat Paulꝰ klerlich / ein Christenlich leben dahynn gestellet / das alle werck sollen gericht[441] seyn / dem nehsten zu gutt / Die weyl ein yglicher fur sich selb gnug hatt an seynen glauben / vnd alle andere werck vn̄ leben yhm vbrig seyn / seynem nehstē damit auß freyer lieb zu dienen / Dartzu furet er ein / Christū zu eynem exempell[442] vnd (C3r) sagt: Seyt also gesynnet / wie yhrs[443] seht yn Christo. Wilcher ob er wol voll gottlicher form ware vnd fur sich selb gnug hatte / vnd yhm sein leben / wircken vnd leydenn nicht nott ware / das er da mit frum odder seligk wurd.[444] Dennoch hatt er sich des alles geeußert / vnd geperdet[445] wie ein knecht / allerley gethan vnd gelidenn[446] / nichts angesehen / denn[447] vnßer beßtis / vn̄ alßo ob er wol frey ware / doch vmb vnßer willenn ein knecht wordenn.[448]

---

[440] = NHG *ermahne, erinnere*, 'remind of' (+ genitive).

[441] = NHG *gerichtet*.

[442] = NHG *führt er Christus als Exempel an*.

[443] Abbreviation of *yhr es*.

[444] 'ware', 'hatte', 'wurd' are a series of subjunctive forms (*wäre, hätte, würde*) which in NHG would be rendered as indicatives *obwohl er war, hatte, wurde*.

[445] = NHG *entäußert und gebärdet*.

[446] = NHG *gelitten*.

[447] = NHG *außer*.

[448] = NHG *geworden ist*.

'I remind you of all the consolation which you have in Christ and all the consolation which you have from our love to you and all the fellowship that you have with all spiritual, righteous Christians; you should want to make my heart completely rejoice by willingly being of one mind from now on, to show love towards one another, serve one another, and looking out not for yourself, nor for what is yours, but for others and for what others need'.[449]

Look, here Paul has clearly set forth a Christian life, that all works should be directed to the benefit of others, since everybody has enough in their faith and has all their other works and their whole life to spare for serving their neighbours with love freely given.

Furthermore, he introduces Christ as an example, and says: 'Be of just the same mind as you see in Christ, who, although he was fully in the form of God and had enough for himself and had no need of his life, works, and passion to become righteous or saved through them, still he divested himself of everything and acted like a servant, did and suffered many things, had regard for nothing but what is best for us, and so although he himself was free, he nevertheless became a servant for our sake'.[450]

---

[449] KJV Philippians 2,1–4: 'If *there be* therefore any consolation in Christ, if any comfort of love, if any fellowship of the Spirit, if any bowels and mercies, Fulfil ye my joy, that ye be likeminded, having the same love, being of one accord, of one mind. Let nothing be done through strife or vainglory; but in lowliness of mind let each esteem other better than themselves. Look not every man on his own things, but every man also on the things of others.'

[450] KJV Philippians 2,5–7: 'Let this mind be in you, which was also in Christ Jesus: Who, being in the form of God, thought it not robbery to be equal with God: But made himself of no reputation, and took upon him the form of a servant, and was made in the likeness of men.'

¶ Czum .xxvij. Alßo soll ein Christen mensch / wie Christus seyn heubt[451] / voll vnd satt / yhm auch benugen lassen an[452] seynem glaubenn / den selben ymer mehrenn / wilcher seyn leben / frumkeit vnd seligkeyt ist / der yhm gibt allis was Christ⁹ vnd gott hat / wie droben gesagt ist. Vnd S. Paul Gal. 2. spricht / Was ich noch ynn dem corper lebe / das lebe ich ynn dem glauben Christi gottis sohn.

Vnd ob er nu gantz frey ist[453] / sich widderūb williglich eynē diener machen[454] seynem nehsten zu helffenn / mit yhm faren[455] / vnd handeln / wie gott mit yhm durch Christū handlet[456] hatt / vnd das allis vmbsonst / nichts darynnen suchen denn gottliches wolgefallenn[457] / vnd alßo denckenn. Wolan meyn gott hatt mir vnwirdigen vordampten menschen[458] / on alle vordienst / lauterlich vmbsonst vñ auß eytel barmhertzickeit[459] gebeñ / durch vnd ynn Christo / vollen reychtumb aller frumkeit vnd selickeit / das ich hynfurt[460] / nichts mehr bedarff / denn glauben es sey also.

Ey so will ich solchem vatter[461] der mich mit seynen vberschwenglichen gutterñ alßo vbirschuttet hatt / widerumb / frey / frͤolich vnd vmbsonst thun was yhm wolgefellet / Vnnd gegen meynem nehsten auch werden ein Christen / wie Christus mir worden ist / vnd nichts mehr thun / denn was ich nur sehe / yhm nott / nͤutzlich vnd seliglich sey[462] / die weyl ich doch / durch meynenn glauben / allis dings yn Christo gnug habe.

---

[451] = NHG *Haupt.*

[452] 'yhm … benugen lassen an' = NHG *sich genügen lassen an.*

[453] = NHG *obwohl er nun ganz frei ist.*

[454] 'soll' is understood with 'machen'.

[455] 'faren' = NHG *verfahren, umgehen.*

[456] = NHG *gehandelt.*

[457] = NHG *darin suchen als göttliches Wohlgefallen.*

[458] = NHG *unwürdigen, verdampten Menschen*, in apposition to 'mir'.

[459] = NHG *völlig umsonst und aus reiner Barmherzigkeit.*

[460] = NHG *sodass ich hinfort.*

[461] Indirect object of 'thun'.

[462] = NHG *ihm notwendig, nützlich und zur Seligkeit dienend sei,* refers to 'meynem nehsten'.

27 So a Christian should, like Christ their head,[463] be fully satisfied, be content in their faith, and always increase it because it is their life, righteousness, and salvation, which gives them everything that Christ and God have, as has been stated above. And as St Paul says in Galatians 2: 'What I now live in the flesh I live in the faith of Christ, the Son of God'.[464] And although they are now completely free, they should make themselves into a willing servant in order to help their neighbour, and behave and treat their neighbour as God has treated them through Christ, and do all this freely, seeking nothing from it other than God's pleasure, and should think: 'Well then, my God has given me, unworthy, damnable person, without any of my own merits, for nothing in return and out of pure mercy, through and in Christ, the full riches of all righteousness and salvation, so that henceforth I need nothing other than to believe that it is so.

Oh, then, for such a father, who has showered me with His abundant goods, freely, joyfully, and without reward, I will in return do what is pleasing to Him. And I will also be a Christian to my neighbour, just as Christ has been to me, and I will do nothing other than what I can see is necessary, useful, and salutary for them, since I have sufficiency in everything in Christ through my faith'.[465]

---

[463] KJV Ephesians 5,15 'But speaking the truth in love, may grow up into him in all things, which is the head, *even* Christ.'

[464] KJV Galatians 2,20: 'I am crucified with Christ: nevertheless I live; yet not I, but Christ liveth in me: and the life which I now live in the flesh I live by the faith of the Son of God, who loved me, and gave himself for me.'

[465] KJV 2 Corinthians 12,9: 'My grace is sufficient for thee.'

Sih also fleusset[466] auß dem glauben die lieb vñ lust zu gott / vnd auß der lieb / ein frey / willig / frolich lebeñ dem nehsten zu dienē vmbsonst. Denn zu gleych wie vnser nehst nott leydet / vnd vnßers vbrigenn bedarff[467] / alßo haben wir fur gott nott geliden vnd seyner gnaden bedurfft. Darumb wie vns gott hatt durch Christum vmbsonst geholffen / alßo sollen wir / durch den leyp / vnd seyne werck / nit anders den dem nehsten helffen. Also sehen wir wie eyn hoch edliß leben sey vmb[468] ein Christlich leben / das (C3v) leyder nu ynn aller welt / nit allein nyderligt / sondernn auch nit mehr bekandt ist noch gepredigt wirt.

---

[466] = NHG *Sieh, so fließt.*

[467] = NHG *in gleicher Weise wie unser Nächster Not leidet und unseres Überflusses bedarf.*

[468] 'vmb' here has the sense 'in', but need not be translated.

Behold, in this way love and longing for God flow out of faith, and from this love flows a free, willing, joyful life serving one's neighbour without reward. For just as our neighbour suffers want and needs to partake in our abundance, so it was with us when we suffered want before God and were in need of His grace. Therefore, just as God helped us without reward through Christ, so we should through our body and its works do nothing other than help our neighbour. So we can see what a high, noble life the Christian life is, which sadly is now laid low throughout the world, but also is no longer known nor preached.

¶ Czum .xxviij. Alßo leßen wir Luce. 2. Das die Junpfraw Maria zur kirchen gieng nach den sechs wochen vnd ließ sich reynigen nach dem gesetz / wie alle ander weyber / ßo sie doch nit gleych mit yhn vnreyn war / noch schuldig dˀ selben reynigung / bedurfft yhr[469] auch nit. Aber sie thetts[470] auß freyer lieb / das sie die andere weyber nit vorachtet[471] / sondernn mit dem hauffen[472] bliebe.

Alßo ließ S. Pauel / S. Timotheũ beschneytten / nit das es nott were / sonderñ das[473] er den schwachglaubigen Juden nit vrsach gebe / zu bosen gedanckeñ / der doch widderumb Titũ nit wollt lassen beschneyttẽ / da mã drauff dringen wolt / er must beschnitten seyn / vnd were nott[474] zur seligkeit. Vnd Christus Matt. 17. Da võ seynen Jůngern ward die tzinß pfennig gefoddert[475] / disputiert er mit S. Peter / ob nit kůnigs kynder frey weren zynß zu geben. Vnd sanct Peter / ja sagt. Hieß er yhn doch hynn gehen an dz mehr[476] vnd sprach / Auff[477] das wir sie nit ergernñ / ßo gang hyn[478] / den ersten fisch du fehist / den nym vnd yn seynem maull wirstu finden eynen pfennig / den gib fur mich vñ dich. Das ist ein feyn exempell / zu dißer lere / da Christus / sich vnd die seynen freye kůnigs kinder nennett / die keynis dings bedurffen / vnd doch sich vnterlessit[479] williglich/ dienet vnd gibt den tzynß.

---

[469] = NHG *obwohl sie doch nicht gleichermaßen mit ihnen unrein war, noch verpflichtet* ('schuldig' + genitive) *zu derselben Reinigung, sie* ('yhr' = genitive governed by 'bedurfft', referring to 'der selben reynigung') *auch nicht bedurfte.*

[470] = NHG *tat es.*

[471] = NHG *verachtete.*

[472] 'the crowd, the majority'.

[473] Introduces a purpose clause.

[474] = NHG *notwendig.*

[475] = NHG *die Zinspfennige gefordert wurden.*

[476] = NHG *Meer.*

[477] = NHG *So.*

[478] = NHG *Auf dass wir sie* (i.e. collectors of the temple tax) *nicht ärgern, so gehe hin.*

[479] = NHG *sich herablassen, demütigen*, DWB s.v. 6, 'submit'.

28 Thus, we read in Luke 2 that the Virgin Mary went to church after the six weeks and submitted to purification according to the law, like any other woman, although she was not impure like them nor obliged to do the same purification, nor did she need it.[480] But she did it out of love freely given, so as not to be scornful of the other women, but in order to remain part of the group. In the same way, St Paul had Timothy circumcised not because it was necessary but in order not to give those Jews of little faith any reason to think evil thoughts.[481] Conversely, he did not want Titus to be circumcised when people were trying to insist that he had to be circumcised and that this was necessary for salvation.[482]

And Christ in Matthew 17 argued with St Peter when tribute money was demanded from his disciples, whether the king's children were not free to pay tribute. And St Peter said yes, but he asked him to go to the sea and said: 'Lest we offend them, go there, take up the first fish that you catch, and in its mouth you will find a penny: give it for me and you'.[483] It is a good example of this teaching, since Christ calls himself and those who belong to him free children of the king, who need nothing, but still readily submit, serve, and pay the tribute.

---

[480] KJV Luke 2,22: 'And when the days of her purification according to the law of Moses were accomplished, they brought him to Jerusalem, to present *him* to the Lord.' According to Leviticus 12,2–8 ('the law'), following the birth of a son, the mother was required to wait 40 days before going to the temple to offer a sacrifice for her purification.

[481] KJV Acts 16,3: 'Him would Paul have to go forth with him; and took and circumcised him because of the Jews which were in those quarters: for they knew all that his father was a Greek.'

[482] KJV Galatians 2,3: 'But neither Titus, who was with me, being a Greek, was compelled to be circumcised.'

[483] KJV Matthew 17,26–27: 'Jesus saith unto him, Then are the children free. Notwithstanding, lest we should offend them, go thou to the sea, and cast an hook, and take up the fish that first cometh up; and when thou hast opened his mouth, thou shalt find a piece of money: that take, and give unto them for me and thee.'

Wie vill[484] nu das werck / Christo nott war vnd dienet[485] hatt / zu seyner frumkeit oder seligkeit / so vil sein alle ander sein vnd seyner Christen werck yhn not zur seligkeit / sondern sein allis frey dienste / zu willen vñ besserung der andern. Also solten auch aller priester / kloͤster vnd stifft[486] werck gethā sein / das ein yglicher seynis stands vñ ordens werck allein darūb thet / den anderñ zu wilfaren[487] vñ seynen leib zu regieren / den anderñ exempell zu geben auch also[488] zu thun / die auch bedurffenn yhre leyb zu zwingenn / doch altzeit / fursehen das nit da durch frum vnd selig werdeñ / furgenommen werd. Wilchs allein des glaubens vermuͤgen ist. Auff die weyße gepeut[489] auch S. Paul Ro. 13. vñ Tit. 3. Das sie sollen weltlicher gewalt vnterthā vñ bereyt sein / nit das sie da durch frum werdē sollen / sondern das sie den anderñ vnd der vbirkeit[490] da mit frey dieneten / vnd yhren willen thetten auß lieb vñ freyheit. Wer nu dissen vorstand hette / der kund leychtlich sich richtenn / ynn die (C4r) vntzellichen gepotten vnd gesetzen des Babsts[491] / der Bischoff / der kloͤster / der stifft / der fursten vñ herrñ / die etlich tolle prelaten alßo treyben[492] / als weren sie nott zur seligkeit / vnd heyssen es / gepott der kirchen / wie wol vnrecht. Deñ ein freyer Christen spricht alßo. Ich wil fasten / betten / ditz vnd das thun / was gepotten ist / nit dz ichs bedarff oď da durch wolt frum oder selig werden / sondern ich wils dem Babst / Bischoff / der gemeyn / oď meynem mit bruder / herrn zu willen / exempel vnd dienst thun vñ leydeñ / gleych wie mir Christus viel groͤsser ding zu willen thā vnd geliden hatt / des yhm vill weniger nott ware. Vnd ob schon die tyrannē vnrecht thun solchs zu foddern / ßo schadets mir doch nit / die weyl es nit widder gott ist.

---

484 'Wie vill' correlates with 'so vil' = NHG *wie viel ... ebenso viel.*

485 = NHG *gedient.*

486 = NHG *die Werke aller Priester, Klöster und Stifte* (collegiate foundations).

487 = NHG *willfahren, zu Willen sein,* 'satisfy'.

488 = NHG *ebenso.*

489 = NHG *gebietet.*

490 = NHG *Obrigkeit.*

491 = NHG *könnte leicht sich schicken in die unzähligen Gebote und Gesetze des Papsts.*

492 = NHG *verrückte Prälaten so betreiben* ('promote').

Now that work was as necessary for Christ and contributed as much to his salvation as his works and those of his Christians are necessary for their salvation, but rather they are all services freely given for the sake and benefit of others. Similarly, the works of all priests, monasteries, and collegiate institutions should be done in a way that each should do the works appropriate to their position and order solely to satisfy others and to control their own bodies, to set an example to others to act in the same way, since they also need to coerce their bodies, but they always have to take care that this is not undertaken in order to become righteous and saved, since that is only possible for faith.

And in the same way, St Paul demands in Romans 13[493] and Titus 3[494] that they be subject and responsive to worldly power, not to become righteous by this, but freely to serve others and authority, and do their will out of love and freedom. Whoever understood this could easily adjust themselves to the countless commandments and laws of the pope, bishops, monasteries, colleges, princes, and lords, which some mad clergymen promote as if they were necessary for salvation and call them commandments of the church, but quite wrongly.

For a free Christian says thus: 'I want to fast, pray, do this and that which has been commanded, not because I need to or want to become righteous and saved thereby, but because I want to do and suffer this for the sake, example, and service of the pope, bishops, the community or my fellow brother, lord, just as Christ did and suffered many greater things for my sake, which were far less necessary for him. And even though the tyrants act unjustly by demanding such, it will not hurt me since it is not against God'.

---

[493] KJV Romans 13,1–7: 'Let every soul be subject unto the higher powers. ... Render therefore to all their dues: tribute to whom tribute is due; custom to whom custom; fear to whom fear; honour to whom honour.'

[494] KJV Titus 3,1: 'Put them in mind to be subject to principalities and powers, to obey magistrates, to be ready to every good work.'

¶ Czum .xxix. Hierauß mag ein yglicher ein gewiß vrteyl vñ vnterscheydt nehmen / vnter allen wercken vnd gepottenn / auch wilchs[495] blind tolle od̾ recht synnige prelaten sein. Deñ wilchs[496] werck nit dahynauß gericht[497] ist / dem anderñ zu dienen / oder seynen willen zu leydenn / ßo fern er nit zwing/ wider gott zu thun[498] / ßo ists nit ein gut Christlich werck. Daher kumpts / das ich sorg[499] / wenig stifft kirchen / kloͤster / altar / meß / testamēt / Christlich seinn / Datzu auch / die fasten vnd gepett etlichen heyligen / sonderlich gethan. Denn ich furcht / das ynn den allen sampt ein yglicher nur das seyne sucht / vormeynend[500] damit sein sund zu buͤssen vnd seligk werden. Wilchs allis kūpt auß vnwissenheit des glaubens vñ Christlicher freyheit / Vnd etlich blind p̄laten / die leuth da hynn treybeñ vnd solch weßen[501] preyssen / mit ablas schmucken vñ den glauben nym̄er mehr leren. Ich rate dir aber wiltu[502] etwas stifften / betten / fasten / so thu es nit der meynūg / dz du wollist[503] dir etwas guts thū / sondern gibs dahin frey / dz and̾e leuth desselben genißen mugen vñ thu es yhn zu gut / so bistu ein rechter Christē / wz sollē dir dein guͤtter vñ gute werck die dir uͤbrig sein / dein leyb zu regieren vñ vorsorgen / so du gnug hast am glaubeñ / daryn dir gott alle ding geben hat. Sihe also mussen gottis gutter fliessen auß eynē / yn den andern vñ gemeyn werdē. dz ein yglicher sich seynis nehstē also annehm / als were erß[504] selb

[495] = NHG *welche* ('which'), referring to 'prelaten'.

[496] Here 'whatever', 'any … which'.

[497] = NHG *darauf ausgerichtet*.

[498] Parenthesis = NHG *sofern er nicht dazu zwinge, gegen Gott zu handeln.*

[499] = NHG *Daher kommt es, dass ich besorge* ('worry, fear').

[500] = NHG *vermeinend / in der Meinung*.

[501] = NHG *Wesen*, here 'behaviour'.

[502] = NHG *willst du*; this is the beginning of a conditional clause.

[503] 2 singular present subjunctive of *wellen* (= NHG *wollen*).

[504] Abbreviation of *er es*; *es* is used, despite referring to 'seynis nehsten'.

29 From this, every person may form a sure opinion and distinction between all works and commandments, and also identify which are blind, foolish, or right-thinking prelates. For any work that does not aim to serve somebody else or suffer their will, so long as it does not force one to act against God, is not a good Christian work.

This is why I fear that few collegiate church, abbeys, altars, masses, or legacies are Christian, nor the fasts and prayers specifically for various saints. For I fear that in all these, people only seek their own advantage, thinking that by this they may atone for their sin and attain salvation. All this comes from ignorance of faith and of Christian freedom. And some blind prelates urge people on in this, and praise such activity, tricking themelves out with indulgences, and no longer preach faith. But I advise you that if you want to endow something, to pray, to fast, do not so on the assumption that you are thereby going to do something good for yourself, but do it freely, so that other people may have the enjoyment of it, and do it for their benefit; then you are a true Christian. What use are your goods and good works, which you have over and above what you require to control and take care of your body, since you have all you need in faith, through which God has given you everything? Behold, therefore, God's good things must flow from each other and become common to all, so that everyone should receive their neighbour as themselves.

Auß Chrō fliessen sie yn vns / dʼ sich vnser hatt angenōmen ynn seynē leben̄ / als were er dz gewesen / dz wir sein.[505] Auß vns sollen sie fliessen / yn die / so yr bedurffen.[506] Auch so gar / dz ich muß auch (C4v) meynenn glaubenn vnd gerechtickeyt / fur meynenn nehsten setzen fur gott / seyne sund zu decken / auff mich nehmen vnd nit anders thun / denn als weren sie meyn eygen / eben wie Christꝰ vns allen than hatt. Sich[507] das ist die natur der liebe / wo sie warhafftig ist / Da ist sie aber warhafftig / wo der glaub warhafftig ist. Darumb gibt der heylig Apostell / der lieb zu eygen[508] 1. Cor. 13. Das sie nit sucht das yhre / sondern / was des nehsten ist.

---

505 = NHG *als wäre er das gewesen, was wir sind.*

506 = NHG *zu denen, die ihrer bedürfen* ('to those who need them').

507 = NHG *Sieh.*

508 = NHG *schreibt der Liebe zu* ('attributes to love').

From Christ, who has received us into his life as though he were as we are, they flow into us. From us they should flow to those who need them. And indeed so much so, that I should place my faith and justification before God on behalf of my neighbour in order to cover their sins, to take them on myself, and act as though they were my own, just as Christ has done for us all. Behold, this is the nature of love, where it is true. But love is true where faith is true. This is why the holy apostle says of love in I Corinthians 13 that it 'does not seek its own benefit, but what is advantageous for its neighbour'.[509]

[509] I Corinthians 13 describes the properties of love as we should show to one another. The KJV uses the term 'charity' rather than 'love'. KJV I Corinthians 13,5: '[Charity] Doth not behave itself unseemly, seeketh not her own, is not easily provoked, thinketh no evil.'

¶ Czum .xxx. Aus dem allenn folget der beschluß / das eyn Christen mensch lebt nit ynn yhm selb / sondern ynn Christo vñ seynem nehstenn / ynn Christo durch den glauben / ym nehsten / durch die liebe / durch den glauben feret[510] er vber sich yn gott / auß gott feret er widder vnter sich durch die liebe / vnd bleybt doch ymmer ynn gott vñ gottlicher liebe / Gleych wie Christus sagt Johan. 1. Ihr werdet noch sehen den hymell offen stehn / vñ die Engell auff vnd absteygenn vbir den Sun des menschenn.[511]
Sihe das ist / die rechte / geystliche / Christliche freyheyt / die das hertz frey macht / von allen sundenn / gesetzen / vnd gepotten / wilch alle andere freyheyt vbirtrifft / wie der hymell die erdenñ / Wilch geb vns gott recht zuuorstehen vnd behaltenn /

AMEN.

---

[510] = NHG *fährt.*
[511] = NHG *Menschensohn.*

30 The conclusion that follows from all this is that Christians do not live within themselves, but in Christ and in their neighbour. In Christ through the faith, in their neighbour through love; by faith they move above themselves to God, from God they move below themselves through love, but remaining always in God and in divine love. Just as Christ says in John I: 'You will see the heaven open and the angels ascending and descending upon the Son of Man'.[512]

Behold, that is true, spiritual, Christian freedom, which sets the heart free from all sins, laws, and commandments, which surpasses all other freedom as the heaven the earth. May God give us to understand and keep them rightly.

Amen.[513]

---

[512] KJV John 1,51: 'And he saith unto him, Verily, verily, I say unto you, Hereafter ye shall see heaven open, and the angels of God ascending and descending upon the Son of man.'

[513] This ties back to the beginning of the text, reading 'Ihesus'. The structure of the text was intended by Luther to mirror the structure of a prayer, hence the ending with 'AMEN'.

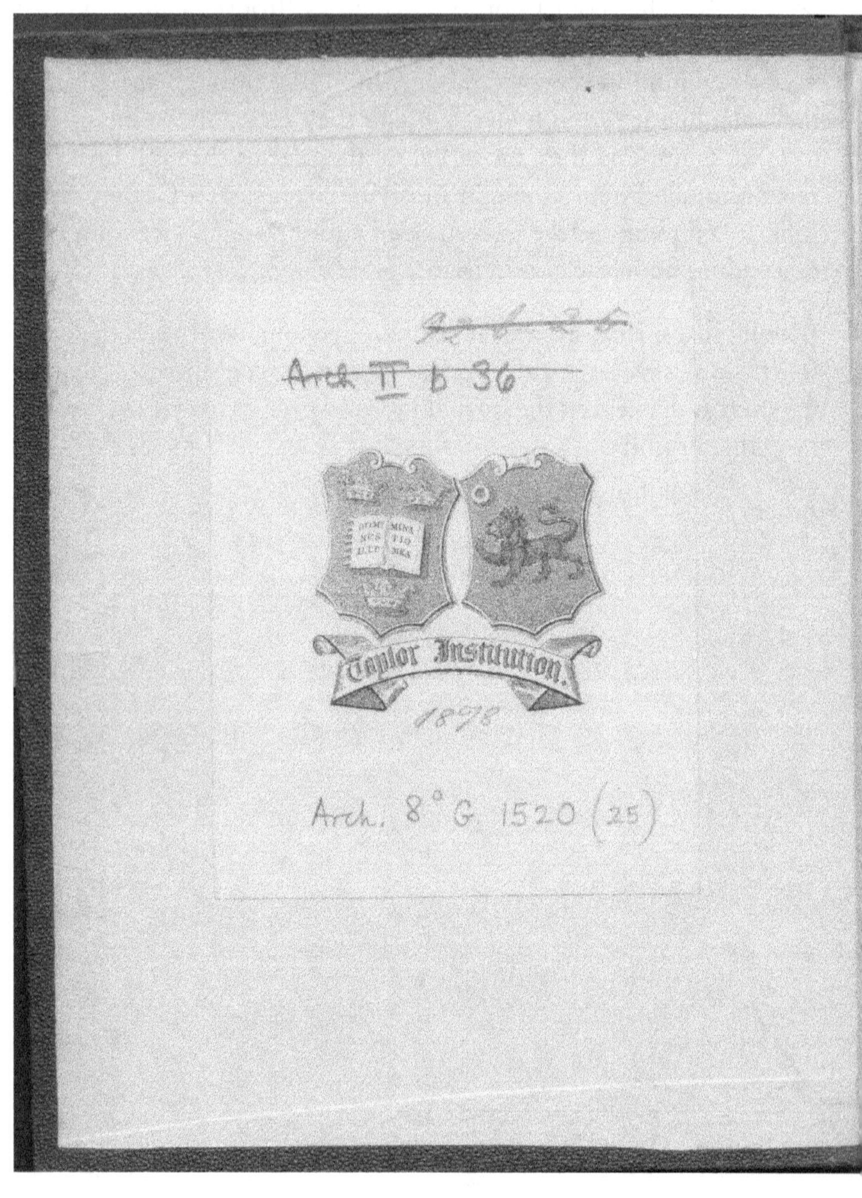

Upper Pastedown ARCH.8°.G.1520(25) with Bookplate
For a description of this edition and the Taylorian copy cf. chapter 4.1.

Von der Freyheyt
eyniſz Chriſten
menſchen.

Martinus Luther.

Vuittembergae.
Anno Domini
1 5 2 0.

Title page

A1v

Dem fursichtigen vnd weyßen hern

Hieronymo Mülphordt Stadvogt zu Zwyckaw meynem besondern günstigen freund vnd Patron Empiete ich genanst D. Martinus Luther August. meyne willige dienst vnnd allis guttis.

¶ Fursichtiger weyßer Herr/vnd Günstiger freund/der wirdig Magister Johan Egran/ewr löblichen stat Prediger/hat mir hoch gepreysset ewr lieb vnd lust/ßo yhr zu der heyligen schrifft traget/wilch yhr auch emßlich bekennen vnd fur den menschen zu preyßen nit nachlasset. Derhalben er begeret/mich mit euch bekennet zu machen/byn ich gar leychtlich willig vnd frölich des beredt/denn es mir eyn sondere freudt ist/zu hören/wo die gottlich warheyt geliebt wirt/der leyder ßo vill/vnd die am meysten/die sich yhres titels auffwerffen/mit aller gewalt vnd list widderstreben/wie wol es alßo seyn muß/das an Christum/zu eynem ergernis vnd zeychen gesetzt/dem widdersprochen werden muß/vill sich stossen/fallen/vnd auffstahen mussen. Darumb hab ich an zu heben vnßer kundschafft vnd freuntschafft/diß tractatell vnnd Sermon euch wollen zuschreyben/ym deutschē/wilchs ich latinisch dem Bapst hab zugeschrieben/damit fur ydeman/meyner lere vnd schreyben/von dem Bapstum/nit eyn vorweyßlich/als ich hoff/vrsach angetzeygt. Befill mich hie mit/euch/vnd allsampt/gottlichen gnaden. A M E N. Zu Wittenbergk. 1 5 2 0.

A2r (fol. 2r)

Jhesus.

Zum ersten. Das wir grundlich mügen erkennen/ was eyn Christen mensch sey/ vñ wie es gethā sey/ vmb die freyheyt/ die yhm Christus erworben vñ geben hatt/ davon S. Paulus viel schreybt/ will ich setzen/ dyße zween beschluß.

Eyn Christen mensch ist eyn freyer herr/ über alle ding / vnd niemandt vnterthan.

Eyn Christen mensch ist eyn dienstpar knecht aller ding vnd yderman vnterthan.

Diße zween beschlüß seynd klerlich sanct Paulus. 1. Cor. 12. Ich byn frey yn allen dingen/ vñ hab mich eynß ydermā knecht gemacht. Itē Ro. 13. Ihr solt niemand ettwz vorpflichtet seyn/ denn dz yr euch vnternāder liebet. Lieb aber/ die ist/ dienstpar/ vñ vnterthan dem das sie lieb hatt. Alßo auch von Christo Gal. 4. Gott hatt seynen ßon außgesandt/ von eynem weyb geporn vnd dem gesetz vnterthan gemacht.

¶ Czum andern/ Diße zwo widderstendige rede/ der freyheyt vnd dienstparkeyt zuuornehmen/ sollen wir gedencken/ das eyn yglich Christen mensch ist zweyerley natur/ geystlicher vñ leyplicher. Nach der seelen wirt er eyn geystlich/ new/ ynnerlich mensch genennet/ nach dem fleysch vnd blut wirt er eyn leyplich alt vnd eußerlich mensch genennet. Vnd vmb dißes vnterschiedß willen/ werden von yhm gesagt yn der schrifft/ die do stracks widdernander seyn/ wie ich itzt gesagt/ von der freyheyt vnd dienstparkeit.

¶ Czum dritten/ So nhemen wir fur vns den ynnwendigen geystlichen menschen/ zusehen was datzu gehöre/ dz er eyn frum frey/ Christen mensch sey vnd heysse. So ists offenbar/ das keyn eußerlich ding mag yhn frey/ noch frum machen/ wie es mag ymmer genennet werden/ denn seyn frumkeyt vñ freyheyt/ widerumb seyn boßheyt vnd gefenckniß/ seyn nit leyplich noch eußerlich. Was hilffts die seelen/ das der leyp/ vngefangen/ frisch vnd gesund ist/ yssett/ trinckt/ lebt/ wie er will? Widderumb was schadet das der seelen/ das der leyp/ gefangen krang vnd matt

A2v (fol. 2v)

ist/hungert/dürstet vnd leydet/wie er nit gerne wolt. Dißer ding reychet keyniß/biß an die seelen/sie zu befreyhen oder fahen/ frum oder böße zu machen.

¶ Czum vierden/ Alßo hilffet es die seele nichts/ ob der leyp heylige kleyder anlegt/wie die priester vñ geystlichen thun/auch nit ob er ynn den kirchen vnd heyligen stetten sey. Auch nit ob er mit heyligẽ dingẽ vmbgah. Auch nit ob er leyplich bette/faste/walle/vnd alle gute werck thue/die durch vnd ynn dem leybe geschehen mochten ewiglich. Es muß noch allis etwas anders seyn/das der seelen bringe vnd gebe frumkeyt vnd freyheyt. Denn alle diße obgenanten stuck/ werck vnd weyßen/mag auch an sich haben vnd üben/eyn bößer mensch/eyn gleyßner vnd heuchler. Auch durch solch weßen keyn ander volck/ denn eyttell gleyßner werden. Widderumb/schadet es der seelen nichts/ob ð leyp vnheylige kleyder tregt/an vnheyligen örten ist/yßt/trinckt/wallet/bettet nit/vnd lesst alle die werck onstehen/die die obgenanten gleyßner thun.

¶ Czum funfften/Hatt die seele keyn ander dinck/widder yn hymel noch auff erden darynnen/sie lebe/frum/frey/ vnd Christen sey/denn das heylig Euãgeliũ/das wort gottis von Christo geprediget. Wie er selb sagt. Joh.11. Ich byn dz leben vñ auffersthung/ wer do glaubt yn mich/ der lebet ewiglich. Item.17. Ich byn der weg/die warheyt/ vnd das leben. Item Matt.4. Der mensch lebet nit alleyn von dem brot/ sondern von allen worten die do gehen von dem mund gottis. So mussen wir nu gewiß seyn/ das die seele kan allis dings emperen on des worts gottis/vnd on das wort gottis/ist yhr mit keynem ding beholffen. Wo sie aber das wort hatt/ßo darff sie auch keynes andern dings mehr/sondern/sie hat in dem wort/gnugde/speiß freud/frid/licht/kunst/gerechtickeyt/warheyt/weyßheyt/freyheit vnd allis gutt überschwenglich. Alßo leßen wir ym Psalter sonderlich ym.118.psalm/das der prophet nit mehr schreyet/den nach dem gottis wort. Vnd yn ð schrifft die aller hochste plag vnd gottis zorn gehalten wirt/ ßo er seyn wort von den menschen nympt/ Widderumb keyn grösser gnade/ wo er seyn wort hyn sendet/wie psalmus.104.stet. Er hat seyn wort auß gesandt/damit er yhn hatt geholffen. Vnd Christ⁹ umb keyns

andern ampts geholffen/den zu predigen das wort gottis kum
men ist. Auch alle Apostell/Bischoff/ priester vñ gantzer geyst
licher stand/alleyn vmb des worts willen ist beruffen vnd eyn-
gesetzt/wie woll es nu leyder anders gaht.
¶ Czum sechsten/ Fragistu aber/ wilchs ist denn das wort
das solch grosse gnad gibt. Vnd wie sol ichs gebrauchen? Ant
wort. Es ist nit anders/ deñ die predigt von Christo geschehen
wie das Euangeliũ ynnehelt. Wilche soll seyn/ vnd ist alßo ge
than/das du hörist deynen gott zu dir reden/ Wie alle deyn le-
ben vnd werck/nichts seyn fur gott/ sondern müßsist/ mit allem
dem das ynn dir ist ewiglich vorterben. Wilchs ßo du recht
glaubst/wie du schuldig bist/so mustu an dir selber vortzwey
ffelnñ/vnd bekennen/das war sey der spruch Osee. O Jsrael yn
dir ist nichts/denn deyn vorterben/ alleyn aber yn mir steht deyn
hulff. Das du aber auß dir vnd von dir/ das ist auß deynem
vorterben kömen mügist/ ßo setzt er dir fur/ seynen lieben ßon
Jhesum Christũ/vnd lessit dir durch seyn lebendigs trostlichs
wort sagen. Du solt ynn den selben mit festem glauben dich er-
geben/vnd frisch ynn yhn vortrawen. So sollen dir vmb des-
selben glaubens willen/alle deyne sund vorgeben/alle deyn vor-
terben vberwunden seyn/vnd du gerecht/ warhafftig/ befridet/
frum/vñ alle gebott erfullet seyn/võ allen dingen frey sein. Wie
S. Paulus sagt. Ro. i. Ein rechtfertiger Christen/ lebt nur von
seynem glauben. Vnd Ro. x. Christus ist das ende vnd fülle
aller gebot/denen/die ynn yhn glauben.
¶ Czũ siebenden. Drumb solt das billich aller Christen ey-
nigs werck vnd übung seyn/das sie das wort vñ Christũ wol
ynn sich bildeten/solchen glauben stetig vbeten vñ sterckteñ. Deñ
keyn ander werck/ mag eynen Christen machen. Wie Christus
Joh. 6. zu den Juden sagt/da sie yhn fragten/was sie fur werck
thun solten/dz sie gottlich vñ Christlich werck thetten. Sprach
er. Das ist das eynige gotliche werck/das yhr glaubt yn denen/
den gott gesandt hatt. Wilchen gott der vatter allein auch dar
tzu vorordnet hatt. Darũb ists gar ein vberschwencklich reych-
tumb/ein rechter glaub yn Christo/ denn er mit sich bringt alle
seligkeit/vnd abnympt alle vnseligkeyt. Wie Mar. vlt. Wer do
glaubt vnd taufft ist/ der wirt selig. Wer nit glaubt/ der wirt

A3v

vordampt. Darumb der prophet Isa. x. Den reychtumb des selben glaubens ansach vnd sprach. Gott wirt eyn kurtz summa machen auff erden/vnd die kurtz summa wirt/wie ein syndflut eynfliessen die gerechtickeit/das ist/der glaub/darynn kurtzlich aller gebot erfullung steht/ wirt vberflussig rechtfertigē alle die yhn haben/ das sie nichts mehr bedurffen / das sie gerecht vnd frum seyn. Alßo sagt S. Pauel Ro. x. Das man von hertzen glaubt/das macht eynen gerecht vnd frum.

¶ Czū achten/ Wie gaht es aber zu / das der glaub allein mag frum machen / vnd on alle werck ßo vberschwencklich reychtumb geben/ßo doch souill gesetz/gebot/werck/stend vnd weyße vns furgeschrieben seyn/ynn der schrifft. Hie ist fleyßsig zu mercken/vnd yhe mit ernst zubehalten/dz allein der glaub on alle werck frum/frey/vñ selig machet/wie wir hernach mehr hören werden Vnd ist zu wissen/das die gantze heylige schrifft/ wirt yn zweyerley wort geteyllet/wilche seyn. Gebot oder gesetz gottis/vnd vorheyschen oder zusagunge. Die gebott leren vnd schreyben vns fur/ mancherley gutte werck aber damit seyn sie noch nit geschehen. Sie weyßen wol/ sie helffen aber nit/ leren was man thun soll/geben aber keyn sterck dartzu. Darūb seyn sie nur dartzu geordnet/das der mensch drynnen sehe sein vnuormügen zu dem gutten / vnd lerne an yhm selbs vortzweyffeln. Vnd darumb heyssen sie auch das alte testament/vnd gehören alle ynß alte testament. Als/das gebott/Du solt nit böß begird haben/beweysset das wir allesampt sunder seyn/ vnd kein mensch vormag/zu sein on böße begirde/ er thue was er will / Darauß er lernet an yhm selbs vortzagen vnd anderßwo zu suchen hulff/das er on böße begird sey/vnnd alßo das gebott erfulle/ durch eynen andern/das er auß yhm selb nit vormag/ alßo sein auch alle andere gebott/vns vnmuglich.

¶ Czū neunden/ Wen nu der mensch auß den gebotten sein vnuormügen gelernet vñ empfunden hatt / das yhm nu angst wirt/wie er dem gebott gnug thue. Seyntemal das gebot muß erfullet seyn/ oder er muß vordampt seyn. So ist er recht gedemütiget vnd zu nicht worden/ ynn seynen augen / findet nichts yn yhm damit er müg frum werden. Dan ßo kūpt das ander wort. Die gottlich vorheyschung vnd zusagung/ vnd spricht/

wiltu alle gepott erfullen / deyner bößen begirde vnd sund loß
werden / wie die gebott zwyngen vnd foddern. Sihe da / glaub
in Christũ / yn wilchem ich dir zusag / alle gnad / gerechtickeyt /
frid vñ freyheyt / glaubstu so hastu / glaubstu nit / so hastu nit.
Den das dir vnmuglich ist / mit allen wercken d' gebott / der vill
vnd doch keyn nutz seyn mussen / das wirt dir leycht vnd kurtz /
durch den glauben. Den ich hab kurtzlich / yn den glauben ge-
stellet alle ding / das / wer yhn hat / sol alle ding haben vnd selig
seyn / wer yhn nit hatt / soll nichts haben. Alßo geben die zusa-
gung gottis / was die gepott erfoddern / vnd volnbringen / was
die gepott heyssen / auff das es allis gottis eygen sey. Gepot vñ
erfullung / er heysset allein / er erfullet auch alleyn. Darumb seyn
die zusagung gottis / wort des newen testaments vnd gehoren
auch yns newe testament.

¶ Czum tzehenden / Nu seyn diße vnd alle gottis wort / hey-
lig / warhafftig / gerecht / fridsam / frey vnd aller gůtte voll / dar-
umb wer yhn mit eynem rechten glauben anhangt / des seele
wirt mit yhm voreynigt / ßo gantz vnd gar / das alle tugent des
worts / auch eygen werden der seelen / Vnd alßo durch den glau-
ben / die seele von dem gottis wort / heylig / gerecht / warhafftig /
fridsam / frey / vnd aller gůtte voll / eyn warhafftig kind gottis
wirt / wie Johan. 1. sagt. Er hatt yhn geben / das sie mugen kyn-
der gottis werden alle die ynn seynem namen glauben.
Hierauß leychtlich zu mercken ist / warumb der glaub ßo vill
vormag / vnd das keyne gutte werck yhm gleych seyn mugen /
Den keyn gut werck / hanget an dem gottlichen wort / wie der
glaub / kan auch nit yn der seelen seyn / sondern alleyn das wort
vnd glaube regirn / yn der seelen / Wie dz wort ist / ßo wirt auch
die seele võ yhm / gleych / als das eyssen wirt glutrodt wie das
fewr auß der voreynigung mit dem fewr. Alßo sehen wir / das an
dem glaubenn eyn Christen mensch gnug hatt / darff keynis
wercks / das er frum sey / darff er den keynis wercks mehr / ßo ist
er gewißlich entpunden von allen gepotten vnd gesetzen / ist er
entpũden / so ist er gewißlich frey / Das ist die Christlich freiheit /
der eynige glaub / der do macht / nit das wir můssig gahn oder
übell thun mugen / sondern das wir keynis wercks bedurffen zur
frumkeyt vnd seligkeyt zu erlangen / dauon wir mehr hernach
sagen wollen.

Czum eylfften

A4v (fol. 4v)

¶ Czū eylfften/ Weytter ists mit dem glauben alßo gethan/ das/ wilcher dem andern glaubt/ der glaubt/ yhm darumb. das er yhn fur eynen frumen warhafftigen man achtet/ wilchs die gröste ehre ist/ die ein mensch dem andern thun kan/ als widder umb die gröste schmach ist/ ßo er yhn fur eynen loßen lugenhafftigen leychtfertigen man achtet. Alßo auch wenn die seele gottis wort festiglich glaubt/ ßo helt sie yhn fur warhafftig/ frum vñ gerecht/ da mit sie yhm thut die aller grössiste ehre, die sie yhm thun kann/ denn da gibt sie yhm recht/ da lessit sie yhm recht/ da ehret sie seynen namen/ vnd lessit mit yhr handeln wie er will/ deñ sie zweyffelt nit er sey frum/ warhafftig ynn allen seynen worten. Widderumb kan man gott keyn grössere vnehre auffthun/ deñ yhm nit glauben/ damit die seel yhn fur eynen vntuchtigen lugenhafftigen leychtfertigen helt/ vñ ßouil an yhr ist/ yhn vorleugnet mit solchem vnglauben/ vnd ein abgott yhres eygens synn/ ym hertzen widder gott auffricht/ alß wolt sie es besser wissenn deñ er. Wenn denn gott sihet/ das yhm die seel/ warheit gibt vnd alßo ehret durch yhren glauben/ ßo ehret er sie widderumb/ vnd helt sie auch fur frum vnd warhafftig/ vnd sie ist auch frum vnd warhafftig durch solchen glauben/ denn das man gott die warheyt vñ frumkeit gebe/ das ist recht vnd warheit/ vnnd macht recht vnd warhafftig. Die weyll es war ist vnd recht/ das gotte die warheit geben werd. Wilchs die nit thun/ die nit glauben/ vnd doch sich mit vielen gutten wercken/ treyben vnd mühen.

¶ Czum zwölfften/ Nit allein gibt der glaub ßouil/ das die seel/ dem gottlichen wort gleych wirt aller gnaden voll/ frey/ vñ selig/ sondernn voreynigt auch die seele mit Christo/ als eyne brawt mit yhrem breudgam. Auß wilcher ehe folget/ wie S. Paulus sagt/ das Christus vñ die seel/ eyn leyb werden/ ßo werden auch beyder gutter/ fall/ vnfall vnd alle ding gemeyn/ das was Christus hatt/ das ist eygen/ der glaubigen seele/ was die seele hatt/ wirt eygen Christi. So hatt Christus alle gütter vnd seligkeit/ die seyn der seelen eygen. So hatt die seel alle vntugent vnd sund auff yhr/ die werden Christi eygen. Hie hebt sich nu der frölich wechßel vnd streytt/ Die weyl Christus ist gott vnd mensch/ wilcher noch nie gesundigt hatt/ vnd seyne frumkeyt

vnuͤbirwindlich/ewig/vnd almechtig ist/ ßo er denn der glau-
bigen seelen sund/ durch yhren braudring/das ist/ d̕ glaub/yhm
selbs eygen macht vnd nit anders thut/den̄ als hett er sie gethā/
ßo mussen die sund ynn yhm vorschlunden vn̄ erseufft werden/
Denn sein vnuͤbirwindlich gerechtigkeyt/ ist allen sunden zu-
starck/also wirt die seele vō allen yhren sunden/lauterlich durch
yhrē malschatzts/das ist des glaubens halben/ledig vnd frey/
vnd begabt/mit der ewigen gerechtickeit yhrs breudgams Chri-
sti. Ist nu das nit ein froliche wirtschafft/da der reyche/edle/
frummer breudgam Christus/das arm voracht boßes hurlein
zur ehe nympt/vnd sie entledigt von allem ubell/zieret mit allen
gutern. So ists nit muglich/das die sund sie vordampne/den̄
sie ligen nu auff Christo/vn̄ sein ynn yhm vorschlunden/so hat
sie ßo ein reyche gerechtickeyt ynn yhrem breutgam/das sie aber-
mals/wider alle sund bestahn mag/ob sie schon auff yhr legē.
Dauon sagt Paulus.1.Cor.15. Gott sey lob vnd danck der vns
hatt gegeben ein solch ubirwindung ynn Christo Jhesu/ ynn
wilcher vorschlunden ist/ der todt mit der sund.

¶ Czu dreytzehenden/ Hie sichstu aber/ auß wilchem grund
dem glauben ßouil billich zugeschrieben wirt/das er alle gepott
erfullet/vnd on alle andere werck frum macht. Denn du sihest
hie/das er das erste gepott erfullet alleine da gepotten wirt/ Du
solt eynen gott ehren. Wenn du nu eytell gutt werck werist/biß
auff die versenn/ ßo werestu dennoch nit frum vnd gebist gott
noch keyn ehre/ vnd alßo erfullistu das aller erst gepott nicht.
Denn gott mag nicht geehret werden/ yhm werd dan/ warheyt
vnd allis gut zu geschrieben/wie er denn warlich ist/Das thun
aber keyn gutte werck/ sondern allein der glaube des hertzen.
Darumb ist er allein/die gerechtickeit des menschen vnd aller ge
pott erfullung. Den wer das erste haubt gepott erfullet/der er
fullet gewißlich vnd leychtlich auch alle ander gepott. Die
werck aber seyn todte ding/ kunden nit ehren noch loben gott/
wie wol sie mugen geschehen/vnd lassen sich thun gott zu ehren
vn̄ lob/aber wir suchē hie den/d̕ nit gethan wirt/als die werck/
sondern den selbthetter vnd werckmeyster/der gott ehret/vnd die
werck thut. Das ist niemāt dan der glaub des hertzen/der ist
das haubt vnd gantzis weßens der frumkeyt/ darumb es eyn

B1v (fol. 5r)

ferlich finster rede ist. Wenn man leret / die gottis gepott mit wercken zu erfullen / ßo die erfullung fur allen wercken / durch den glauben muß geschehen seyn / vnd die werck folgen nach der erfullung / wie wir hörenn werdenn.

¶ Czum viertzehenden / Weytter zu sehen / was wir yn Christo haben / vnd wie groß gutt sey / ein rechter glaube. Ist zu wissenn / das fur vnd ynn dem altenn testament / gott yhm auß zog vnd furbehilt alle erste menliche geburt / von menschen vñ von thierren / Vnd die erste geburt war köstlich vnd hatt zwey grosse förteyll fur allen anderñ kinderñ / nemlich die hirschafft vnd priesterschafft odder kunigreych vnd priesterthum / alßo das auff erden / das erste gepornn kneblin / was eyn herr vbir alle seyne bruder vnd ein pfaff odder Babst fur gott. Durch wilche figur bedeutt ist Jhesus Christus / der eygentlich / die selb erste menlich geburt ist gottis vatters / von der Junpfrawen Marie. Darumb ist er ein kunig vñ priester / doch geystlich. denn seyn reych ist nit yrdnisch noch yn yderrnischen / sonderñ yn geystlichen guttern / als da seyn / warheyt / weyßheyt / frid / freud / seligkeyt ꝛc. Damit aber nit außgezogen ist zeytlich gutt / denn es ist yhm alle ding vnterworffen / ynn hymell / erdenn vnd helle / wie wol man yhn nit sicht / das macht / das er geystlich / vnsichtlich regirt.

Alßo auch seyn priesterthum steht nit ynn den eußerlichenn geperdenn / vnd kleydern / wie wir bey den menschen sehen / ßonderñ es steht ym geyst vnsichtlich / alßo / das er fur gottis augen on vnterlaß / fur die seynen steht vnd sich selb opffert vnd allis thut / was eyn frum priester thun soll. Er bittet fur vns / Wie S. paul. Ro. 8. sagt. So leret er vns ynnwendig ym hertzen / wilchs sein zwey eygentliche recht ampt eyniß priesters Denn alßo bitten vnd leren auch eußerlich menschlich zeytlich priester.

¶ Czum funfftzehenden / Wie nu Christus die erste geburtt hatt / mit yhrer ehre vnd wirdickeit / alßo / teyllet er sie mit allenn seynen Christen / das sie durch den glauben / mussen auch alle kunige vnd priester seyn / mit Christo / Wie S. Petrus sagt. 1. Pet. 2. Ihr seyt ein priesterlich kunigreych / vñ ein kuniglich priesterthū.

Vnd das geht alßo zu/das ein Christen mensch durch den glauben ßo hoch erhaben wirt vbir alle ding / das er aller eyn herr wirt geystlich/denn es kan yhm kein ding nit schaden zur seligkeit. Ja es muß yhm alles vnterthan seyn vnd helffen zur seligkeyt/Wie S.Paulus leret Ro.8.Alle ding müssen helffenn den außerwelten/zu yhrem besten/es sey leben/sterben/sund/frumkeit gut vñ bößes/wie man es nennen kan. Item.1.Cor.3.Alle ding seynd ewr/es sey das leben oder ꝺ todt/kegenwertig oder zukünfftig ꝛc. Nit das wir aller ding leyplich mechtig seyn/sie zu besitzen oder zu brauchen / wie die menschen auff erdē / denn wir müssen sterben leyplich vnd mag niemant dem todt entfliehen/ ßo müssen wir auch viel andern dingen vnterligē / wie wir yn Christo vñ seynen heyligen sehen/ Denn diß ist ein geystliche hirschafft/die do regiert/yn der leyplichen vnterdruckung/ das ist/ ich kann mich on allen dingen bessern nach der seelen/das auch der todt vnd leyden / müssen mir dienen vnd nützlich seyn zur seligkeyt / das ist gar ein hohe ehrliche wirdickeit vnd eyn recht almechtige hirschafft/ein geystliche künigreych / da keyn ding ist ßo gut/ßo böße/es muß mir dienen zu gut/ßo ich glaube/vñ darff seyn doch nit / sondern meyn glaub ist mir gnugsam. Sihe wie ist das ein köstlich freyheyt vnd gewalt der Christen.

¶ Czum sechtzehenden/ Vbir das seyn wir priester/das ist noch vil mehr/denn künig sein/darumb/das das priesterthum vns wirdig macht fur gott zu tretten vnd fur andere zu bitten/ Denn fur gottis augen zu stehn vnd bitten/gepürt niemāt denn den priestern. Alßo hatt vns Christꝰ erworben/das wir mügen geystlich/fur ein ander tretten vñ bitten/ wie ein priester fur das volck leyplich tritt vnd bittet. Wer aber nit glaubt yn Christū dem dienet keyn ding zu gut / ist ein knecht aller ding / muß sich aller ding ergern. Datzu ist sein gepett nit angenehm/ kumpt auch nit fur gottis augen/ Wer mag nu außdencken/ die ehre vnd höhe eyniß Christen menschen: durch seyn künigreych ist er aller ding mechtig/ durch sein priesterthū ist er gottis mechtig/ denn gott thut was er bittet vnd wil/wie do stet geschrieben im psalter. Gott thut den willen der/die yhn furchten/vnd erhöret/ yhr gepett/ zu wilchen ehren er nur allein durch den glauben vnd

B2v (fol. 6v)

durch keyn werck kumpt. Darauß mā clar sihet/wie eyn Christen mensch frey ist von allen dingen vnd vbir alle ding / alßo das er keyner gutter werck/datzu bedarff/das er frum vnd seligk sey/sondern der glaub bringts ym alles vber flußsig. Vnd wo er ßo töricht were vnd meynet/durch ein gutt werck/frum/frey/selig odder Christen werden / ßo vorlür er den glauben mit allen dingen/Gleych als/đ hund/der ein stuck fleysch ym mund trug vnd nach dem schemen ym wasser schnapt/damit/fleysch vnd schem vorlör.

¶ Czum siebentzenden fragistu/ Was ist den fur ein vnterscheydt,/ zwischen den priestern vnd leyen ynn der Christenheyt/ ßo sie alle priester seyn? Antwort/ Es ist dem wortlin priester/ pfaff/geystlich vnd des gleychen vnrecht geschehen/das sie von dem gemeynen hauffen seyn getzogen/auff den kleynen hauffen den man itzt nennet geystlichen stand. Die heylige schrifft/ gibt keynen andern vnterscheyd/denn das sie/die gelereten odder geweyhetē/ nēnet ministros/seruos/oeconomos/das ist/diener/ knecht/schaffner/die do sollen/ den andern/ Christū/ glauben/ vnd Christliche freyheit predigen/Denn ob wir wol alle gleych priester seyn/ßo kunden wir doch nit alle dienen odder schaffen vnd predigen. Alßo sagt S. Paulus.1. Cor. 4. Wir wollen nichts mehr von den leuthen gehalten seyn/denn Christꝰ diener/ vnd schaffner des Euangelij. Aber nu ist auß der scheffnerey worden eyn solch weltlich/eußerliche/prechtige/forchtsam hirschafft vnd gewalt/das yhr die recht weltlich macht/ ynn keynen weg mag gleychen/gerad als weren die leyen etwas anders denn Christenleuth / damit hyngenummen ist der gantz vorstand Christlicher gnad/freyheit/glaubens/vnd allis was wir von Christo habē/vnd Christꝰ selbs/haben dafur vbirkūmen/ viel menschen gesetz vnd werck/seyn gantz knecht wordenn/der aller vntüchtigsten leuth auff erden.

¶ Czum achtzehenden/Auß dem allen lernen wir/das es nit gnug sey gepredigt/Wen man Christus leben vnd werck oben hynn vnd nur als ein histori vnd Cronicken geschicht predigt/ schweyg denn/ßo man seyn gar schweygt/ vnd das geystlich recht oder ander menschen gesetz vn̄ lere predigt. Er ist auch vill/die Christū alßo predigen/vnd leßen / das sie ein mit leyden

vbir yhn habenn / mit den Juden zurnñ odder ſonſt mehr kyn-
diſch weyß/ drynnen vben. Aber er ſoll vnd muß alßo predige
ſein/ dz mir vñ dir/ der glaub drauß erwachß vñ erhalten werd-
Wilcher glaub da durch erwechſt vnd erhalten wirt. Wen mir
geſagt wirt. Warumb Chriſtus kūmen ſey/ wie man ſein brau-
chen vnd nieſſen ſoll/ was er mir bracht vnd geben hat/ das ge-
ſchicht/ wo man recht außlegt / die Chriſtlich freyheit / die wir
von yhm haben/ vnd wie wir künig vnd prieſter ſeyn/ aller ding
mechtig. Vnd allis was wir thun/ das fur gottis augen an-
genehm/ vnd erhöret ſey/ wie ich biß her geſagt hab. Dañ wo
ein hertz alßo Chriſtũ höret/ das muß frölich werden von gan-
tzem grund/ troſt empfahen/ vñ ſüß werden gegen Chriſto/ yhn
widderumb lieb zuhaben. Dahyn es nymmer mehr mit geſetzē
odder werck kummen mag/ Deñ wer wil eynem ſolchen her-
tzen ſchaden thun / oder erſchreckenn? felt die ſund vnd der todt
daher/ ßo glaubt es Chriſt⁹ frumkeit ſey ſein/ vnd ſein ſund ſein
nymmer ſein/ ſondern Chriſti/ ßo muß die ſund vorſchwinden/
fur Chriſtus frumkeit/ ynn dem glauben/ wie droben geſagt iſt/
vnd lernet/ mit dem Apoſtell dem todt vnd ſund trotz bieten/ vñ
ſagen. Wo iſt nu du todt deyn ſig? Wo iſt nu todt dein ſpieß?
deyn ſpieß/ iſt die ſund. Aber gott ſey lob vnd danck / der vns
hatt geben den ſieg/ durch Jheſum Chriſtũ vnſern herñ. Vnd
der todt iſt erſeufft ynn ſeynem ſieg ꝛc.

¶ Czum neuntzehenden/ Das ſey nu gnug geſagt / von dem
ynnerlichen menſchen/ von ſeyner freyheit/ vnd der heubt gerech-
tickeit/ wilch keynis geſetzs noch gutten wercks bedarff/ ya yhr
ſchedlich iſt/ ſo yemant da durch wolt rechfertig zu werdē ſich
vormeſſenn. Nu kummen wir auffs ander teyll/ auff den eu-
ſſerlichen menſchen Hie wollen wir antworten allen denen/ die
ſich ergern auß den vorigen reden vñ pflegen zuſprechen Ey ſo
denn der glaub alle ding iſt vnd gilt allein gnugſam frum zu-
machen. Warūb ſein denn die gutten werck gepotten? ſo wol-
len wir gutter ding ſein/ vnd nichts thun. Neyn lieber menſch
nicht alſo. Es wer wol/ alſo/ wen du allein ein ynnerlich men-
ſch werist/ vnd gantz geyſtlich vnd ynnerlich worden/ wilchs
nit geſchicht biß am Jüngſten tag. Es iſt vñ bleybt auff erdē
nur ein anheben vñ zu nehmen/ wilchs wirt in yhener welt vol-

8

frücht. DahER heyssets der Apostell primitias spirit⁹/das sein die ersten frücht des geysts/drumb gehört hie her/ das droben gesagt ist. Ein Christē mensch/ist ein dienstpar knecht/vñ ydermā vnterthan/gleych/wo er frey ist/darff er nichts thun/wo er knecht ist/muß er allerley thun. Wie dz zugahe wollen wir sehē.

¶ Czum zwentzigsten/Ob wol der mensch ynwendig nach der seelen durch den glauben gnugsam rechtfertig ist/ vnd alles hatt was er haben soll/on das der selb glaub vñ gnugde/muß ymer zunehmen/biß ynn yhenes leben. So bleybt er doch noch ynn dißem leyplichen lebenn auff erdenn/vnd muß seynen eygen leyp regiern vnd mit leuthen vmbgahen. Da heben sich nu die werck an/hie muß er nit müssig gehn/da muß furwar der leyb mit fasten/ wachen/ erbeytten vnd mit aller messiger zucht getrieben/ vñ geübt sein/ das er dem ynnerlichen menschen vñ dem glauben gehorsam vnd gleychformig werde/ nit hyndere noch widderstreb/ wie sein art ist/wo er nit getzwungen wirt/deñ der ynnerliche mensch ist mit gott eyniß/frölich vnd lustig / vmb Christus willen/der yhm ßouil than hat/vñ stett alle seyn lußt darynn/das er widderumb mocht gott auch vmbsonst dienen ynn freyer lieb/ßo findt er ynn seynem fleysch eynen widerspenstigen willen/der wil der welt dienen vñ suchen was yhn lustet Das mag der glaub nit leyden/vnd legt sich mit lußt/an seynen halß yhn zu dempfen vñ weren. Wie S. Pauel sagt Ro. 7. Ich hab ein lust/yn gottis willen nach meynem ynnerñ menschen/ ßo find ich eynen anderñ willen ynn meynem fleysch / der wil mich mit sunden gefangē nehmen. Item ich zuchtige meynen leyp vñ treib yhn zu gehorsam/auff das ich nit selbs vorwerfflich werde/der die andern leren soll. Item Gal. 5. Alle die Christū angehören/creutzigen yhr fleysch mit seynen bößen lüsten.

¶ Czū eyn vnd zwentzigsten/Aber die selben werck/ müssen nit geschehn ynn der meynung / das da durch der mensch frum werd fur gott/deñ die falsch meynung kan der glaub nit leydē/ der alleyn ist vñ sein muß die frumkeyt fur gott/sonderñ nur yn der meynung/das der leyp gehorsam werde/vnd gereynigt von seynen bosen lüsten/vñ dz aug nur sehe/auff die bosen lüsten/sie auß zu treyben/Deñ die weyl die seel durch den glauben reyn ist/ vñ gott liebet/wolt sie gern das auch also alle ding reyn weren

zuuor yhr eygen leyp/vnd yderman gott/mit yhr liebt vnd lobt/
So geschichts/das d̃ mensch seyns eygen leyps halben nit kan
müßsig gehen/vñ muß vil gutter werck drober vben/das er yhn
zwinge/vnd doch die werck nit das rechte gutt seyn/dauon er
frum vnd gerecht sey fur gott/ ßondern thue sie auß freyer lieb
vmbsonst/got zu gefallen/nichts darynn anders gesucht noch
angesehen/denn das es gott also gefellet/wilchs willen er gerne
thet auffs allerbeste. Darauß denn ein yglicher kan selbs neh=
men die maß vnd bescheydenheit den leyp zu Casteyen/Denn er
fastet/wachet/erbeyt/ ßouiell er sicht dem leyp nott seyn/ seynen
muttwillen zu dempffen. Die andern aber/die do meynen mit
wercken frum zu werden/ haben keyn acht auff die casteyung/
sondern sehen nur auff die werck/vnd meynen/wen sie der selben
nur viel vnd groß thun/ ßo sey es wol than vnd sie frum wür=
den/zu weyllen zu brechen die köpff vnd vorterben yhr leybe drü=
ber/das ist ein grosse torheyt/vñ vnuorstand Christlichs lebens
vnd glaubens/das sie on glauben/ durch werck frum vnd se=
lig werden wollen.

¶ Czum zwey vnd zwentzigsten/ Das wir des etlich gleych
niß geben. Soll man die werck eynis Christen menschen der
durch seynen glaubē/vñ auß lautern gnaden gottis/vmbsonst
ist rechtfertig vnd selig worden/ nit anders achten/ den wie die
werck Adam vnd Eue ym paradiß geweßen weren/ Dauon
Geñ.2. stett geschrieben. Das gott den geschaffenen menschen/
setzt ynß paradiß/das er dasselb erbeytten vnd hutten solt.
Nu war Adam von gott frum vnd wol geschaffen/ on sund/
das er durch seyn erbeytten vnd hutten nit durfft frum vñ recht
fertig werden/doch das er nit müssig gieng/ gab yhm gott zu
schaffen/ das paradeys zu pflantzen/ bawen vnd bewarenn.
Wilchs weren eytell frey werck geweßen/vmb keynß dings wil=
len gethan/denn allein gott zu gefallen/ vnd nit vmb frumkeyt
zu erlangen/ die er zuuor hett/ wilch vns auch allen naturlich
were angeborn geweßenn. Alßo auch eynis glaubigen men=
schen werck/wilcher durch seynen glauben ist widderumb ynß
paradiß gesetzt/vnd von newen geschaffen/darff keyner werck
frum zu werden/sondern das er nit müssig gahe vnd seynen leyb
erbeytt vnd beware/ seyn yhm solche freye werck zu thun alleyn
gott zu gefallenn befolhen. Item

Item gleych wie eyn geweyheter Bischoff/ wen der kirchen weyhet/ fermelt odder sonst seynis ampts werck ubet/ ßo machen yhn die selben werck nit zu eynem bischoff/ Ja wenn er nit zuvor ein Bischoff geweyhet were/ ßo tuchte der selben werck keyniß und were eytell narrn werck. Alßo eyn Christen/ der durch den glauben geweyhet/ gutte werck thut/ wirt durch die selben nit besser oder mehr geweyhet (wilch nit denn des glauben mehrung thut) zu eynem Christen/ Ja wenn er nit zuvor glaubet und Christen were/ ßo gulten alle seyne werck nichts/ sondern weren/ eytell nerrisch/ strefflich vordamplich sund.

¶ Czum drey und zweintzigsten/ Drumb seyn die zween spruch war. Gutte frum werck machen nymmer mehr ein guten frummen man/ sondern eyn gutt frum man/ macht gutte frum werck Bösse werck machen nymmer mehr eynen bößen man/ sondern ein bößer man macht bösse werck/ alßo/ das allweg/ die person zuvor muß gut und frum sein vor allen gutten wercken/ und gutte werck folgen und außgahn/ von der frumen gutten person. Gleych wie Christus sagt. Ein bößer bawm tregt keyn gutte frucht. Ein gutter bawm tregt keynn bosse frucht. Nu ists offenbar/ das die frucht tragen nit den bawm/ ßo wachßen auch die bawm nit auff den fruchten/ sondern widerumb/ die bawm tragen die frucht/ und die frucht wachßen auff den bawmen. Wie nu die bawm mussen ehe seyn/ den die frucht/ und die frucht machen nit die bawm widder gutte noch böse/ sondern die bawm machen die fruchte. Alßo muß der mensch ynn der person zuvor frum oder bösse seyn/ ehe er gutte oder bösse werck thut/ Und seyne werck machen yhn nit gutt odder bösse/ sondern er macht gutt odder bösse werck. Des gleychen sehen wir ynn allen hand wercken. Ein gutt oder bösse hauß macht keynen gutten oder bößen zymmerman/ sondern ein gutter oder boßer zymmerman/ macht ein böß oder gutt hauß/ keyn werck macht eynenn meyster/ damach das werck ist/ sondern wie der meyster ist/ damach ist sein werck auch. Alßo seyn die werck des menschen auch/ wie es mit yhm stett ym glauben odder unglauben/ damach seind seyne werck gutt oder bösse. Und nit widerumb/ wie seyne werck stehn damach sey er frum odder glaubig/ die werck/ gleych wie sie nie glaubig machen/ ßo machen sie auch nit frum.

Aber der glaub gleych wie er frum macht/ ßo macht er auch gutte werck. So dañ die werck niemant frum machen/ vnd der mensch zuuor muß frum ſein/ ehe er wirckt/ ſo iſts offenbar/ das allein der glaub auß lautern gnaden/ durch Chriſtū vnd ſeyn wort/ die perſon gnugſam frum vnd ſelig machet. Vnd das keyn werck/ keyn gepott/ eynem Chriſten nott ſey zur ſeligkeit/ ſondern er frey iſt von allen gepotten/ vñ auß lauterer freyheit/ vmb ſonſt thut/ alls was er thut/ nichts damit geſucht ſeyneß nutzs oder ſelickeyt/ Denn er ſchon ſatt vnd ſelig iſt/ durch ſeynem glaubenn/ vnd gottis gnaden/ ſonderñ nur gott darynnen gefallen.

¶ Czum. xxiiij. Widdervmb dem/ der on glauben iſt/ iſt kein gutt werck furderlich zur frumkeyt vnd ſeligkeit/ Widdervmb keyn boße werck yhn boße vnd vordampt machen/ ſonderñ der vnglaub/ der die perſon vnd den bawm böß macht der thutt boße vnd vordampte werck. Darumb wen man frum odder boße wirt/ hebet ſichs nit an den wercken an/ ſondern an dem glauben/ Wie der Weyße man ſagt. Anfang aller ſund/ iſt von gotte weychen vnd yhm nit trawen. Alſo leret auch Chriſt' wie man nit an den wercken muß anheben vñ ſagt. Entweder macht den bawm gutt vnd ſeyne fruchte gutt/ oder macht den bawm boſe/ vnd ſeyne früchte böße/ als ſolt er ſagen/ wer gutte frücht haben wil/ muß zuuor an dem bawm anheben/ vnd den ſelben gutt ſetzen. Alßo wer do wil gutte werck thun/ muß nit an den wercken an heben/ ſondern an der perſon/ die die werck thun ſoll. Die perſon aber macht niemant gut/ denn allein der glaub/ vnd niemand macht ſie boße denn allein der vnglaub. Das iſt wol war/ die werck machen eynen frum odder boße fur den menſchen/ das iſt/ ſie zeygen eußerlich an/ wer frum od boſe ſey. Wie Chriſtus ſagt. Matt. 7. Auß yhren früchten ſollet yhr ſie erkennen. Aber das iſt alles/ ym ſcheyn vnd eußerlich. Wilchs anſehenn yrre macht viel leuth/ die do ſchreyben vnd leren/ wie man gutte werck thun ſoll vnd frum werdenn. ßo ſie doch/ des glaubens nymmer gedenckenn/ gahn dahynn/ vnd furet ymmer ein blind den anderñ/ marterñ ſich mit vielen wercken vnd kuñmen doch nymmer zu der rechten frumkeit/ von wilchen Sanct Pauel ſagt. 2. Timo. 3. Sie haben eynen ſcheyn der frumkeyt/

C1v (fol. 9v)

aber der grund ist nit da/ gehn hynn vnd lernen yñer vñ ymmer vnd kummen doch nymmer zur erkentniß der waren frumkeit. Wer nu mit den selben blinden nit will yrren/ muß weytter sehen/ den ynn die werck/ gepott/ odder lere der werck. Er muß ynn die person sehen fur allen dingen/ wie die frum werd. Die wirt aber nit durch gepott vnd werck/ sondernn durch gottis wort (das ist/ durch seyne vorheyschung der gnadenn) vnd den glaubenn/ frum vnd selig/ auff das bestehe seyn gottliche ehre/ das er vns nit durch vnser werck/ sondern durch seyn gnedigs wort vmbsonst vnd lauter barmhertzickeit selig mache.

¶ Czũ. xxv. Auß dißem allen ist leychtlich zuuorstehen/ wie gutte werck zu vorwerffen vñ nit zuuorwerffen seyn. Vnd wie man alle lere vorstahn soll/ die do gutte werck leren/ dann wo der falsch anhang/ vñ die vorkerete meynũg [illegible]yn ist/ das durch die werck/ wir frum vnd selig werden wollen/ seyn sie schon nit gutt/ vnd gantz vordamlich/ deñ sie seyn nit frey/ vnd schmehen die gnad gottis/ die allein durch den glauben frum vnd seligk macht/ wilchs die werck nit vormügen/ vñ nehmẽ es yhn doch fur zu thun/ vnd damit der gnaden/ ynn yhr werck vnd ehre greyffenn. Drumb vorwerffen wir die gutte werck/ nit vmb yhrer willen/ ßondernn/ vmb des selben boßen zusatzs vnd falscher vorkerter meynung willen. Wilche macht/ das sie nur gutt scheynen/ vnd seyn doch nit gutt/ betriegen sich vnd yderman damit/ gleych wie die reyssend wolff/ ynn schaffs kleydernn.

Aber der selb boße zusatz vnd vorkerete meynung/ ynn den werckenn/ ist vnübirwindlich/ wo der glaub nit ist. Er muß sein/ ynn dem selben wirckheyligenn/ biß der glaub kum vnd vorstöre yhn/ die natur vormag yhn/ von yhr selb nit auß treybenn. Ja auch nit erkennen/ sondernn sie helt yhn fur eyn köstlich/ selig dingk/ drumb werden yhr auch ßo viel da durch vorfuret.

Derhalben/ obs woll gutt ist/ von rewen/ beychten/ / gnugthun/ schreyben vnd predigenn/ ßo man aber nit weytter feret biß zum glauben/ sein es gewißlich/ eitel teuffelische/ vorfurische lere. Mã muß nit eynerley allein p̃digen/ sondern alle beyde wort gottis/ Die gepot/ sol mã predigen/ die sunder zur schrecken vñ yhr sund zu offenbarnn/ das sie rewe haben vnd sich bekeren. Aber da soll es nit bleyben/ mã muß/ das ander wort/ Die zusagũg der gna-

C2r (fol. 10r)

den auch predigen/den glauben zu leren/on wilchem die gepott
rew vnd allis ander vorgebenß geschicht. Es sein wol noch
blieben prediger/die rew der sund vñ gnad ꝑdigen/aber sie strey-
chen die gepott vnd zusagung gottis nit auß/das mã lere/ wo
her vnd wie die rew /vnd gnad kumme. Denn die rew/fleust
auß den gepotten/der glaub / auß den zusagung gottis / vnd
alßo wirt d͛ mensch/durch den glauben gotlicher wort gerecht-
fertiget vnd erhaben/der durch die furcht gottis gepottis gede-
mütiget/vnd ynn seyn erkentniß kummen ist.

¶ Czum. xxvi. Das sey von den wercken gesagt ynn gemeyn
vnd die ein Christen mensch gegen seynem eygen leybe üben sol.
Nu wollen wir von mehr wercken sagen / die er gegen andere
menschen thut. Denn der mensch lebt nit allein / ynn seynem
leybe/sondern auch vnter anderm menschen auff erdenn. Dar-
umb kan er nit on werck sein gegen die selbenn / er muß yhe mit
yhn zu reden vnd zu schaffen habenn/ wie wol yhm der selben
werck keyns nodt ist zur frumkeit vnd seligkeyt. Drumb soll
seyne meynung ynn allen werckenn frey vnd nur dahynn gericht
seyn / das er andern leutten damit diene vnd nütz sey. Nichts
anders yhm furbilde/denn was den andern nott ist/das heyssit
denn ein warhaffteig Christen leben/ vnd da geht der glaub mit
lust vnd lieb ynß werck/als S. Paulus leret die Galatas.
Denn zu den Philippen / do er sie geleret hatte/wie sie alle gnad
vnd gnugde hettenn durch yhren glauben yn Christo / leret er sie
weytter vnd sagt. Jch vorman euch allis trosts / den yhr ynn
Christo habt/vnd allis trosts/ den yhr habt von vnßer liebe zu
euch/ vñ aller gemeinschafft/die yhr habt mit allen geystlichen
frumen Christen/yhr wolt meyn hertz erfrewen volkömlich/ vñ
das damit/das yhr hynfurt/wollet eyniß synnes seyn/ eyner ge-
gen dem andern lieb ertzeygen/eyner dem andern dienen / vnd ein
yglicher acht haben/nit auff sich noch auff das seyne/sondern
auff den andern/vnd was dem selben nott sey. Sihe da hat
Paulꝰ klerlich/ein Christenlich leben dahynn gestellet / das alle
werck sollen gericht seyn/dem nehsten zu gutt/ Die weyl ein yg-
licher fur sich selb gnug hatt an seynen glauben/vñ alle andere
werck vñ leben yhm vbrig seyn/seynem nehstẽ damit auß freyer
lieb zu dienen/Dartzu furet er ein/Christũ zu eynem exempell vnd

C2v (fol. 10v)

sagt. Seyt also gesynnet/ wie yhrs seht yn Christo. Wilcher ob er wol voll gottlicher form ware vnd fur sich selb gnug hatte/ vnd yhm sein leben/ wircken vnd leydenn nicht nott ware/ das er da mit frum odder seligk wurd. Dennoch hatt er sich des alles geeussert/ vnd geperdet wie ein knecht/ allerley gethan vnd gelidenn/ nichts angesehen/ denn vnßer bestis/ vñ alßo ob er wol frey ware/ doch vmb vnßer willenn ein knecht wordenn.

¶ Czum.xxvij. Alßo soll ein Christen mensch/ wie Christus seyn heubt/ voll vnd satt/ yhm auch benugen lassen an seynem glaubenn/ den selben ymer mehrenn/ wilcher seyn leben/ frumkeit vnd seligkeyt ist/ der yhm gibt allis was Christꝰ vnd gott hat/ wie droben gesagt ist. Vnd S. Paul Gal. i. spricht/ Was ich noch ynn dem corper lebe/ das lebe ich ynn dem glauben Christi gottis sohn. Vnd ob er nu gantz frey ist/ sich widderũb williglich eynẽ diener machen seynem nehsten zu helffenn/ mit yhm faren/ vnd handeln/ wie gott mit yhm durch Christũ handlet hatt/ vnd das allis vmbsonst/ nichts darynnen suchen denn gottliches wolgefallenn/ vnd alßo denckenn. Wolan meyn gott hatt mir vnwirdigen vordampten menschen/ on alle vordienst/ lauterlich vmbsonst vñ auß eytel barmhertzickeit gebẽ/ durch vnd ynn Christo/ vollen reychtumb aller frumkeit vnd selickeit/ das ich hynfurt/ nichts mehr bedarff/ denn glauben es sey also. Ey so will ich solchem vatter der mich mit seynen vberschwenglichen gutterñ alßo vbirschuttet hatt/ widerumb/ frey/ frölich vnd vmbsonst thun was yhm wolgefellet/ Vnnd gegen meynem nehsten auch werden ein Christen/ wie Christus mir worden ist/ vnd nichts mehr thun/ denn was ich nur sehe/ yhm nott/ nützlich vnd seliglich sey/ die weyl ich doch/ durch meynenn glauben/ allis dings yn Christo gnug habe. Sih also fleusset auß dem glauben die lieb vñ lust zu gott/ vnd auß der lieb/ ein frey/ willig/ frolich lebẽ dem nehsten zu dienẽ vmbsonst. Denn zu gleych wie vnser nehst nott leydet/ vnd vnßers vbrigenn bedarff/ alßo haben wir fur gott nott geliden vnd seyner gnaden bedurfft. Darumb wie vns gott hatt durch Christum vmbsonst geholffen/ alßo sollen wir/ durch den leyp/ vnd seyne werck/ nit anders den dem nehsten helffen. Also sehen wir wie eyn hoch edliß leben sey vmb ein Christlich leben/ das

leyder nu ynn aller welt / nit allein nyderligt/sondernn auch nit
mehr bekandt ist noch gepredigt wirt.
¶ Czum.xxviij. Alßo leßen wir Luce.2. Das die Junpfraw
Maria zur kirchen gieng nach den sechs wochen vnd ließ sich
reynigen nach dem gesetz/ wie alle ander weyber/ ßo sie doch nit
gleych mit yhn vnreyn war/noch schuldig d̕ selben reynigung/
bedurfft yhr auch nit. Aber sie thetts auß freyer lieb/ das sie die
andere weyber nit vorachtet/sondernn mit dem hauffen bliebe.
Alßo ließ S.Pauel/S.Timotheū beschneytten/nit das es nott
were/sondern̄ das er den schwachglaubigen Juden nit vrsach
gebe/ zu bosen gedancken̄ / der doch widderumb Titū nit wollt
lassen beschneyttē/da mā drauff dringen wolt/er must beschnit
seyn/vnd were nott zur seligkeit. Vnd Christus Matt.17. Da
vō seynen Jüngern ward die tzinß pfennig gefoddert/disputiert
er mit S.Peter/ob nit kunigs kynder frey weren zynß zu geben.
Vnd sanct Peter/ ia sagt. Hieß er yhn doch hynn gehen an dz
mehr vnd sprach/ Auff das wir sie nit ergernn̄/ ßo gang hyn/
den ersten fisch du fehist/den nym vnd yn seynem maull wirstu
finden eynen pfennig/den gib fur mich vn̄ dich. Das ist ein feyn
exempell/zu dißer lere/da Christus/sich vnd die seynen freye kū-
nigs kinder nennett/ die keynis dings bedurffen / vnd doch sich
vnterlessit williglich / dienet vnd gibt den tzynß. Wie vill nu
das werck/Christo nott war vnd dienet hatt/zu seyner frumkeit
oder seligkeit/so vil sein alle ander sein vnd seyner Christen werck
yhn not zur seligkeit/sondern sein allis frey dienste/zu willen vn̄
besserung der andern. Also solten auch aller priester / klöster vnd
stifft werck gethā sein/das ein yglicher seynis stands vn̄ ordens
werck allein darūb thet / den andern̄ zu wilfaren vn̄ seynen leib
zu regieren/den andern̄ exempell zu geben auch also zu thun / die
auch bedurffenn yhre leyb zu zwingenn/ doch alzeit / fursehen
das nit da durch frum vnd selig werden̄ / furgenommen werd.
Wilchs allein des glaubens vormügen ist. Auff die weyße ge-
pent auch S. Paul Ro.13. vn̄ Tit.3. Das sie sollen weltlicher
gewalt vnterthā vn̄ bereyt sein/nit das sie da durch frum werdē
sollen / sondern das sie den andern̄ vnd der vbirkeit da mit frey
dieneten vnd yhren willen thetten auß lieb vn̄ freyheit. Wer nu
dissen vorstand hette/der kund leychtlich sich richtenn / ynn die

vnnzellichen gepotten vnd gesetzen des Babsts / der Bischoff/
der klöster/der stifft/der fursten vñ herñ/ die etlich tolle p̄latē
alßo treyben/als weren sie nott zur seligkeit/ vnd heyssen es/ge-
pott der kirchen/wie wol vnrecht. Deñ ein freyer Christen spri-
cht alßo. Ich wil fasten/betten/ditz vnd das thun / was ge-
potten ist/nit dz ichs bedarff od᷑ da durch wolt frum oder selig
werden/sondern ich wils dem Babst/Bischoff/der gemeyn/od᷑
meynem mit bruder/herrn zu willen/exempel vnd dienst thun vñ
leydeñ/gleych wie mir Christus viel grösser ding zu willen thā
vnd gelidden hatt / des yhm vill weniger nott ware. Vnd ob
schon die tyrannē vnrecht thun solchs zu foddern/ßo schadets
mir doch nit / die weyl es nit widder gott ist.

¶ Czum.xxix. Hierauß mag ein yglicher ein gewiß vrteyl vñ
vnterscheydt nehmen/ vnter allen wercken vnd gepottenn/ auch
wilchs blind tolle od᷑ recht synnige p̄laten sein. Deñ wilchs
werck nit dahynauß gericht ist/dem anderñ zu dienen/ oder sey-
nen willen zu leydenn/ßo fern er nit zwingt/wider gott zu thun/
ßo ists nit ein gut Christlich werck. Daher kumpts / das ich
sorg/wenig stifft kirchen/klöster/altar/meß/testamēt/ Christ-
lich seinn/Datzu auch/ die fasten vnd gepett etlichen heyligen/
sonderlich gethan. Denn ich furcht/ das ynn den allen sampt
ein yglicher nur das seyne sucht/vormeynend damit sein sind zu
büssen vnd seligk werden. Wilchs allis kūpt auß vnwissenheit
des glaubens vñ Christlicher freyheit/Vnd etlich blind p̄laten/
die leuth da hynn treybeñ vnd solch weßen preyssen/mit ablas
schmucken vñ den glauben nymer mehr leren. Ich rate dir aber
wiltu etwas stifften/betten/fasten/so thu es nit der meynūg/ dz
du wollist dir etwas guts thū/sondern gibs dahin frey/dz ande
leuth desselben genießen mugen vñ thu es yhn zu gut/so bistu ein
rechter Christē/ wz sollē dir dein gütter vñ gute werck die dir üb
rig sein / dein leyb zu regieren vñ vorsorgen/so du gnug hast am
glaubeñ/daryn dir gott alle ding geben hat. Sihe also mussen
gottis gutter fliessen auß eynē/yn den andern vñ gemeyn werdē.
dz ein yglicher sich seynis nehstē also annehm/als were erß selb
Auß Chrō fliessen sie yn vns/d᷑ sich vnser hatt angenōmen ynn
seynē lebeñ/ als were er dz gewesen/dz wir sein. Auß vns sollen
sie fliessen/yn die/so yr bedurffen. Auch so gar/dz ich muß auch

meynenn glaubenn vnd gerechtickeyt, fur meynenn nehsten setzen
fur gott/ seyne sund zu decken/ auff mich nehmen vnd nit anders
thun/ denn als weren sie meyn eygen/ eben wie Christus vns allen
than hatt. Sich das ist die natur der liebe/ wo sie warhaff-
tig ist/ Da ist sie aber warhafftig/ wo der glaub warhafftig
ist. Darumb gibt der heylig Apostell/ der lieb zu eygen. 1. Cor. 13
Das sie nit sucht das yhre/ sondern/ was des nehsten ist.

¶ Czum. xxx. Auß dem allem folget der beschluß/ das eyn
Christen mensch lebt nit ynn yhm selb/ sondern ynn Christo vñ
seynem nehstem/ ynn Christo durch den glauben/ ym nehsten/
durch die liebe/ durch den glauben feret er vber sich yn gott/ auß
gott feret er widder vnter sich durch die liebe/ vnd bleybt doch
ymmer ynn gott vñ gottlicher liebe/ Gleych wie Christus sagt
Johan. 1. Ihr werdet noch sehen den hymell offen stehn/ vñ die
Engell auff vnd absteygenn vbir den Sun des menschenn.
Sihe das ist/ die rechte/ geystliche/ Christliche freyheyt/ die das
hertz frey macht/ von allen sundenn/ gesetzen/ vnd gepotten/
wilch alle andere freyheyt vbirtrifft/ wie der hymell die erdenn/
Wilch geb vns gott recht zuuorstehen vnd behaltenn/

A M E N.

C4v (fol. 12v)

www.ingramcontent.com/pod-product-compliance
Lightning Source LLC
Chambersburg PA
CBHW070459120726
47910CB00003B/1070

* 9 7 8 0 9 9 5 4 5 6 4 5 7 *